Curriculum
in the Postmodern
Condition

Studies in the
Postmodern Theory of Education

Joe L. Kincheloe and Shirley R. Steinberg
General Editors

Vol. 103

PETER LANG
New York • Washington, D.C./Baltimore • Boston • Bern
Frankfurt am Main • Berlin • Brussels • Vienna • Oxford

Alicia de Alba, Edgar González–Gaudiano,
Colin Lankshear, & Michael Peters

Curriculum
in the **Postmodern**
Condition

PETER LANG
New York • Washington, D.C./Baltimore • Boston • Bern
Frankfurt am Main • Berlin • Brussels • Vienna • Oxford

Library of Congress Cataloging-in-Publication Data

de Alba, Alicia.
Curriculum in the postmodern condition / Alicia de Alba ... [et al.].
p. cm. — (Counterpoints; vol. 103)
Includes bibliographical references (p.) and index.
1. Curriculum planning—social aspects. 2. Postmodernism and education.
3. Postmodernism. I. de Alba, Alicia. II. Counterpoints (New York, N.Y.); vol. 103.
LB2806.15.C694   374'.001—dc21   99-058774
ISBN 0-8204-4176-7
ISSN 1058-1634

Die Deutsche Bibliothek-CIP-Einheitsaufnahme

de Alba, Alicia:
Curriculum in the postmodern condition / Alicia de Alba ...
–New York; Washington, D.C./Baltimore; Boston; Bern; Frankfurt am Main;
Berlin; Brussels; Vienna; Oxford: Lang.
(Counterpoints; Vol. 103)
ISBN 0-8204-4176-7

Cover design by Lisa Dillon

The paper in this book meets the guidelines for permanence and durability
of the Committee on Production Guidelines for Book Longevity
of the Council of Library Resources.

© 2000 Peter Lang Publishing, Inc., New York

All rights reserved.
Reprint or reproduction, even partially, in all forms such as microfilm,
xerography, microfiche, microcard, and offset strictly prohibited.

Printed in the United States of America.

Contents

Introduction

Curriculum in the Postmodern Condition

I

To talk of the curriculum in the *postmodern condition* is to locate it within its appropriate contemporary historical and philosophical contexts. Attempts to characterize these contexts have, however, been fraught with all kinds of difficulty. Any such attempts to provide narratives of world history, or non-ideological descriptions of the emergence of a distinct philosophical ethos are contestable and open to interpretation. Nonetheless, it is important that conceptions of the curriculum be related to their historical and philosophical contexts. Indeed, such "reflexive contextualization" is especially important in an age of rapid and ongoing space-time compressions (see Harvey 1989), in which space annihilates time. It is crucial that the curriculum both reflect its cultural age—its socio-historical context—*and* at the same time provide some critical purchase on these developments. These statements sound like the formulation of the truism: when it comes to curriculum philosophy, always historicize!

The problem with historicizing curriculum is that it almost inevitably generates attempts to narrativize world history, to tell stories about "progress," "development," and "change." Typically, these stories have their own built-in ends or teleologies, which change according to who is telling the story, to whom, and for what political purpose. Even so, philosophers, sociologists, and historians widely agree that highly significant social, technological, economic and political change has occurred since the end of World War II. Moreover, they agree that this change in some way or other bespeaks a new sensibility and worldview: that these technological and socio-political transformations amount to a sea change. The terms "postmodernism" and "the postmodern" have, albeit grudgingly in many cases, become widely accepted as catchwords indicating this new sensibility, style, ethos, or disposition. Foreshadowing our argument, we will argue that "postmodernism," by contrast, is not concerned with venerating the old because it is closer to the sacred (religious origins and texts)—traditionalism—or with valorizing the present simply because it is newer. Indeed, postmodernism is both critical of attitudes to time as human creations and agonistic in relation to its sources.

II

Philosophers generally define "postmodernism" by reference to its parent term, "modernism." Modernism has two uses. The first is *aesthetic*, referring to movements in the arts from around the end of the nineteenth century. The second use is *historical* and *philosophical*. Here it refers to "the modern" in the sense of "modernity": the age or period following the medieval period. The relationship between these two senses can be expressed simply by saying talk of modernism and the modern involves a self-conscious break with the old, the classical, and the traditional, asserting instead an emphasis on the new or the present. Furthermore, we might say it also involves the general belief or underlying assumption—contrary to classicalism or traditionalism—that the modern is in some sense *better than* the old since, in the sequence of historical development, it comes *later*. From a philosophical standpoint, then, modernism in philosophy begins with the Renaissance—with the thought of Francis Bacon in England and René Descartes in France.

In the first sense referring to developments in the arts from the end of the nineteenth century, modernism is typically used to characterize the methods, style, or attitude of modern artists and, in particular, a style in which the artist deliberately breaks away from classical and traditional methods of expression based on realism and naturalism. Silverman describes modernism as follows:

> [M]odernism in art, literature, and philosophy involved novelty, break with tradition, progress, continuous development, knowledge derived from either the position of the subject or from claims to objectivity. . . . [It] involved a shift . . . to the stream of consciousness, lived and internal time-consciousness, transcendental subjectivity, narrated remembrance and awareness (1996, 353).

In philosophy (and theology), modernism can be seen as a movement sustained by a belief in the advancement of knowledge and human progress premised on experience and scientific method. It is epitomized, perhaps, by Immanuel Kant's "critical" philosophy and by the idea that advancement in knowledge comes with subjecting traditional beliefs to criticism.

"Postmodernism" likewise has two broad meanings, related to these specific senses of modernism. It is used in an *aesthetic* sense to refer to developments in the arts occurring subsequently or in reaction to modernism. Secondly, it is used in a *historical* and/or *philosophical* sense to refer to a period ("postmodernity") or an ethos ("the postmodern"). It could be argued that in its second sense postmodernism represents a transformation of modernity or a radical shift in the system of values and practices underlying modernity. This is, in fact, the way the Oxford English Dictionary defines postmodernism, giving its root meaning and etymology as follows:

post-modern, a. Also post-Modern. Etymology: post- B. 1 b.
Subsequent to, or later than, what is 'modern'; spec. in the arts, esp. Archit., applied to a movement in reaction against that designated 'modern' (cf. modern a. 2 h). Hence post-modernism, post-modernist a. and sb.

Speaking of the application of the term postmodern to the human sciences, Ermarth suggests that:

[P]ostmodernism can be recognized by two key assumptions. First, the assumption that there is no common denominator—in "nature" or "truth" or "God" or "the future"—that guarantees either the One-ness of the world or the possibility of natural or objective thought. Second, the assumption that all human systems operate like language, being self-reflexive rather than referential systems—systems of differential function which are powerful but finite, and which construct and maintain meaning and value (1998: 587).

Discussing its relevance to political philosophy, Lilly claims that postmodernism

aims at exposing how, in modern, liberal democracies, the construction of political identity and the operationalization of basic values take place through the deployment of conceptual binaries such as we/them, responsible/irresponsible, rational/irrational, legitimate/illegitimate, normal/abnormal, and so on. . . . [P]ostmodernists draw attention to the ways in which the boundary between . . . [these] terms is socially reproduced and policed (1998, 591).

These scholars reflect the tendency—which has become a common strategy—to treat postmodernism synonymously with poststructuralism, or to use postmodernism as the all-embracing term. Yet this is not a position we would endorse. We believe that poststructuralism should be distinquished both from postmodernism and from its predecessor movement, structuralism. Although there are philosophical and historical overlaps between the two movements, it is important to distinguish between the two in order to appreciate their respective intellectual and cultural genealogies, their theoretical trajectories and applications. Poststructuralism has often been confused with its kinship term, postmodernism, and indeed some critics have argued that the latter term, through patterns of established usage, has come to subsume poststructuralism. We maintain there is an important set of differences that can be most easily understood by recognizing the difference between their *theoretical objects of study*. Poststructuralism takes as its theoretical object "structuralism," whereas postmodernism takes as its theoretical object "modernism." What is often confusing is that some poststructuralist thinkers, such as Jean-François Lyotard, actively engage with the term postmodernism, while others, such as Michel Foucault, pretend they do not know to what it refers. Lyotard is, perhaps, the most famous of contemporary philosophers who refers to postmodernism in both an aesthetic and historical/philosophical sense. Jean-François Lyotard is considered by most commentators, justly or not, as the preeminent non-Marxist philosopher of "the postmodern condition" (sometimes referred to as "postmodernity"). His *The Postmodern Condition: A Report on Knowledge* (1984), originally published in Paris in 1979, became an instant cause célèbre. The book crystallized in an original interpretation a study of the status and development of knowledge, science, and technology in advanced capitalist societies. Arguably, no contemporary work in curriculum philosophy that aims at teasing out the significance of the "postmodern condition" can afford to ignore Lyotard's work, and it is to his analysis of the "postmodern condition" that we now briefly turn.

III

The Postmodern Condition was important for a number of reasons. It developed a philosophical interpretation of the changing state of knowledge, science, and education in the most highly developed societies, reviewing and synthesizing research on contemporary science within the broader context of the sociology of postindustrial society and studies of postmodern culture. Lyotard brought together for the first time diverse threads and previously separate literatures in an analysis that many commentators and critics believed signaled an epochal break not only with the so-called modern era but also with various traditionally modern ways of viewing the world.

The strength and originality of *The Postmodern Condition*, considered in its own right and on its own merits, is reason enough for educators to devote time and effort to understanding and analyzing Lyotard's major working hypothesis: "[T]he status of knowledge is altered as societies enter what is known as the postindustrial age and cultures enter what is known as the postmodern age" (1984, 3). He uses the term postmodern condition to describe the state of knowledge and the problem of its legitimation in the most highly developed societies. In this he follows sociologists and critics who have used the term to designate the state of Western culture "following the transformations which, since the end of the nineteenth century, have altered the game rules for science, literature and the arts" (Lyotard 1984, 3). Lyotard places these transformations within the context of the crisis of narratives, especially those Enlightenment metanarratives concerning meaning, truth, and emancipation that have been used to legitimate both the rules of knowledge of the sciences and the foundations of modern institutions.

By "transformations" Lyotard is referring to the effects of the new technologies since the 1950s and their combined impact on the two principal functions of knowledge—research and the transmission of learning. Significantly, he maintains, the leading sciences and technologies have all been based on language-related developments—theories of linguistics, cybernetics, informatics, computer languages, telematics, theories of algebra—and their miniaturization and commercialization. In this context, Lyotard argues that the status of knowledge is permanently altered: Its availability as an international commodity becomes the basis for national and commercial advantage within the global economy; its computerized use in the military is the basis for enhanced state security and international monitoring. Knowledge, as he acknowledges, has already become the principal force of production, changing the composition of the work force in developed countries. The commercialization of knowledge and its new forms of media circulation, he suggests, will raise new ethico-legal problems between the nation-state and the information-rich multinationals, and will widen the gap between the so-called developed and Third Worlds.

Here is a *critical* account theorizing the status of knowledge and education in the postmodern condition that focuses upon the most highly developed societies. It constitutes a seminal contribution and important point of departure to what has become known—in part due to Lyotard's work—as the modernity/postmodernity debate, a debate that has involved many of the most prominent contemporary philosophers and social theorists (see Peters 1995a and Peters 1996a for illustrative examples).

It is a book that directly addresses the concerns of education, perhaps more so than any other single poststructuralist text. It does so in a way that bears on the future status and role of education and knowledge in what has proved to be a stunningly prophetic analysis. Many of the features of Lyotard's analysis of the "postmodern condition"—an analysis now twenty years old—appear today to be accepted aspects of our experiences in Western societies.

He writes in a now famous formulation of the *modern*:

> I will use the term *modern* to designate any science that legitimates itself with reference to a metadiscourse . . . making explicit appeal to some grand narrative, such as the dialectics of the Spirit, the hermeneutics of meaning, the emancipation of the rational or working subject, or the creation of wealth (Lyotard 1984, xxii).

By contrast, he defines *postmodern* simply as "incredulity toward metanarratives" (xxiv). In *The Postmodern Condition*, Lyotard was concerned with the grand narratives that had grown out of the Enlightenment and had come to mark modernity. In *The Postmodern Explained to Children*, Lyotard mentions specifically

> the progressive emancipation of reason and freedom, the progressive or catastrophic emancipation of labour . . . , the enrichment of all through the progress of capitalist technoscience, and even . . . the salvation of creatures through the conversion of souls to the Christian narrative of martyred love (1992, 29).

Grand narratives, then, are the stories that cultures tell themselves about their own practices and beliefs in order to legitimate them. They function as a unified single story that purports to legitimate or found a set of practices, a cultural self-image, discourse, or institution (see Peters 1995a).

Lyotard (1984), in his very first footnote, acknowledges the sources for his notion of "the postmodern": the sociology of postindustrial society (mentioning the work of Daniel Bell and Alain Touraine, the literary criticism of Ihab Hassan, studies of "performance" in postmodern culture by Michel Benamou and Charles Caramello, and M. Köhler's essay). These are useful sources to note because, taken together, they combine elements of the changing mode of economic and social organization of advanced societies with certain changes in culture. Lyotard suggests that the status of knowledge is altered as societies enter the postindustrial age and cultures enter the postmodern age. Some sociologists have begun to talk of this transition in terms of "postmodernization," similar to the way that sociologists of a previous generation analyzed the transition from the traditional to the modern in terms of "modernization."

If we take the definition Lyotard provided in his essay "Answering the Question: What Is Postmodernism?" (appended to the English translation of *The Postmodern Condition*), we would be driven to accept that postmodernism is "not modernism at its end but in the nascent state, and this state is constant. I have said and will say again the postmodern signifies not the end of modernism, but another relation to modernism" (1984, 79). What he is suggesting is that postmodernism as a movement in the arts is a continuation of modernism by other means—the search for the new and the avant-garde experimentalism remain. That is, postmodernism entertains an ambivalent relation to modernism, considered as a category in aesthetics, and it defines a style, an attitude, or an ethos rather than a period (that is, something that comes *after* modernism). In this sense, there are clearly many postmodernisms in the sense of defining a style in the arts, and although they may come and go, the *postmodern*, as an episteme, a philosophical stance, or historical periodization, like the *modern*, is here to stay.

IV

This account of the postmodern, although brief, nonetheless provides a basis for considering curriculum in the postmodern condition. We need to put some flesh on the bones of our account, however. We begin this task by characterizing the philosophical changes referred to by "the postmodern condition" presented as a cluster of concepts. These concepts are then related briefly to the curriculum.

If we approach curriculum in a conventional way, we can think of programs of study in terms of dimensions such as content and skills, or bodies of knowledge and processes of knowing. Any curriculum statement or theory must refer to *what* students are (expected) to learn and *how* they are expected to go about learning, *what* teachers are to teach and *how* they are to teach it. From a slightly different perspective, we may think in terms of curriculum as having to deal with both the *structure* and *content* of knowledge. In addition, of course, curriculum theory and curriculum planning must include a *normative* dimension, which provides reasons for what is included and excluded and for the kinds of approaches and processes to be taken. The key point to be made about the cluster concepts of postmodern philosophy we have identified is that they issue profound challenges to the ways educators have typically thought in the past and, to a disconcerting extent, *continue* to think about curriculum.

Table 1 The Cluster Concepts of Postmodern Philosophy

Anti-foundationalism	• Suspicion of transcendental arguments and viewpoints
	• Suspicion of metanarratives
	• Rejection of canonical descriptions and final vocabularies
	• Perspectivism and multiplicity
Post-epistemological standpoint	• Rejection of the picture of knowledge as accurate representation
	• Rejection of truth as correspondence to reality
	• Standpoint, nonfoundational, or "ecological" epistemology
Anti–naive realism	• Anti-realism about meaning and reference
	• The nonreferentiality of language
	• The naturalizing tendency in language
	• The diagnosis and critique of binarism
Anti-essentialism and the self	• The critique of the metaphysics of presence
	• Substitution of genealogical narratives for ontology
	• The cultural construction of subjectivity
	• The discursive production of the self
	• Analysis of technologies of self
Analysis of power/ knowledge	• The critique of the metaphysics of presence
	• Questioning of the problematic of the humanist subject
	• Substitution of genealogical narratives for ontology
	• The cultural construction of subjectivity
	• The discursive production of the self
	• Analysis of technologies of self
Boundary crossings	• Erasure of boundaries between literature and philosophy
	• Interdisciplinarity and multidisciplinarity

Formal educational theory, policy, and practice with respect to curricular content and processes, skills, and knowledge is comprehensively outdated. It assumes and builds upon *categories* and *modus operandi* that no longer apply. Although approximations to elements of postmodern philosophical insight are occasionally touched upon in notions of prioritizing "learning how to learn" over "fixed bodies of content," the ways in which such ideas are taken up in curriculum development and classroom practice are typically superficial and underinformed. For example, the idea that *information* has somehow displaced *knowledge* all too frequently degenerates into flaccid forms of relativism or is reduced to inane cliched formulae such as the idea that the teacher's role has evolved from that of "sage on the stage" to "guide on the side." Although such notions have a basis in very real and significant conditions of change, they are less than adequate responses, and may well play into the hands of those who would do away with teachers and schools altogether (see Perelman 1992) or otherwise whittle away at access to education as a vital dimension of the social wage.

Deep contradictions exist in curriculum planning and policy right now that demand attention. For instance, at a time when knowledge and skills seem genuinely to be up for grabs in radical ways, much policy and planning seems intent on screwing them down more tightly and defining them more narrowly than has been common in recent times. The postmodern world simultaneously demands and delivers increased "metaknowledge"—often in ways that elude us. For instance, diminished welfare bureaucracies demand that users possess a metaknowledge of how services and institutions are organized in order to be able to access services and "opportunities." Powerful ways of operating new technologies presuppose that users can relegate "basic skills" of operation to relatively subordinate positions in order to get on with "the real business" of their application: symbolic manipulation, innovation, design, and so on. Yet our curricula are becoming overwhelmed by practices of diagnosis, intervention, and remediation grounded not merely in "basic skills," but in *old and outmoded* forms of basic skills—and developers and producers of "quick-fix" programs for remedial education and professional development are experiencing a boom. Although it remains important for today's learners to master "basic" forms of skill and acquire a sound base of "cultural literacy," this curriculum is predicated on the grounds that it genuinely offers bases of and pathways to "metalevel" planes of understanding and performance (Gee 1996; Gee, Hull, and Lankshear 1996; Rogoff 1990; Rogoff 1995). The problem here, of course, is that what is genuinely "basic" in these terms has undergone major changes, yet prevailing curriculum theory, policy, and practice insist on preserving a misguided investment in old ways and old frameworks.

We find curriculum still being construed very much in terms of "packages" of skills and content at a time when a metaphor like "platforms" seems much more apposite (this idea was developed in conversation with Richard Smith). In "techspeak" a platform refers to an undergirding operating logic or operating system upon which diverse, more immediate computing applications are based. In this sense, DOS, Mac, UNIX and so on provide examples of different platforms. The postmodern philosophical concepts of anti-foundationalism and post-epistemological standpoint invoke logics and sensibilities that privilege active pursuit of *ways of looking at the world* rather than absorbing *predefined content and skills* grounded in extant worldviews. The learner who masters "platforms" can proactively generate interpretations and frame designs that in turn generate their own learning and innovation agendas and, ultimately, worldviews.

Such approaches do not eliminate standards and criteria. Far from it. Some platforms work better than others. The educational question for curriculum is how to distinguish between these platforms and how to understand their underlying principles. "Off the shelf" and "one size fits all" approaches to curriculum policy and design, although they have some scope for flexibility, subvert an understanding of the underlying principles of skills "platforms." The problem is that if teachers are to become oriented toward platform logic and away from packages, they need to understand and grasp the characteristically postmodern structure of knowledge. This possibility is systematically undermined by approaches that favor more of the same.

Parallel points could be developed for each of the concepts of postmodern philosophy we have identified above. But that would be secondary to our main point, which is to grasp that the concepts of postmodern philosophy that were developed as a means for understanding that the temperament of the times inhabit different categorical space and categorically different space from modernist mindsets and categories.

Our cluster concepts provide a sense of how far our current ways of engaging with curriculum in theory, policy, and practice conflict *categorically* with the age. Educationists still widely think in terms of subject territories and continue to frame academic and professional training in such terms. Curriculum planning, policy development, and curriculum resourcing continue to be undertaken within familiar subject domains rather than in forms of collaboration and reciprocal informing that transcend traditional disciplinary parameters in fruitful and timely ways. A recent study (Lankshear et al. 1997, Vol. 1) found curriculum and resourcing policies for technology being developed mainly in isolation from literacy. On what possible grounds, one wonders, could this be justified—at any time, let alone under present conditions? Likewise, what grounds are there in the so-called information age for continuing to stipulate subject content ranges for school year levels as closely as we typically do? Would it not make altogether more sense to encourage approaches that have learners, teachers, and other relevant experts work together to generate information, organize and analyze this information, compile reliable databases, and the like on a model of the school as an information base for its community? (Chris Bigum, personal communication). This would involve learners being apprenticed to expert—mature, "insider"—approaches to gathering, compiling, organizing, analyzing, storing, and disseminating information rather than "learning" from pre-packaged content.

The definition of curriculum as a structured series of learning opportunities highlights the constructed nature of the curriculum based on a conception of knowledge—its organization into disciplines—and learning theory

(Cherryholmes 1988, 133). It also serves to draw attention to the curriculum as a values-driven *selection* of material or course content that operates to both include and exclude certain traditions of knowledge, particular perspectives, and sets of values.

The cluster concepts of postmodern philosophy outlined above cut across modernist epistemological assumptions and learning theory based on these assumptions. They provide grounds for questioning the foundationalist conception of knowledge (inherited from Descartes and the Enlightenment) as well as the organization and structure of knowledge as disciplines. The nonfoundationalist, post-epistemological, and nonrepresentational view, then, contains a deep-seated critique of modern views of knowledge and curriculum. Together with the cluster we call anti-essentialism, postmodern philosophy provides grounds for challenging humanist constructions of the self as a unified entity that is transparent to itself and as the fount of all knowledge and moral action. Just as it sows radical doubt—where there had existed for so long certainty and total faith—in the ideal of the sovereign subject, postmodern philosophy at the same time also creates doubt around the reality of the learning subject: the child, the toddler, the pupil, the student. This adds weight to the importance of genealogical investigation of subjectivities and representations of students, youth, and adult learners.

The postmodern critique of the modern constitution of the curriculum in terms of nonfoundationalism and anti-essentialism, and the ways in which we recognize the curriculum as particular historical constructions of power/knowledge, raise profound challenges to mainstream curriculum theory, policy, and practice. In the chapters that follow we begin to explore the significance of these curriculum challenges in relation to notions of science, technology and environment, as well as to conventional wisdom about literacy.

V

Attempting to present a historical narrative of postmodernity is, perhaps, even more difficult than characterizing the postmodern ethos in philosophical terms. In this case, rather than providing a narrative we will construct what we have called snapshot scenarios. These scenarios are based on what now are commonly thought to be some of the most important changes as societies shift from industrial to postindustrial, and then to information societies/economies.

Scenario planning has emerged during the past forty to fifty years as a generic technique to stimulate thinking about the future in the context of strategic planning (Cowan 1998). It was initially used in military planning, and was subsequently adapted for use in business environments (Wack 1985a; Wack 1985b; Schwartz 1991; van der Heijden 1996) and, most recently, for planning political futures in such countries as post-apartheid South Africa, Colombia, Japan, Canada, and Cyprus (Cowan 1998). We offer a modified version here as a way of thinking about curriculum in the postmodern condition.

Scenarios are succinct narratives that describe possible futures and alternative paths toward the future based on plausible hypotheses and assumptions. The idea behind scenarios is to start thinking about the future now in order to be better prepared for what comes later. Proponents of scenario planning make it very clear that scenarios are not predictions. Rather, they aim to perceive futures in the present. In Rowan and Bigum's words they are a

> means for rehearsing a number of possible futures. Building scenarios is a way of asking important "what if" questions: a means of helping groups of people change the way they think about a problem. In other words, they are a means of learning (1997, 73).

If we take the issue of curriculum, the question is What kinds of things should we be learning and teaching now in order to prepare learners as well as possible for handling what comes in the future, *and* to be able to act better now as well as later in order to create more viable futures? When we look at much current educational policy, planning, and curriculum development it is easy to see a lot of the past enshrined in guidelines and plans and a lot of unwarranted certainty assumed and expressed about things relevant to the world in which today's learners will live—an assuredness and taken-for-grantedness about the relevance of particular forms of content, skills, worldviews, etc., that are at odds with what we know and don't know about the future worlds of students (74).

Scenario planning is very much about challenging the kinds of mindsets that underwrite such certainty and assuredness and is about "reperceiving the world" (76) and promoting more open, flexible, proactive stances toward the future. As Cowan and colleagues put it, the process and activity of scenario planning is designed to facilitate conversation about what is going on and what might occur in the world around us so that we might "make better decisions about what we ought to do or avoid doing" (1998, 8). Developing scenarios that perceive possible futures in the present can help us "avoid situations in which events take us by surprise." They encourage us to question "conventional predictions of the future," help us to recognize "signs of change" when they occur, and establish standards for evaluating "continued use of different strategies under different conditions." Most important, they provide a means of organizing our knowledge and understanding of future environments within which the decisions we take today will be played out (Rowan and Bigum 1997, 76).

Within typical approaches to scenario planning a key goal is to aim for making policies and decisions now that are likely to prove sufficiently robust when they are played out across several possible futures. Rather than predicting the future, a range of possible futures are entertained and policies and decisions in the "now" are framed that will optimize options and outcomes no matter which of the anticipated futures eventually pans out (most approximately).

Hence, scenarios must narrate particular and credible worlds given forces and influences currently evident and known to us that are likely to steer the future in one direction or another. A popular way of doing this is to bring together participants to the present policymaking or decision-making exercise and have them frame a focusing question or theme within the area they are concerned with. If, for instance, our concern is with designing current courses in literacy education and technology for in-service teachers in training, we might frame the question of what learning and teaching of literacy and technology might look like in educational settings for elementary school-age children fifteen years hence.

Once the question is framed, participants try to identify driving forces they see as operating and as being important in terms of their question or theme. When these have been thought through, participants identify those forces or influences that seem more or less predetermined: that will play out in more or less known ways. Participants then identify less predictable influences, or uncertainties: key variables in shaping the future that could play out in quite different ways, but ones for which we genuinely can't be confident one way or another about how they will play out. From this latter set, one or two are selected as "critical uncertainties" (Rowan and Bigum 1997, 81). These are forces or influences that seem especially important in terms of the focusing question or theme but that are genuinely up for grabs and unpredictable. The critical uncertainties are then dimensionalized by plotting credible poles: between possibilities that, at one pole are not too bland and, at the other, not too off the wall. These become raw materials for building scenarios: accessible, catchy, but punchy and fruitful stories about which we can think in ways that suggest decisions and policy directions *now*.

Although the scenario snapshots we offer here are not strictly like this—they have not been framed as closely or by participants within formal and focused scenario planning forums—they nonetheless provide a standpoint for thinking about curriculum in the postmodern condition in relation to current curriculum policies, directions, decisions, guidelines, and class-room implementations. Our point here is that there currently exists a lot of information and understanding about postmodernity *that is not being taken seriously into account in curriculum development and planning*, but that *ought to be taken thus into account*. Indeed, it is very easy to read from the following snapshot scenarios the extent to which much current curriculum work is oblivious to the possibilities and implications of even these partially framed and underdeveloped scenarios.

Just as the cluster concepts developed from our philosophical account of postmodernity provide a basis for critiquing and reconceptualizing curriculum, so these snapshot scenarios provide useful tools for reconsidering curriculum in theory, policy, and practice. As tools and reference points, they augment our philosophical perspective in five key and inter-related ways.

First, they provide analytical tools that we can use for comparing current curriculum theory and practice with the circumstances and demands of the postmodern condition. To the extent that our scenarios capture conditions, circumstances and their implied requirements for effective living and participation under present and foreseeable future conditions, they provide a kind of checklist against which to assess curriculum. We can use them as a benchmark, asking how far existing curriculum arrangements reflect the themes captured in the scenarios.

Second, they augment the cluster concepts in terms of reappraising the disciplinary and subject-oriented nature of curriculum theory and practice. To what extent, in other words, can the issues and demands inherent in the scenario snapshots be framed, understood, and addressed conceptually, theoretically, and practically by the kind of learning enabled by existing curricula?

Third, they might be approached in terms of defining and structuring components of an embryonic experimental curriculum for the upper secondary school or university. From this standpoint, the scenarios can be seen as identifying foci, problems, issues, and themes that collectively might well define a coherent program of study for students in higher levels of formal programs. The sorts of foci, issues, and themes involved would, once unpacked, provide guidelines for structuring knowledge and inquiry, generating relevant information, and acquiring appropriate methodical tools of inquiry and criteria for using them well.

Table 2 Seven Snapshot Scenarios

Snapshot Scenario 1: Globalization
- World economic integration with technological changes in telecommunications, information, and transport
- (Political) promotion of free trade and the reduction in trade protection
- Weakening of the nation-state and growth of local mafias, especially in Eastern bloc countries
- Decline of the state and growth of multinationals brings a growing importance of the city (and hinterland) as the political administrative and governing unit
- Imposition of structural adjustment policies on Third World countries
- Emergence of a one-superpower hegemony but also the consolidation of China and world Islamization
- Growth of religious and ethnic nationalisms
- Increased gaps between richer and poorer, in terms of both economic and cultural/informational capital
- Instability of the unregulated global financial system (financial collapse of the Asian "tiger" economies and economies of Soviet Union and Brazil)

Snapshot Scenario 2: Changes in Economic Processes
- Shift from industrial to service and/or information economy
- Increased importance of property in general, including the technology of reproduction, intellectual property, and genetic engineering
- Declining power of labor unions
- Development of flex-time work arrangements (i.e., growth of part-time work) and the emergence of the "flexible worker"
- Casualization of work and increasing levels of unemployment, especially in the Third World
- Transformation from late capitalism to transnational managerial capitalism and finance capitalism
- Shift to "knowledge industries" and global information economies
- The increasing substitution of capital for labor (and nonreversibility of the substitution principle)
- The growing importance of symbolic economies and the manipulation of symbolic systems and processes

Snapshot Scenario 3: Knowledge Production and Formation
- Increased specialization of academic fields, discourses, languages
- Commercialization of schools and universities
- Commodification of knowledge
- Shift from knowledge to knowledge management
- Exponential growth of knowledge and emergence of the knowledge industries (quaternary, quintary—e.g., culture and ethics industries)
- New legal, ethical, and political problems generated by language-based techno-knowledge developments over simulacra (e.g., patents, copies)
- The growing differentiation of new knowledge groups and classes
- The decline of state-centered knowledge institutions and the growth of private and corporate think-tanks, foundations, and institutes
- The radical concordance and convergence of media and media ownership

Table 2 Continued

Snapshot Scenario 4: Mathematical/Physical Processes
- Increased incommensurabilities, including languages, teleologies, and scripts
- Problematizing of space-time and stable categorizations
- Development of mathematics of nonclassical spaces (monster curves, fractals, catastrophe theory, chaos theory, eccentric or abject spaces)
- Inclusion of disorder in mathematics and physics
- Development of intermaths
- Development of postmodern science with an accent on local determinisms, paralogy, undecidability, incompleteness, and openness
- The many worlds interpretation in physics
- Importance of implicate order and dissipative structures
- The conception of the participatory universe

Snapshot Scenario 5: Ecological Sustainability
- Destabilization of whole ecosystems, often eliciting managerial or fundamentalist responses
- Development of apocalyptic and survivalist ideologies and subcultures
- Increased reduction of DNA variability and increased toxicity of the planet
- Massive plant and animal extinctions
- Deep pollution of local and usually urban environments
- Increased "natural" catastrophes (e.g., flooding) as the result of human interference
- Growth of shack cities (barrios, favelas, colonias without sewage, water, electricity) and shack cultures
- Massive depletion of world rain forest belts, clean water, and air
- Development of germ banks and eco-banks
- Experiments with human-made environments, e.g., biosphere
- Emergence of ecoterrorism
- Strategic national biosecurity
- Global viral environments

Snapshot Scenario 6: Info-Communication Processes
- Movement from analog to digital processing technologies
- Predominance of entertainment and edutainment forms over traditional news or "straight" information-based programming
- Worldwide growth of the Internet and darknet locations
- Discursive development of communication subcultures based on the mode of reception
- Totalization of universal (computational) languages and simultaneous development of idiolects
- Commodification of all semiotics and symbol creation
- Microelectronic expansion of the virtual body, tending toward full seamlessness
- Greater automation and autonomy of "intelligent," seventh-generation robots for all tasks, including translation
- Growth of "resistance" technological subcultures (e.g., hacking, cracking, pirate radio and television, phone phreaking)

Table 2 Continued

Snapshot Scenario 7: Cultural Changes
- Interpenetration of traditional spheres and models of public and private relationships in areas of the sexual, the civic, the social, and the institutional
- Emancipation increasingly tied to communication and communicative strategies
- "Transgressive" sexualities and problematization of gender within queer theory/feminist debates
- New forms of hybrid art-tech/tech-art
- Cultural and ecological tourism as a museum-preservationist model of nature and culture
- The importance of the simulacrum and all simulation and modeling processes
- Body-cyborg interactions and compilations/combinations
- Importance of cybernetic epistemologies
- Emergence of virtual cultures and subcultures
- Growth of diasporic populations
- Renaissance of ethnic traditions and knowledges
- Growing importance of displaced populations and refugees

Fourth, were we not to wholly—or largely—abandon more traditional subject/disciplinary approaches, the scenarios could usefully provide a series of themes that could be developed in ways that could be explored via traditional subjects. For example, subject areas might pick up on themes that run across all seven snapshots; that is, the snapshot scenarios become ways of weaving together an interdisciplinary study.

Finally, the scenarios provide a series of working hypotheses for anticipating or thinking about the future of the curriculum: What would the curriculum look like if we developed each of these scenario snapshots in terms of appropriate pedagogy, techniques of inquiry, thematic emphases, conceptions of resources and learning technologies, ideals of expertise and of authentic practice, and so on? For example, if we were to take up the options in the first snapshot scenario and begin to rethink how we might reposition the curriculum to take account of developments referred to under the label of globalization in a way that promotes a critical view we might arrive at something like the following (see Table 3) as an agenda for a curriculum for alternative globalizations. How would the traditional curriculum pursue this agenda?

We do not have the space here to develop this agenda further, but simply advance it as an example of the confusion into which globalization throws the traditional curriculum; we pose this as a problem—how best to develop a curriculum that reflects *and engages* in critical and reflective

Table 3 An Agenda for the Curriculum of Alternative Globalizations

Promoting and developing a global social contract	• Promoting sustainable development
	• Promoting ecological standards
	• Consolidating the democratic process
	• Enhancing development of international labor markets
	• Promoting world trade union rights
	• Monitoring the social dimension of global and regional trade agreements
Promoting and encouraging global governance	• Building standards of global governance
	• Protecting the public institutions of civil society
	• Developing transparency and accountability of international forums and world institutions
	• Developing approaches to institutions of an international civil community
	• Encouraging greater North/South dialogue and better world representation
Promoting and developing cultural globalization	• Promoting cultural diversity and exchange
	• Developing genuine multicultural structures and processes
	• Promoting and enhancing the notion of cultural rights
	• Protecting indigenous property rights
	• Promoting political and cultural self-determination

ways those changes referred to as globalization. Similar questions, we would argue, need to be asked about each of the snapshot scenarios.

VI

In this book we take some initial steps toward rethinking curriculum in the postmodern condition. These are very much first steps. Indeed, we see the ideas and approach sketched in this Introduction as providing the basis for building an entire research program during the years to come. In this initial exploratory foray, we have brought together four researcher-scholars whose intellectual, political-ethical, and practical-pedagogical interests and circumstances lend themselves fruitfully to this task.

Our approach here has been to take primary individual responsibility for different chapters. The native English-speaking authors have assumed responsibility for overseeing translation and have played the main role in dealing with editorial and stylistic aspects. The roles will be reversed for any subsequent projects grounded in Spanish. We have reviewed each other's chapters and contributed as fully as possible to smoothing out unnecessary differences in authorial voice. During the production of this book, Alicia de Alba was working mainly in England. Edgar González-Gaudiano was working in México. Colin Lankshear was working mainly in Australia, with periods in the United States and México. Michael Peters was working mainly in New Zealand, with periods in the United States, Australia, and Europe. We coordinated via e-mail—for lengthy periods on an almost daily basis. Alicia de Alba was primarily responsible for Chapter 6; Edgar González-Gaudiano for Chapters 2 and 3; Colin Lankshear for Chapters 7 and 8; Michael Peters for Chapters 1, 4, and 5. Colin Lankshear and Michael Peters were primarily responsible for the Introduction. Notwithstanding these divisions of labor, we regard ourselves as a collaborating writing collective, hence individual chapters have not been assigned to individual authors.

Subsequent chapters address aspects of our theme as follows. In Chapter 1 we deal with the notion of the enterprise curriculum, or the curriculum of competition. Here the national context is New Zealand, a small country with a dependent economy that since the early 1980s has undergone radical neoliberal social and economic changes in a shift away from a welfare state to a fully consumer-driven society with a minimum "safety net." In a brief period of rapid neoliberal reform, successive New Zealand governments floated the exchange rate; abolished all subsidies to manufacturers and producers; dismantled tariffs, corporatized, commercialized and, then, privatized state trading organizations in massive state assets sales totaling over $15 billion; commercialized health and education (and the residual public sector) and introduced user charges; and moved historically away from national wage bargaining and industrial arbitration to anti-union employment contracts legislation. Education has not been immune to the changes; it has followed suit in terms of the implementation of so-called principles of new public management. In this chapter, adopting a Foucauldian approach to understanding neoliberalism that conceptually makes the link between the question of governance and self-governance or regulation, we chart the reforms to the curriculum and the way these changes reflect the ethos of competition. Here the focus falls upon the development of what we call the "entrepreneurial self." New Zealand provides an example of a deliberate neoliberal reconstruction of culture—away from the so-called welfare state "culture of dependency" to a culture of "self-reliance"—through the curriculum that demonstrates a politically reactionary understanding of postmodernity.

Chapter 2 examines the field of environmental education with particular reference to the vexed issue of sustainable development. Problems associated with trying to define the parameters of environmental education threaten the very sustainability of the field itself. These must be addressed in ways that resist attempts to standardize pedagogical responses. We argue that the sustainability of environmental education is itself closely linked to the direction taken by controversies surrounding sustainable development. The argument draws out aspects of the scenarios concerned with globalization and ecological sustainability in ways that reflect the concepts of anti-foundationalism, post-epistemological standpoint, and disciplinary boundary-crossing from postmodern philosophy.

These emphases are further taken up and extended in Chapter 3 in relation to the professionalization of environmental educators. The process of professionalizing environmental education is seen as linked to possibilities for consolidating research processes and directions in the field and, to this extent, to opportunities for constructing preferred discourses of environmental education. Without research there is no field, and without a field there is no prospect of professionalization. Just as professionalization of the field is associated with research, so too is it associated with curriculum development. The chapter concludes by proposing a framework for an environmental educator's study plan.

Chapter 4, entitled "Postmodern Science in Aotearoa/New Zealand? Conservation, Cosmology and Critique," begins with a first-person narrative concerning whaling in New Zealand and poses the question why the value reversal has occurred. New Zealand's coastline was the site of American, French, British whaling activity from the late eighteenth century through to the mid-twentieth century. In a period of some two and a half centuries the values have changed from exploitation of a species to near extinction to their active protection, often by populations of whole townships and, nationally, by volunteers who at their own expense travel to the site of recently stranded whale populations to care for them and try to save them. This chapter provides an analysis of science, first in its colonial guise as a discourse that intricately interweaves scientific classification and understanding with Christianity and capitalism and second, more speculatively, in its "postmodern guise," where science as a reason of state does not actively work to conserve indigenous species. An account of the way in which postmodern science, as developed by Stephen Toulmin and others, promotes a new ethical responsibility in science and is seen to be part of a return to cosmological holism is provided alongside a postmodern account of science that is explicitly political. Science in both senses contrasts strongly with classically modern views of science that are taught as part of curricula in the West.

Chapter 5 begins to tease out these issues more explicitly in terms of the curriculum; it first reviews and discusses in a critical light the influential account given by William Doll of postmodern perspectives of the curriculum, and then by contrast develops a poststructuralist critique of this "constructive postmodern" view of science as one that pays too much attention to developments "internal" to science itself, and not enough—if at all—to political factors, or we might say, the historical and philosophical sense of "the postmodern" in the sense elaborated earlier in this Introduction. The critique proceeds along three main lines, linking with earlier themes: neoliberal governmentality as the politico-economic context within which national and global economic and social "reforms" have been made; the so-called information society as another globalizing context that needs to be taken account of in curriculum development; and, finally, what has been called "the crisis of cultural authority," by which is meant not only the discovery of the plurality of cultures, or "postcolonialism" and the philosophy of decolonization, but also the development and proliferation of postwar youth subcultures and the rise of the new social movements. An account of the postmodern, it might be argued, could easily be developed in terms of one of these three lines of inquiry, or all three. Certainly, it would seem that an account of the curriculum which failed to notice the growth of youth subcultures would be making a serious mistake.

Chapter 6 frames and explores the question How do we constitute the curriculum-society link within the context of societies that are caught in the generalized structural crisis of postmodernity and that lack wide and ambitious socio-political projects? It draws on theory from Laclau, Lacan, Derrida, Wittgenstein, and Lyotard to describe the conditions that have severed earlier constitutions of the curriculum-society link, and that face those who would seek to reestablish a link and (re)constitute themselves as subjects of curricular overdetermination. The chapter goes beyond describing and analyzing the related crises in the curriculum specifically and social structure more generally. In addition, it offers conceptual and theoretical tools with which to take up the challenge of constituting anew the curriculum-society link. Among these, the concepts of social traits and contours are basic. Six key social traits and contours—poverty, "swiftness," globalization, democracy, development, and difference—are identified and discussed and their curriculum implications noted.

Chapters 7 and 8 explore a range of postmodern developments in literacy from a critical perspective. The emphasis in Chapter 7 is on constructions of literacy within contemporary education policy proposals intended to guide literacy education within the school curriculum. Five main constructions of literacy are identified. Each is spelled out in terms resonant with key elements of scenarios concerned with information and communication processes, cultural changes, knowledge production and formation, and globalization. Particular attention is paid to policy formulations of literacy in relation to Lyotard's account of performativity. Major features of the varying constructions of literacy are subjected to critique and an alternative ideal of literacy sketched—one that is more in line with the kinds of demands anticipated in the scenarios and the proposed agenda for a curriculum that reflects and engages changes referred to by "globalization."

The focus in Chapter 8 is on technological literacies understood in terms of practices mediated by contemporary information and communications technologies. In the first half of the chapter a range of quite typical practices of technological literacy produced within classroom curriculum settings are described and analyzed. The second half of the chapter describes and analyzes a quite different range of discursive practices involving new technologies associated with cultural activities in a community youth space. The two sets of practices are treated as postmodern variants of technological literacies that illustrate some deeply contradictory tendencies within postmodernity.

Chapter 1

Neoliberalism, the Enterprise Curriculum, and the Constitution of Self in Aotearoa/New Zealand[1]

Introduction

The question What are the relations of governance between neoliberalism and education? provides the basis for this chapter. Our approach to this question is premised on Michel Foucault's lectures on the notion of governmentality and recent work undertaken by neo-Foucauldians.

We adopt this perspective for several reasons. First, a neo-Foucauldian approach to the sociology of governance avoids interpreting liberalism as an ideology, political philosophy, or an economic theory and reconfigures it as a form of governmentality with an emphasis on the question of how power is exercised.[2] Second, such an approach makes central the notion of the self-limiting state which, in contrast to the administrative (or "police") state, brings together in productive ways questions of ethics and technique, through the responsibilization of moral agents and the active reconstruction of the relation between government and self-government. Third, it proposes an investigation of neoliberalism as an intensification of an economy of moral regulation first developed by liberals, and not merely or primarily as a political reaction to big government or the so-called bureaucratic welfare state of the postwar Keynesian settlement. Indeed, some who adopt this approach see welfarism as an aberrant episode that has little to do with liberalism per se. Fourth, the approach enables an understanding of the distinctive features of neoliberalism. It understands neoliberalism in terms of its replacement of the natural and spontaneous order characteristic of Hayekian liberalism with "*artificially arranged or contrived forms of the free, entrepreneurial, and competitive*

Figure 1 Elements of Neoliberal Governmentality

1. **Classical liberalism as a *critique of state reason*:** A political doctrine concerning the self-limiting state; the limits of government are related to the limits of state reason, that is, its power to know; a permanent critique of the activity of rule and government.

2. ***Natural* versus *contrived* forms of the market:** Hayek's notion of natural laws based on spontaneously ordered institutions in the physical (crystals, galaxies) and social (morality, language, market) worlds has been replaced with an emphasis on the market as an artifact or culturally derived form and (growing out of the catallaxy approach) a *constitutional* perspective that focuses on the judicio-legal rules governing the framework within the game of enterprise is played.

3. **The politics-as-exchange innovation of public choice theory ("the marketization of the state"):** The extension of Hayek's spontaneous order conception (catallactics) of the institution of the market beyond simple exchange to complex exchange and finally to *all processes of voluntary agreement* among persons.

4. **The relation between government and self-government:** Liberalism as a doctrine that positively requires that individuals be free in order to govern; government as the community of free, autonomous, self-regulating individuals; responsibilization of individuals as moral agents; the neoliberal revival of *homo economicus* (based on assumptions of individuality, rationality and self-interest) as an all-embracing redescription of the social as a form of the economic.

5. **A new relation between government and management:** The rise of the new managerialism, new public management; the shift from *policy* and *administration* to *management*; emulation of private sector management styles; the emphasis on "freedom to manage" and the promotion of "self-managing" (that is, quasi-autonomous) individuals and entities.

6. **A "degovernmentalization" of the state (considered as a positive technique of government):** Government through the market, including promotion of consumer-driven forms of social provision (health, education, welfare), "contracting out," and privatization.

7. **The promotion of a new relationship between government and knowledge:** "Government at a distance" developed through relations of forms of expertise (expert systems) and politics; development of new forms of social accounting; an actuarial rationality; referendums and intensive opinion polling made possible through the new information and computing technologies; privatization and individualization of "risk management"; development of new forms of prudentialism.

8. **An economic theory of democracy (the marketization of democracy):** an emerging structural parallel between economic and political systems—political parties have become entrepreneurs in a vote-seeking political marketplace; professional media consultants use policies to sell candidates as image products; voters have become passive individual consumers. In short, democracy has become commodified at the cost of the project of political liberalism and the state has become subordinated to the market.

9. **The replacement of "the social" by "the community":** The decentralization, devolution and delegation of power/authority/responsibility from the center to the region, the local institution, the community; the invocation of the notion of social capital.

Figure 1   Continued

10.   **Cultural reconstruction as deliberate policy goal (the marketization of
the social):** The development of an enterprise society; privatization of the public
sector; the development of quasi-markets; marketization of education and health;
a curriculum of competition and enterprise.

conduct of economic-rational individuals" (Burchell 1996, 23). And, further, it understands neoliberalism through the development of *"a new
relation between expertise and politics,"* especially in the realm of welfare, where an actuarial rationality and new forms of prudentialism manifest and constitute themselves discursively in the language of "purchaser-
provider," audit, performance, and "risk management" (for a schematic
account of neoliberal governmentality, see Figure 1).

We build on this approach and these broad understandings to address
the issue of neoliberalism and the governance of education. Our argument proceeds in three sections. The first section briefly examines Michel
Foucault's notion of "governmentality" and the developments of this term
by neo-Foucauldians. The second section elaborates liberalism and
neoliberalism as forms of the *critique of state reason.* Following the
work of Michel Foucault and Colin Gordon, it tracks three versions of
neoliberalism, all of which appear to be committed to institutionalizing
the game of enterprise as a generalized principle for the organization of
society as a whole. The third section investigates the development of the
liberal mode of government, and its contemporary neoliberal modes in
relation to the notion of an enterprise culture and an enterprise curriculum.

In developing these arguments, particularly with the New Zealand experience in view, we have in mind the force of Gordon's restatement of
Foucault's criticism and challenge to the left:

> In a nutshell, he [Foucault] suggests that recent neoliberalism, understood . . . as
> a novel set of notions about the art of government, is a considerably more original
> and challenging phenomenon than the left's critical culture has had the courage
> to acknowledge, and that its political challenge is one that the left is singularly ill-
> equipped to respond to, the more so since, as Foucault contends, socialism itself
> does not possess and has never possessed its own distinctive form of government
> (1991, 6).

As he says elsewhere (Gordon 1996, 267), quoting Foucault's words
to a Paris audience in the late 1970s, "[Y]ou cannot hope to contest
successfully for electoral victory if you cannot show that you know how to

govern; at present, although you have hardly noticed this, others have acquired a more convincing claim than you to possess such knowledge."

Foucault's "Governmentality" and Neo-Foucauldianism

Michel Foucault (1991a) coins the term "governmentality" in an article of the same name, in which he begins to examine the problematic of government by analyzing the series security, population, government. He maintains that there was an explosion of interest on the "art of government" in the sixteenth century that was motivated by diverse questions: the government of oneself (personal conduct); the government of souls (pastoral doctrine); the government of children (problematic of pedagogy). At the intersection of two competing tendencies—state centralization and a logic of dispersion—the problematic of government can be located; a problematic that poses questions of the how of government and seeks "to articulate a kind of rationality which was intrinsic to the art of government without subordinating it to the problematic of the prince and of his relationship to the principality of which he is lord and master" (Foucault 1991a, 89).

Foucault identifies the introduction of economy—that is, "the correct manner of managing goods and wealth within the family"—into political practice as the essential aspect of the establishment of the art of government in the sixteenth century (92). This usage of political economy remained stable through into the eighteenth century; it signified "wise government of the family for the common welfare of all," although the word no longer stood for a form of government but rather designated a field of intervention (92). Foucault maintains that it was in the late sixteenth and early seventeenth centuries that the art of government crystallized for the first time around the notion of "reason of state" understood in a positive sense: "the state is governed according to rational principles which are intrinsic to it and which cannot be derived solely from natural or divine laws or the principles of wisdom and prudence; the state, like nature, has its own proper form of government, albeit of a different sort" (97). By the term "governmentality" Foucault means three things:

1. The ensemble formed by the institutions, procedures, analyses, and reflections; the calculations and tactics that allow the exercise of this very specific, albeit complex, form of power, which has as its principal form of knowledge political economy and as its essential technical means apparatuses of security.

2. The tendency which, over a long period and throughout the West, has steadily led toward the preeminence of this type of power that may be called government over all other forms (sovereignty, discipline, etc.) resulting, on the one hand, in the formation of a whole series of specific governmental apparatuses, and, on the other, in the development of a whole complex of *savoirs*.

3. The process, or rather the result of the process, through which the state of justice of the Middle Ages, transformed into the administrative state during the fifteenth and sixteenth centuries, gradually became "governmentalized."

In elaborating these themes Foucault, clearly, is concentrating his analytical energies on understanding the *pluralized* forms of government, its *complexity*, and its *techniques*. Our modernity, he says, is characterized by the governmentalization of the state. He is interested in the question of *how* power is exercised. In outlining the three aspects of governmentality he is implicitly providing a critique of the contemporary tendencies to overvalue the problem of the state and to reduce it to a unity or singularity based on a certain functionality.

David Burchell describes the importance of Foucault's work in this area. He indicates that in Foucault's account classical liberalism occupies a position in relation to a set of discourses about government. This has its beginnings

> both in the "reason of state" (*ragione di stato*) literature of the later Italian renaissance, and in the emergence of the "science of police" (*polizeiwissenschaft*) in seventeenth century Germany. It is here, Foucault argues, that the modern art of governmental reasoning emerges, out of a series of doctrines which insist that the exercise of state authority has its own distinctive form of internal political reason (reason of state), and that this reason can be turned into a kind of science (police) (1997, 375).

Burchell indicates the way in which liberalism in Foucault's accounts stands in ambiguous relation to this literature and tradition; it is both heir and critique. Here the notion of economy enters into political science in two ways. On the one hand it speaks of a form of government informed by the precepts of political economy. On the other, it speaks of a government concerned to economize its own efforts and costs, where government has become its own problem. It is in the latter sense, established as a distinctively modern form or style of government by Adam Smith, that we can speak properly of the *critique of state reason*.

By neo-Foucauldian we are referring here mainly to the British/Austra-
lian neo-Foucauldians (for example, Gordon 1991; Burchell 1993; Rose
1993), as distinct from both the French and U.S. neo-Foucauldians, and
as exemplified in a recent edited collection called *Foucault and Political
Reason* (Barry et al. 1996).[3] This approach centers on Foucault's concept of governmentality as a means of mapping the history of the present
and understands the rationality of government as both permitting and
requiring the practice of freedom of its subjects. In other words, government in this sense only becomes possible at the point at which policing
and administration stops, at the point at which the relations between
government and self-government coincide and coalesce. As Barry and
colleagues argue, in this sense, the emphasis is centered upon "the extent
to which freedom has become, in our so-called 'free societies', a resource
for, and not merely a hindrance to, government" (1996, 8).

In this context it is interesting to survey the reasons advanced by Gordon (1996, 263) for the very limited British "reception" of Foucault, especially by a Left political culture that saw in Foucault not only a pronounced aversion to theorizing the state per se, but, more so, "an
unwillingness to take the side of society against the State." Foucault's
English-speaking contemporaries, such as the social historian E. P.
Thompson and the literary theorist Raymond Williams, who thought of
themselves as Gramscian "organic intellectuals," saw their task as preserving or reconstructing a democratic common culture. Foucault, by
contrast, openly displayed a "mistrust of the social bond" in his work,
which indicated "a clear refusal . . . to recognize in civil society—as defined by Left or Right—a principle of good opposable to the evil of the
State" (ibid.). Gordon provided a genealogy of the British neo-Foucauldians:
Jacques Donzelot, Robert Castel, Pasquale Pasquino, and others of
Foucault's friends, once their work was translated in the late 1970s, offered to a small group on the British Left a new critical approach to "the
social," which was both different and more powerful than neo-Marxist
theories of ideology. By "the social" Gordon meant the twentieth century
development of the welfare state. "These analyses," he noted, "made
possible a reading of the 'social' as the terrain, the objective and even the
invention of a series of governmental techniques and knowledges" (Gordon
1996, 264).[4]

Building on this reinterpretation of political subjectivity and the importance of individual autonomy, choice, and action for liberal governance,
the neo-Foucauldian approach also follows Foucault in charting at the
molecular level of institutions the exercise of power in the overlap and

interpenetration of techniques of domination and technologies of the self. Such an analysis decenters a preoccupation with the state per se to refocus our attention on arteries and tributaries of the positive exercise of power by the state through the disciplines and the institutions that comprise "society." Thus, there develops in this analysis an understanding of the technical in relation to politics—for example, of systems of expertise—that discursively shape society into an object of government. In relation to Nikolas Rose's (1996) essay, Barry and colleagues remarked on the importance of the opportunities for governing at a distance through forms of expertise that do not assume an overt repression or coercion:

> Of key importance to neoliberalism, for example, is the development of techniques of auditing, accounting and management that enable a "market" for public services to be established autonomously from central control. Neoliberalism, in these terms, involves less a retreat from government "intervention" than a re-inscription of the techniques and forms of expertise required for the exercise of government (Barry et al. 1996, 14).

We can understand more of the distinctiveness of the neo-Foucauldian approach to liberalism by contrasting it with two alternative contemporary approaches. It can be contrasted, on the one hand, with Stuart Hall's neo-Gramscian approach to Thatcherism as ideology and, on the other, with Habermas's variant of the Frankfurt School's understanding of technocratic reason. Although these are not, of course, global or comprehensive comparisons, they demonstrate important differences in orientation.

According to the editors of Barry and colleagues, by recasting Thatcherism in ideological terms Hall is prevented from understanding, technically, the advances in the art of government represented by Thatcherism. They argue: "Above all, it is a mistake to see neoliberalism as simply a negative political response to the welfarism or corporatism of previous decades" (Barry et al. 1996, 11). From this standpoint, Hall's approach smacks of a reductive and reactive logic and fails to comprehend the way in which a so-called retreat from the state can be construed as a regovernmentalization through other means.

The argument from Habermas and the Frankfurt School has taught us to view technocratic reason as emanating outside civil society—as part of the state—and as being directed at its citizens for purposes of social control and administration. Habermas talks of technocratic reason and the scientization of politics in terms of the increasing administration of society as a whole and the colonization of the life-world. Against this view, the neo-Foucauldian approach refuses a view of the technical and technocratic reason as something purely negative that necessarily originates from an outside source that is then applied to us in a coercive fashion. Instead, technical reason is seen as a practice we engage in willingly in the process of producing ourselves as "free" subjects of a certain kind.

Liberalism as a Critique of State Reason

Gordon (1991, 15) argues that, given a Foucauldian interpretation, classical liberalism can be characterized in Kantian terms as a *critique of state reason*. By this he meant that liberalism is essentially a political doctrine concerning the limits of the state. In terms of this interpretation of the doctrine, the limits of government are intrinsically related to the limits of state reason: that is, to its power to know. In its modern sense, the art of government, considered broadly as the administration of a population inhabiting a territory, depends on its knowledge of that territory and its inhabitants that is made possible by the new sciences of statistics and management (see, for example, Hacking 1991).

An important part of this interpretation of liberalism assumes the freedom of the individual, for power is defined precisely in relation to the freedom of the individual to act. Gordon provides the following succinct elaboration:

> Foucault does seem to have been (at least) intrigued by the properties of liberalism as a form of knowledge calculated to limit power by persuading government of its own incapacity; by the notion of the rule of law as the architecture of a pluralist social space; and by the German neoliberals' way of conceiving the social market as a game of freedom sustained by government artifice and invention (1991, 47).

In this view, the intellectual history of the *problem-space* of liberal government is a history of the acknowledgment and successive interpretation of the unknowability for "man" or the sovereign of the totality: the economy as a whole or society as a whole. Foucault emphasizes the rule of law in liberal thought as a technical form of government designed to establish conditions of security for which individual liberty is a necessary condition. Such liberty, then, is seen not only as the means to secure the rights of individuals against the abuses of the sovereign but also as a central defining characteristic of governmental rationality itself, for it ensures the participation of the governed in the establishment of a system of law that is a necessary precondition for a governed economy.

Gordon traces three versions of neoliberalism that were given some attention by Foucault in his course of lectures at the Collège de France during 1979. He mentioned the versions of neoliberalism that took root in postwar West Germany (*Ordoliberalen*), the United States (the Chicago School), and France. These new forms do not represent an innocent return to liberalism's main articles of faith. In other words, the historical revival of liberalism in the present is not simply an exercise in nostalgia, that represents a simple and naive return to past principles. There are major differences between past and present forms of liberalism: Neoliberalism, in other words, displays an innovative interpretative strategy in restyling basic principles to accommodate new exigencies. What they have in common, as Burchell claims, "is a question concerning the extent to which competitive, optimizing market relations and behaviour can serve as a principle not only for limiting governmental intervention, but also for rationalizing government itself" (1993, 270).

Gordon attributes to *Ordoliberalen* the capacity to generate new meanings to the market considered as a form of governmentality. He emphasizes, for instance, that under this form of neoliberal governmentality the market is no longer thought of as a natural or spontaneous institution, contra Hayek.[5] Rather the market is seen as an evolving social construct that must be protected and that requires, therefore, a positive institutional and juridical framework for the game of enterprise to function fully. As Burchell clearly indicates, forms of neoliberalism differ from earlier forms of liberalism:

> [T]hey do not regard the market as an already existing quasi-natural reality situated in a kind of economic reserve in a space marked off, secured and supervised by the State. Rather, the market exists, and can only exist, under certain political, legal and institutional conditions that must be actively constructed by government (1993: 270–71).

For early liberalism the limitation of government was tied to the rationality of the free conduct of governed individuals themselves. For neoliberalism, by contrast, "the rational principle for regulating and limiting governmental activity must be determined by reference to *artificially* arranged or contrived forms of the free, *entrepreneurial* and *competitive* conduct of economic-rational individuals" (Burchell 1993, 271). Burchell depicts neoliberalism, following the work of Donzelot, as promoting "an *autonomization* of society through the invention and proliferation of new quasi-economic models of action for the independent conduct of its activities." He concludes by suggesting that "the generalization of an 'enterprise form' to *all* forms of conduct . . . constitutes the essential characteristic of this style of government: the promotion of an enterprise culture" (Burchell 1993, 274–75).

As Gordon (1991, 42) comments, the major problem for *Ordoliberalen* "is not the anti-social effects of the economic market, but the anti-competitive effects of society." All three versions of neoliberalism to which Gordon refers are, to a greater or lesser extent, committed to institutionalizing the game of enterprise as a generalized principle for the organization of society as a whole. In all versions this feature is seen to take the form of a kind of individualism that involves fashioning one's life as the enterprise of oneself: the individual becomes, as Gordon notes, "the entrepreneur of himself or herself" (44). This notion is traced in terms of the French version's emphasis on the care of the self, especially in relation to the right to permanent retraining. It also surfaces in the United States in the human capital interpretation of work, by which work is construed in terms of two components, a genetic endowment and an acquired set of aptitudes that are produced as a result of private investment in education and the like.

Gordon views the human capital interpretation of work as the most radical because it proposes "a global redescription of the social as a form of the economic." His interpretation is worth quoting at some length:

> This operation works by a progressive enlargement of the territory of economic theory by a series of redefinitions of its object, starting out from the neo-classical formula that economics concerns the study of all behaviors involving the allocation of scarce resources to alternative ends. Now it is proposed that economics concerns *all purposive conduct* entailing strategic choice between alternative paths, means and instruments; or yet more broadly, all rational conduct (including rational thought, as a variety of rational conduct); or again, finally, all conduct, rational or irrational, which responds to its environment in a non-random fashion or "recognizes reality" (1991, 43).

This progressive enlargement is based on the behavioral postulate known as *homo economicus*: the modern rediscovery of the main tenant of classical liberal economics, that people should be treated as rational utility maximizers in all of their behavior. In other words, individuals are modeled as seeking to further their own interests (defined in terms of measured net wealth positions) in politics as in other aspects of behavior.

On this basis, neoliberal governments have argued for a minimal state that has been confined to the determination of individual rights construed in consumerist terms and for the maximum exposure of all providers to competition or contestability as a means of minimizing monopoly power and maximizing consumer influence on the quality and type of services provided. Neoliberalism depends on the development of a set of practices of self-government whereby the individual learns to refashion himself or herself as the entrepreneur of oneself—the "enterprising self"—and so learns the fiduciary art of restyling the self through various forms of personal investment and insurance in a range of welfare fields—health, education, retraining—that are necessary both as a safeguard against risk but also as the preconditions for participation in the competitive society.

The Neoliberal Governance of Welfare and Education

The prevalence of the doctrine of the self-limiting state in many Western states, including Aotearoa/New Zealand, has manifested itself in terms of neoliberal welfare and education policies through an intensification of moral regulation rather than through an overall reduction of levels of welfare and education spending in real terms. Without doubt, in Aotearoa/New Zealand the reduction of the state's trading activities, through privatization programs and the "downsizing" of the public sector, has decreased its power to mediate in the market to achieve the traditional welfare goal of full employment or of equality of opportunity in education.

There is a paradox here. At precisely the point when neoliberals are attempting conceptually to remoralize the link between welfare and employment and to "responsibilize" the individual for investing in education, neoliberal governments have dismantled arrangements for state arbitration in the labor market, substituting an individualized employment contract, and some neoliberal states show signs of moving away from the concept of the minimum wage. This policy move must be mapped against the growth of a permanent underclass, of those who are structurally disadvantaged in terms of access to an increasingly specialized and highly segmented labor market. Intergenerational unemployment now seems an entrenched feature of most western states, with both a femininization and a casualization of the labor force and, often, high rates of youth unemployment, especially in rural areas. Many commentators have discussed the potential deskilling effects of the new information technologies and the redundancy of the unskilled, the semiskilled, and manual laborers in face of greater computerization and autonomization of work.

At the same time, in Aotearoa/New Zealand there has been a cumulative shift in the tax burden away from corporations toward individual wage-earners. Indirect forms of taxation (such as a goods and services tax) and the flat tax structure introduced by some OECD (Organization for Economic Cooperation and Development) countries have ended up favoring corporations and high-income groups at the expense of low- to middle-income groups. The shift to indirect forms, particularly consumer taxes, is seen by policymakers as a way to retain revenue levels in face of an aging population and labor force. This move has both politicized and encouraged political support among different constituencies, notably among middle-income earners, for policies designed to reduce levels of income tax—in fact, more broadly, for viewing a high income-tax level as undue state interference—in exchange for a privatized welfare system in which individuals, through user charges, vouchers, and forms of personal insurance, are forced to take care of themselves.

The state has only been able to begin the process of writing itself out of its traditional responsibilities concerning the welfare state through twin strategies of a greater individualization of society and the responsibilization of individuals and families. Both are often simultaneously achieved through a greater contractualization of society, and particularly by contracting-out state services.

A genealogy of the entrepreneurial self reveals that it is the relationship, promoted by neoliberalism, that one establishes to oneself through forms of personal investment (for example, user charges, student loans) and insurance that becomes the central ethical component of a new individualized and privatized consumer welfare economy. In this novel form of governance, responsibilized individuals are called upon to apply certain management, economic, and actuarial techniques to themselves as subjects of a newly privatized welfare regime.

In this context Burchell's remark that an "enterprise form" is generalized to all forms of conduct and constitutes the distinguishing mark of the style of government, could not be more apt (1993, 275). At one and the same time enterprise and enterprise culture provide the means for analysis and the prescription for change: Education and training are key sectors in promoting national economic competitive advantage and future national prosperity. They are seen increasingly as the passport for welfare recipients to make the transition from dependent, passive welfare consumer to an entrepreneurial self.

In the past, so the neoliberal argument goes, too much emphasis has been placed on social and cultural objectives and insufficient emphasis has been placed on economic goals in education systems. Henceforth, the prescription is for greater investment in education and training as a basis for future economic growth. Such investment in human skills is underwritten by theories of human capital development and human resources management. The major difference from previous welfare state regimes is that education, increasingly at all levels but more so at the level of tertiary education, is no longer driven by public investment but, rather, by *private* investment decisions. The uptake of education and training grants by able-bodied welfare recipients, especially women who are single parents, now becomes mandatory after a given period within countries where neoliberal policies have been adopted, in what some see as a shift from a welfare state to a Schumpetarian workfare state.

The rigidity of the distinction between the private and the public has broken down: commercial and private enterprises exist within or in partnership with many "public" education institutions. Human capital theory is rejuvenated in a privatized rather than statist or public form. The neoliberal state has worked to make individual choice in the tertiary education market the overriding operative principle: Its aim has been to increase diversity—a prerequisite for choice—by abolishing the differences in the missions of the various institutions comprising the tertiary sector and to move to a fully consumer-driven system in which state funding is distributed to individual students by way of entitlements or vouchers rather than to the institutions or "providers" themselves.

Under neoliberalism, questions of national economic survival and competition in the world economy have come increasingly to be seen as questions of cultural reconstruction. The task of reconstructing culture in terms of enterprise has involved remodeling public institutions along commercial lines as corporations and has encouraged the acquisition and use of so-called entrepreneurial qualities. Thus, and in accordance with this new discourse, both the welfare state and education systems have been criticized for leading to a "culture of dependency."

It is against this general background that neoliberal states have abandoned the traditional goals of the universalist welfare state of equality and participation based on social rights in favor of a reduced conception of a "modest safety net" based on targeting social assistance and institutionalizing user charges for social services. In addition, in some OECD countries there have been substantial cuts in welfare benefits, a tightening of eligibility criteria, the introduction of means testing, and a shift toward an increase in policing and surveillance by the state through the development of new information systems to reduce benefit fraud.

This process has been referred to as the emergence of a "shadow" state: the privatization of welfare through contestability of funding and the contracting out of welfare provision to the nongovernmental informal sector comprised of church-based groups, charity organizations, private foundations, and trusts which, increasingly, minister to the "poor" and the "disadvantaged" according to set criteria and performance targets.

Above all, the theme of "responsibilizing the self," a process at once economic and moral, is concomitant with a new tendency to "invest" in the self at crucial points in the life cycle and symbolizes the shift in the regime and governance of welfare under neoliberalism. Risk and responsibility have been thematized in new ways. There has been a shift from a disciplinary technology of power, first, to welfarism—to programs of *social* security as governmentalized risk-management and to new forms of actuarial or insurance-based rationalities—and, second, to new forms of prudentialism (a *privatized* actuarialism) where risk management is forced back onto individuals and satisfied through the market. O'Malley comments, "Within such prudential strategies, then calculative self-interest is articulated with actuarialism to generate risk management as an everyday practice of the self" (1996, 200). The duty to the self—its simultaneous responsibilization as a moral agent and its construction as a calculative rational choice actor—becomes the basis for a series of investment decisions concerning one's health, education, security, employability, and retirement.

The responsibilization of the self and its associated new prudential strategies go hand in hand with two related developments: a substitution of "community" for "society" and the invention of new strategies for government through information (see Figure 1). The first development is significant because it implicitly recognizes a theoretical weakness in the strict neoliberal model of social policy based upon the market alone. Although they do not want to reinvent society (as government has been "reinvented"), neoliberals want to substitute some notion of civil society for the welfare state under the metaphor of community, where civil society means an association of free individuals based on self-rule.[6]

The second line of development issues from the new opportunities for state surveillance and control that accompany the growth of information and communications technologies. In one sense, this can be seen as "government without enclosures" or "government within an open system" (see Deleuze 1995), which promotes more intensified visibility of both private and public spaces than ever before. Such unprecedented high levels of visibility are established through the new security and policing uses to which the video camera has been put in streets, malls, security systems within buildings, and the like and the advent of computerized citizen data, in the forms of "information sharing" across separate government departments and the development of so-called smart card technology for specific purposes (for example, welfare recipients) or for more general "governmental" purposes (for example, New Zealand's community card). Information sharing and the application of new smart card technology have been applied to welfare "problems" of benefit fraud and state calculation of welfare benefits and entitlements.[7]

This movement toward greater control under the theme of responsibilization of self is also seen in a new customized relation (a niche-market welfare) promoted between welfare officers who handle caseloads and recipients. This involves risk-based targeting of services and the shift from an emphasis on a relationship based on professional authority (therapist, counselor, etc.), to an emphasis on self-empowerment and self-help based on training, education, and the development of "personal skills." Increasingly, government strategies signal a shift in orientation from welfare to well-being through the promotion of self-reliance involving market-like incentives in the redefinition of benefit regimes and governmentality associated with forms of "investment" in at-risk children and families.[8]

Neoliberalism represents a continuing critique of state reason; its governance of welfare consists of some strategic innovations in reconceptualizing the exercise of power, most notably the ideas of the responsibilization of self effected through a series of market-like arrangements. These new arrangements provide an increasingly accepted social recipe for individualizing the social by substituting notions of civil society, social capital or community for state. At the same time, however, they carry the combined dangers, on the one hand, of pathologizing and stigmatizing those who are structurally excluded from the labor market, and on the other, of weighing down with debt—of prematurely mortgaging the future lives of—the next generation. The full social consequences of instituting a neoliberal welfare system that individualizes and privatizes current welfare and education by deferring payment to the next generation via loans, user charges, forms of self-investment, and insurance schemes are yet to be investigated.

The Rise of "Enterprise Culture" in Britain and Aotearoa/New Zealand

A notable feature of the early 1990s was the way in which the emphasis on the introduction of the new technologies has given way to a more general discourse that represents issues of economic and institutional reform in cultural terms (Keat and Abercrombie, 1991). In the case of Britain, questions of national economic survival and competition in the world economy came increasingly to be seen under the Conservative governments of Margaret Thatcher and John Major as questions of *cultural* reconstruction. According to Keat and Abercrombie, the idea of an enterprise culture "emerged as a central motif in the political thought and practice of the . . . government" (1991, 1). The task of constructing such a culture has involved remodeling institutions along commercial lines and encouraging the acquisition and use of enterprising qualities. Keat and Abercrombie see the ideological function of the political rhetoric of enterprise as a particular interpretation for making sense of the kind of economic and cultural changes that have been described under the banners of postindustrialism, the information society, postmodernism, and post Fordism. Morris traces the genesis and development of the concept of enterprise from its beginnings in the thinking of the Centre for Policy Studies in the link between Christianity and the "new Conservatism" and in the work of Lord Young. He distinguishes three phases, the latest of which he christens "partnership in cultural engineering." This phase, which represents a massive cultural reconstruction, has concerned policies involving "unprecedented government intervention in education (at all levels)" (1991, 34–35).

By contrast Schwengel provides a snapshot of a more liberal German concept than the British emphasis on enterprise. *Kulturgesellschaft* has a softer focus, containing a utopian element that also attempts to provide "a framework for cultural change beyond corporatist state regulation" (1991, 42). The emphasis on cultural solutions to the problems of the 1990s is worth mentioning here. *Kulturgesellschaft* is based on "promoting direct and early interaction between economy and culture" (42). Unlike enterprise culture it relies on public sector leadership. Schwengel comments:

> Kulturgesellschaft seems to mark a middle way between the "soft" debate on aesthetic modernism and postmodernism, and the "hard" debate on internationalist post Fordist competition in the world market, ecological crisis and the dramatic risks of a class war between the north and the south (1991, 139).

Hence, the emerging German solution also centers on a cultural answer to the issues of rapid technological change and the structural dominance of the service sector. It is, however, less directly ideological and gives more space to the public sector. In an illuminating passage, Schwengel writes:

> We may have a post Fordist theory of production, technology and consumption; we may understand the change from organized capitalism to disorganized institu-

tions of regulation; we may understand the transformation of modernist texture into post modernist figuration. But we have no alternative, political symbolic center as a necessary fiction. A new theory of modernization, which will be one of the most decisive intellectual battlefields between the right and the left in the 1990s, has explicitly to conceptualize the difference between social moderniza- tion and political modernity. The discourses of enterprise culture and Kulturgesellschaft are already providing arguments for both sides (1991, 148).

These debates have become important in Aotearoa/New Zealand. The Porter Project (Crocombe et al. 1991), for instance, focused very clearly on the notion of enterprise culture and the way in which the remolding of the education system is necessary to this end. The minister of education also picked up on this theme, commenting on the way "imperatives of the modern world require a new culture of enterprise and competition in our curriculum" (Smith 1991b, 8). In the New Zealand context this kind of rhetoric has, to a large extent, both grown out of and been supplemented by a Treasury driven emphasis on notions of consumer sovereignty and contestability. The concept of consumer sovereignty provides a particular interpretation of the link between subjectivist theories of values and the market that does not respect the integrity of cultural practices in the public domain. Keat makes the following apposite remark:

> The judgments made by democratic citizens are not regarded, at least in theory, as mere expression of personal preferences, but as resulting from a certain kind of critical engagement with the issues involved in the political sphere. But this is something that requires the acquisition and exercise of a number of skills and capacities, and hence also the availability of a wide range of cultural resources that provide, as it were, the necessary basis for relevant forms of "educative experience." There is thus a crucial role for certain cultural practices in contribut- ing to this process, whose significance is itself at odds with any purely subjective theory of values (1991, 228–29).

Enterprise Culture and the Enterprise Curriculum

Education is one of the newest starships in the New Zealand government's policy fleet. The choice of metaphor is not entirely frivolous, as the fol- lowing quote from Dr. Lockwood Smith, a recent minister of education reveals:

> We can either be slaves of technology, with high unemployment and foreigners providing us with our technological products and services, or we can adapt and face the future with confidence. This is not Star Trek stuff; this is New Zealand over the next three to four years (Smith 1992).

Education thus conceived symbolizes an optimistic future based on the increasing importance of science and technology as the engine of economic growth and the means by which New Zealand can successfully compete in the global economy in years to come. The metaphor also captures and updates the past popular iconography that surrounded an ideology which motivated U.S. educational reformers in the 1960s during the Sputnik catch-up-with-the-Russians debate, the Star Wars scenario of the 1980s, and the more recent Japanese threat to American enterprise. In the era of the "new world order," of structural adjustment policies, of international and regional trade agreements, and of IMF (International Monetary Fund) billion-dollar rescue packages for embattled Asian economies—the focus has shifted away from exploiting fears of imminent destruction in superpower rivalry to the role that education, in conjunction with the new information, computer and communicational technologies, can play in the game of increasing national competitive advantage. The emphasis on possible economic decline in face of international competition and the need to "catch up" with other nations now occupies center ground.

Such a discourse is perhaps less naive, optimistic, and forthright than it once was, given the uncertainty of the prospect for continuous economic growth, of its ecological sustainability, and of its democratic potential for redistributing wealth. Yet it is also both more strategic and effective. The dominance of New Right ideology of the Treasury and the Business Roundtable in the thinking of successive governments in Aotearoa/New Zealand has led to the establishment of the "unprotected" open economy based on the neoliberal paradigm of globalization (as world economic integration), and the abolition of all internal subsidies and external tariffs. Alongside economic globalization, there has been a massive state asset sales program, a wholesale restructuring of the core public sector that has led to the privatization of health and commercialization of education and state housing. In conjunction with these policies there has been, more broadly considered, a deliberate and sustained attempt at cultural reconstruction. At the heart of this attempt is the notion of enterprise culture and the importance of reconstructing education so that it will deliver the necessary research, skills and attitudes required for New Zealand to compete in an increasingly competitive international economy.

The notion of enterprise culture, designed for a postindustrial, information economy of the 1990s, can be seen in poststructuralist terms as the creation of a new metanarrative—a totalizing and unifying story about the prospect of economic growth and development based on the triumvirate of science, technology, and education. This master narrative, which projects a national ideological vision, differs from the social democratic narrative: It does not adopt the language of equality of opportunity and it does not attempt to redress power imbalances or socio-economic inequalities. The new neoliberal metanarrative is based on a vision of the future: one sustained by "excellence," by "technological literacy," by "skills training," by "performance," and by "enterprise."

The code words "enterprise" and "enterprise culture" are major signifiers in this new discourse, which emphasizes that there has been too much emphasis on social and cultural objectives and insufficient emphasis on economic goals in our education system. Henceforth, we must invest heavily in education as a basis for future economic growth by redesigning the system so that it meets the needs of business and industry. The curriculum must also be redesigned to reflect the new realities and the need for the highly skilled flexible worker who possesses requisite skills in management, information handling, communication, problem solving, and decision making. As the metanarrative has grown it has also been transformed to encompass a new emphasis on regional educational standards, portability and transferability of qualifications, performance management of teachers, systems of national testing, and so on.

The sources of the metanarrative, although international in inspiration, have been domesticated for the local scene: the Porter Project *Upgrading New Zealand's Competitive Advantage* (Crocombe et al. 1991), which is informed by Michael Porter's (Harvard Business School) theory of international trade; the notion of enterprise culture as it developed through various phases in Britain under the Thatcher and Major Conservative governments; OECD publications on the new technologies and human resources development; and, more widely, elements of the burgeoning literature on postindustrialism and the new global information economy. Local initiatives have included: the creation of an Enterprise Unit in the Prime Minister's Department and the setting up of the Enterprise Council by Mr. Bolger, the immediate past Prime Minister; the organization by the New Zealand Employers' Federation of a Schools Industry Links Development Board; the Young Persons' Enterprise Scheme operated by the Enterprise New Zealand Trust; and, the Enterprise and Education for Enterprise Conferences held in 1992.

The move to establish an enterprise society in Aotearoa/New Zealand came with the National government's 1991 budget. In her budget speech, Ruth Richardson, the minister of finance at the time, focused clearly on "A Strategy for Enterprise" based on three objectives: the reform of the labor market; the redesigning of the welfare state; and the management of fiscal problems. The first was supposedly accomplished under the Employment Contracts Act (1991), an anti-socialist piece of legislation that effectively dismantled the system of industrial relations based on arbitration, conciliation, and collective bargaining that had been built up over many years. The second involved the move from universalistic premises to the targeting of social assistance and reduced levels of social spending. The third, heavily dependent on the second, focused on reducing the external deficit.

Underlying the budget and the government's enterprise strategy was an explicit assumption that our education and welfare systems have failed us (Richardson 1991, 20, 26): They have allegedly created a "culture of dependency." At the broadest philosophical level the neoliberal answer to these problems was to develop an enterprise culture based on a form of individualism that promots concepts of choice and greater self responsibility. Education was deemed to be "a key investment in our economic future" and the government was committed to providing "an environment that enables businesses and individuals to develop internationally competitive and innovative skills" (20). In this context much is made of student loans, investment in research and development, the reorganization of public sector research, and initiatives to support a more competitive private sector. Government spending at that time was redirected "towards areas important for longer-term economic growth and security, including: larger commitments to investments in *education*, *skills* and *research and development*" (Richardson 1991, 41; emphasis in the original).

The education policy document entitled *Investing in People: Our Greatest Asset* (Smith 1991b) reiterated these claims. The foreword, by the minister of education, began with the assertion that the government came to office with a clear policy "to enhance educational achievement and skill development to meet the needs of the highly competitive, modern global economy." It continued by noting that

> [s]tudies, like the Porter Project, questioned the relevance of our current curriculum with its excessive focus on social issues and poor preparation for the competitive world. It confirmed other recent studies that show inadequate skilling in technology compared with other qualifications (Smith 1991b).

The Prime Minister convened a one day conference in February 1992 "to bring together leaders in education and industry to forge a vision of how these two sectors can better work together to upgrade the New Zealand economy." The three key themes to emerge from the submissions, as analyzed by the Ministry, included the need for

- processes to improve business sector input into the development and implementation of education policy at national and local level;
- mechanisms to encourage and coordinate business-education partnership activity at national and local level; and
- processes to enable the business sector to identify medium- and long-term skills needs for education and training purposes.

There was, however, also a number of prominent themes that emerged around the notion of enterprise culture: the need for business to have a greater say in curriculum formation; suggestions for changes in the processes of teacher training and recruitment to reflect better the world of commerce and business; a variety of proposals for business-education partnerships and better representation of business in tertiary sector decision making. There was an emphasis on performance output measurement of the tertiary sector in terms of more relevant economic criteria, an opening up of the education system to greater competition, and support for total quality management in tertiary institutions. Finally, there was a perceived need for a greater role for government in identifying medium- and long-term skill requirements, the promotion of targets for educational achievement, the creation of educational incentives to support business enterprise development, and review of educational funding to improve accountability or to promote economic growth-related outputs by institutions.

As might be expected at a conference of this nature, no one seriously questioned the appropriateness of business as a model of enterprise for education. There was very little discussion of the notion of enterprise at all, other than in terms of creating closer links between industry and education or modeling education on businesses. This blanket assumption is questionable in the extreme, for several reasons. It promotes the simplistic view that business is enterprising by definition and that education is not. The assumption is erroneous because it assimilates all enterprise in business or industry to one type, yet the reality of the situation is that within the New Zealand business sector there is probably a range of different types of enterprise: some good and some bad, some involve high risk and some do not, some involve sound management practice and some do not, some based on teamwork and some entirely individualistic, some based on a single talent or skill and some based on the right mix of skills, etc.

In other words, the question of what elements make for the successful firm or business is an open one that permits a variety of answers such that none can be legislated upon or generalized. What meaning does the question How enterprising is New Zealand business? really have? Is it possible to ask this question of governments? Does the blanket assumption mean that there is no such thing as enterprise in nonprofit organizations? If we accept that the notion of enterprise is not confined to business that is judged purely in terms of short-term monetary gain, then we might want to recognize other kinds of enterprise that will admit of notions of initiative, sustainable practices or simply of survival in the crudest sense. If it is the case that enterprise is to be defined as business, pure and simple, then the conference should be seen in transparent ideological terms and educators should vigorously resist the notion and its intrusion into education. The notion of enterprise culture can have a number of ideological interpretations; some might be enabling for education, others are pernicious. We must begin to sort out the former from the latter. In the background notes to the conference provided by the Ministry of Education, the following cited statement is found under the section "Objectives in Education":

> A four-year study of ten important world trading nations found that "education and training are decisive in national competitive advantage. . . . In every nation, those industries that were most competitive were often those whose specialized investment in education and training had been unusually great" (Porter 1990, 87).

The comparative analysis of nations, in terms of their education systems, might reveal how meaningless this statement is, and how such comparisons are never innocent or neutral. It might also reveal the empty, ideological nature of a statement that does not take into account very different education and training regimes that characterize the world's most successful economies (see Dale 1991). Education may, indeed, be the starship of the future. It may, intelligently conceived, become the basis of the so-called new economy that provides the requisite skills, abilities, understandings and attitudes necessary for a postindustrial, global, information-based society. Yet the notion of enterprise culture as it has been so far presented will not provide educators or the business sector with either the promise or the policy tools to achieve this new future.

An alternative agenda for pursuing a notion of enterprise culture that is more in line with a conception of social democracy might begin in a more grounded way with the study of the types of enterprise that presently exist. It might turn to focus back on the business sector to elucidate those models of enterprise that currently best service the needs of society and economy in New Zealand by increasing both the level of participation and the welfare of workers through collaborative decision making and profit sharing. In other words, enterprise culture could, alternatively, become an agenda contra the Employment Contracts Act for establishing the conditions necessary for a postindustrial democracy. It might identify how such models operate in different areas of the economy, in small- and large-scale concerns, in new and older industries. Only when educationists and the public more generally can see the benefits of enterprise culture in this way might the notion merit some further and serious consideration. As it is, the notion of enterprise culture has been construed in the narrowest economic sense. It has become part and parcel of a new metanarrative which, in rhetorical terms, presents us with a vision of the future based on a story of the prospect of economic growth. This story, although it gives education pride of place alongside science and technology, reflects the New Right's "creative" appropriation of the postindustrial literature. In essence, the discourse can be seen more as a postindustrialism of reaction than one that explores the social democratic possibilities inherent in postindustrialism.

Notes

1. This chapter is a companion to "Neoliberalism, Welfare Dependency and the Moral Construction of Poverty in New Zealand," *New Zealand Journal of Sociology* 12, no. 1 (1997), 1–34.

2. For an account of Foucault's notion of governmentality, especially in relation to education, see Peters (1994). The first section of the present essay draws on some material from that previously published work. This chapter concentrates on the uses to which Foucault's original notion has since been put.

3. This suggestion comes from Alan Hunt. The chapter draws strongly on his characterization of liberalism and neoliberalism that was advanced in a series of three seminars given at the University of Auckland in May 1996. Besides the editors themselves, the collection edited by Barry, Osborne, and Rose (1996), includes the following contributors: Barry Hindess, Vikki Bell, Ian Hunter, Alan Hunt, Pat O'Malley, Mitchell Dean, and Barbara Cruikshank. (See also Dean 1991; Hindess 1996; Hunter 1994; Hunt and Wickham 1994; Rose 1996). The Anglophone neo-Foucauldians might be distinguished from the French (e.g., Donzelot 1979), and the U.S. neo-Foucauldians. They may also be distinguished from various feminist appropriations of Foucault, which are both too diverse and complex for us to outline here.

4. Gordon (1996, 264) also notes the orthodox Left's criticisms of Foucault, in particular, his lack of a theory of the subject and, therefore, lack of an effective set of strategies of resistance. Both criticisms are often seen as reflecting his Nietzschean "perspectivism" or "relativism." We believe both criticisms are misplaced (see Peters 1997).

5. Although Hayek has been considered as one of the main sources of inspiration for the so-called New Right, he clearly is to be distinguished from the three variants of neoliberalism identified above. Hayek emphasizes, in an *antirational* approach, that many of the institutions that characterize society have arisen and function without design: "[T]he spontaneous collaboration of free men often creates things which are the greater than their individual minds can ever fully comprehend" (Hayek 1949, 70). This is Hayek's celebrated conception of spontaneous order, a reinterpretation of the invisible hand hypothesis, and is used to explain and legitimate the market as the paradigm social institution—allegedly, "a system under which bad men can do least harm." It is from this basic perspective on what Hayek calls "true individualism" that he derives both his defense of private property and the notion of the minimal state. The general principle of private property is to be understood as the endeavor "to make man by the pursuit of his interests contribute as much as possible to the needs of other men." The minimal state is a consequence of the "demand for a strict limitation of all coercive or exclusive power" (Hayek 1949, 16). Hayek effectively summarizes his view of the state thus:

[T]he state, the embodiment of deliberately organized and consciously directed power, ought to be only a small part of the much richer organism which we call "society" and . . . the former ought to provide merely a framework within which free . . . collaboration of men has the maximum of scope (1949, 22).

According to Hayek, the market establishes a workable individualist order because it ensures that the individual's remunerations correspond to the objective results of his or her efforts and of their value to others. The individual, therefore, must be free to choose and it is "inevitable" that he or she must bear the risk attached to their choices, for in consequence he or she is rewarded not according to the goodness or badness of their intentions but solely on the basis of the value of the results to others. Thus, the preservation of individual freedom, in Hayek's view, is incompatible with the notion of distributive justice and, in general, with the notion of equality as it has been progressively interpreted over the period of the development of the welfare state. In other words, the notion of individual freedom subscribed to by Hayek and those who follow him is at odds with the twentieth-century notion of social rights, involving the gradual expansion of citizenship, which served as the basis of the development of the welfare state.

6. On this question see Green, who suggests that "a society of civil associates is based upon three inseparable assumptions: human nature at its best is about assuming personal responsibility for both self-improvement and making the world better for others; people are united not with leadership but when they accept conditions that allow us all to exercise responsibility; and government is understood to be the upholder of these conditions, that is, the conditions for liberty" (1996, vii). See also Peters and Marshall's neo-Foucauldian critique of "community" in their submission to the New Zealand Royal Commission on Social Policy (1988) "Social Policy and the Move to 'Community'," in Peters and Marshall (1996).

7. In the New Zealand context Mark Prebble (1990a and 1990b), a social policy analyst with the Treasury, has headed an investigation of smart-card technology in relation to welfare. See also Henman (1997), who examines the relation between computers and governmentality in Australia's Department of Social Security.

8. This market language of "investment" in at-risk children and families (a monetarist approach to welfare) typifies the approach to welfare in New Zealand (see Department of Social Welfare 1996).

Chapter 2

The Search for Sustainability in Environmental Education[1]

When we observe the precarious advances that have been achieved during the twenty-five year history of environmental education, many questions nag at us. Some are directed toward stringently reexamining the theoretical approximations in vogue which, despite everything, still have not succeeded in clearly defining the parameters in the field of environmental education. This constitutes a challenge that must continue to be explored and debated and that does not entail the pretense of standardizing the pedagogical responses. Still other questions refer to the conditions of the praxis itself and its characteristically low institutional priority.

Nonetheless, we are convinced that the efficiency of the measures to be taken in terms of the quality of their proposals for the target population, their long-term permanence, and their consolidation—that is, that the very sustainability of the field of environmental education—are closely linked to the controversies concerning sustainable development itself. The aim of this chapter is to present a cluster of reflections about how we perceive the field of environmental education with a view toward its sustainability and, more specifically, from the perspective of a developing country.

The Context

Certainly no one can doubt that environmental policy has justified and fortified its international niche during this quarter century. During the World Conservation Congress of the World Conservation Union (IUCN) held in Montreal (October 1996), Canadian Prime Minister Jean Chrétien announced the creation of two new national parks in the Arctic region that together represent a surface area larger than all of Switzerland. This was a praiseworthy decision by the Canadian government that contributes to increasing significantly the world total of protected areas, an attempt to conserve for the future natural spaces representative of the biodiversity of the planet on the part of a nation that possesses 10 percent of the forest resources of the globe and 20 percent of all the fresh water.

Regrettably and invariably, every year an equivalent surface area undergoes desertification in developing countries, according to data from diverse organizations such as the World Resources Institute (WRI), the United Nations Environmental Program (UNEP), the Worldwatch Institute and the like.[2] It can easily be inferred that the degree of deterioration of the environment considerably outstrips the results of measures adopted for its protection. Moreover, in this past quarter century as international concern about the degradation of the planetary environment has come to the fore, the planetary process has not merely reverted, or diminished in its demonstrated rhythms, it has actually suffered an increased rate of degradation. The Canadian government itself is extremely worried about the slow recovery of some fish species, despite a fisheries ban that has already been in effect for two years. This confirms that knowledge about resilience[3] and, in general, knowledge about dynamic ecological processes is far from commanding the precision and predictive capacity that some still believe it has.[4]

We do not, however, embrace a position of neo-Malthusian pessimism. First, we do not consider demographic growth to be the main global problem. That is not to imply, however, that we do not recognize its worrisome dimensions. We believe that the increasing gap between poor and rich is much more serious. Second, pessimism is anti-pedagogic, most of all when it is offered in the terms of those prophets of disaster who cancel out the future.

In industrialized countries ecological pessimism has given rise to a range of postures of diverse ideological-political bent, but which in general terms have been fed by varying doses of a quasi-religious fundamentalism—with which its proponents have claimed to justify restrictive measures against what they consider violations of the rights of other living beings.

Although many restrictive measures are oriented toward industrialization processes and Western life, others are explicitly directed against poverty. Within this controversy poverty is seen from two different perspectives. One perspective considers it the worst of all pollutions (in the sense that it is the cause and consequence of environmental deterioration), recognizes the perverse downward spiral of impoverishment and deterioration to which the dominant styles of development lead, and proposes to attack the structural factors that determine them (CDMAALC 1991).

The other perspective understands poverty only as a cause, placing the main responsibility for the huge environmental deterioration on the very poorest. Here poverty is explained as the direct result of explosive demographic growth (normally explained as an isolated variable), which takes place in the developing countries, and which—according to those who defend these positions—is what hinders them from reaching better levels of well-being.[5] To help developing countries with this problem, family planning programs are fostered under the aegis of new mechanisms subcontracted or organized in order to perform public functions. These have mainly been created by recent political embodiments such as nongovernmental and religious organizations and certain private groups.

Demographic control associated with assistance as a state policy inscribes itself as a form of social Darwinism which has as its point of departure a concept of deficit. Peoples, social classes, ethnic groups, etc. that exceed the acceptable maximum for population growth must be dissuaded in various ways from this behavior, given their manifest inability to do so themselves as their own decision. This view imposes a particular vision of the demographic problem as a universal problem.[6]

On the other hand, we are not convinced either by the techno-economistic optimism of the global free market—as though it truly existed—that promotes solutions without sufficient evidence. The economistic argument that scarce resources will raise prices (thus discouraging their massive use) and its associated technicist plea that the substitution of materials will occur before the collapse of availability of the resources currently used in large-scale productive processes offer no guarantee whatsoever. In the light of the concrete facts of world environmental policy, these last two propositions read like elements of a self-interested discourse that strives to avoid any increases in mandatory restrictions.

Sustainable Development

Sustainable development has appeared as an alternative since it was advocated in 1987 by the report of the World Commission on the Environment and Development (the Brundtland Report), *Our Common Future*. The official concept—satisfying the needs of the present generation without compromising the possibilities of future generations to satisfy theirs—has been subject to various sorts of controversies, related above all to the current asymmetrical distribution of resources and to the timetable, direction, and reach of the processes that have to be set in motion. The majority agrees, however, that this is a proposal that seeks to balance economic growth, environmental protection, and social equity. As might be imagined, this is not such a simple matter. The point of equilibrium among these three components is not only dynamic but varies with differing spatial and temporal circumstances. Moreover, it demands the adoption of global and local policies for which we are not exactly at an optimal moment at present, given recent and current geopolitical readjustments and economic recession.

If we understand sustainable development as "improving the quality of human life while maintaining the carrying capacity of supporting ecosystems" (IUCN 1991, 10)—that is, as emphasizing the ecological components of the problem above the other—then numerous small-scale projects can be reported, based on integrated and "organic" productive processes, usually in rural areas of developing countries.[7] These are very valuable experiences because they attempt to articulate traditional knowledge using gender and community participation approaches. But they do not modify the main stream of development characteristic of the urban areas of industrialization and the concentration of services that set the current pattern of economic processes. Nor do they contribute in ostensible ways to decentering the general principles that rule the international economic-political order.

It would sometimes seem that given the absence in the wealthy countries themselves of the type of proposals "that do work," so widely touted by multinational organizations and nongovernmental organizations (NGOs), a form of sustainable development is being promoted for the rural areas of developing countries based on a concept of quality of life vis-à-vis the sustainable development approach that is advocated for urban areas and developed countries.[8]

Nonetheless, to take up the ideas of Toledo (1996), perhaps what is occurring is that the possibilities for sustainable development really exist only in those enclaves of the planet where Western civilization (urban, industrial, and Eurocentric) has not imposed or has not yet been able to impose and extend its values, practices, enterprises, and actions of modernity and supposed progress. These enclaves coincide with those regions of the globe where contemporary forms of non-Western stock still persist, derived from civilizing processes of a historical character. It is a question of predominantly, though not exclusively rural enclaves in countries such as India, China, Egypt, Indonesia, Peru or México, where the presence of diverse indigenous peoples (farmers and artisans) confirms the presence of different civilizing models distinct from those that originated in Europe.

A discussion of this type could bring us closer to identifying the required conditions for establishing sustainable societies. Is this possible on a global level or does it constitute a proposal which is shown to be feasible only for restricted areas, under conditions such as those described by Toledo?

Proposals exist (Semarnap 1996a, 49–50) that consider the regional dimension as the space par excellence for making sustainability possible. From that standpoint priority regions may be chosen in accordance with criteria of ecological and socio-economic representativity, special public interest, status as a conservation zone because of high biodiversity and the potential for natural resources, the presence of social and nongovernmental organizations, and the availability of studies about the area.

In global terms, and in order to be able to estimate the degree of advancement toward these goals, Semarnap (the Secretariat of Environment, Natural Resources and Fisheries, México) has suggested that concepts about change should integrate the following ideas:

- None of the present development pathways will lead spontaneously to sustainability.
- Nations need to perform an intense social effort in order to change the said pathways directing them toward the creation of sustainability levels.
- All countries, whatever their circumstances are and independent of their level of development, are obliged to display their maximum effort to change. No national circumstance could justify a lack in effort.
- The scope of each national effort must be weighed regarding opportunities and conditions of every country.
- Progress should be made toward more objective methods of recognition and measuring of the effort for change.
- Environmental and natural resources management conditions do not reflect immediately the intensity of the effort for change, since they are usually determined by production processes which have been in place for a long time. Change efforts should emphasize making appropriate changes to causal processes (Semarnap 1996b, 9–10).

The absence of experiences in developed countries or in urban areas of developing countries could be compensated for by modeling studies about the different factors that would have to be modified as a condition for beginning to make the transition toward sustainable development. Even though definitive and conclusive answers cannot be expected here either, such an exercise could at least help us to identify what certainly is not sustainable in those spaces. It seems that in the light of present circumstances we are in a better position to distinguish what is not sustainable from what is.

By this we do not mean to advocate a homogenization of lifestyles that dissolves cultural differences and options, in the way that homogenization is deliberately induced through the globalization of markets and information technology, which both generate new symbolic and cultural balances by propagating a regurgitated form of organization of the totality of the world and its parts.[9] Rather, it is a question of a theoretical and ethico-political problem of the consolidation of standards and maximum levels of aspiration to obtain basic standards of well-being—standards and levels that have been preassigned, according to the terms of the current economic and political geography of globalization.

Economic-political globalization and the exponential technological development of information will generate a phenomenon, the ecological and cultural scope and impacts of which are still not clear[10] and which will contribute simultaneously and paradoxically to resolving some problems and sharpening others (Roszak 1990).

In this regard, three postmodern authors offer us their own visions of the problem. Peter McLaren says that "theories are not simply about different ways of seeing the world, some truer than others, but about individual forms of living" (1993, 44). Gianni Vattimo (1992) affirms that "the images of the world are not simply interpretations of a 'reality' that is a 'given,' but rather constitute the very objectivity of the world" (1992, 9). And finally, Benjamin Arditi (1996) proposes that we have a psychological need to falsify the real as a practical necessity. All knowledge is a falsification of the real, which creates the illusion of being, so that we can rely on a stable foundation. We behave as though it were so. The domestication of the world is a will to power, a will to know, a will to establish a system, to configure an order, to objectify the world: a will to dominate that strives to give form to the world and impose that form upon it.

Critical environmental education cannot participate in academic games that conceive of unequal "sustainable" developments, games that use the facade of cultural relativity to mask the reality that the victims of long-term development are excluded from its benefits by those who enjoy the rewards of that process. This strategy only leads to the globalization of a sustained underdevelopment (González-Gaudiano and de Alba 1994).

Critical environmental education must make an authentic response to a basic principle of social justice: The prosperity of a few must not be sustained by the majority suffering conditions of need.[11]

Any challenges to these systems, including educational challenges, will involve political understanding and activism . . . . Eco-political education is defined as education which can be a basis for the kind of political action needed to challenge unsustainable development (Hickling-Hudson 1994, 20).

Sustainability and Environmental Education

The bibliography that is currently available on sustainable development is overwhelming. We find ideas proposed by different sectors and based on the most varied schools of thought. At least seventy definitions of sustainable development are in circulation (Trzyna 1995). There are also attempts to reconcile this conceptual diversity (Holmberg 1992), although it may be difficult to reconcile definitions that are more closely linked to the need for "greening" processes and products—common among marketers who know how to interpret the tendencies of consumer groups who have buying power—with those that are rooted in the principles of deep ecology, to mention just two cases of divergence.[12]

Typically we environmental educators have not been able to come together on this diversity; we find ourselves full of antagonisms and misinterpretations. Sometimes the fact that diverse positions on the same problem exist has not even been identified. We have indiscriminately used concepts with different approaches and premises or, faced with the absence of the necessary components to adopt decisions of our own, we have faithfully subscribed to the definition proposed by some recognized organization, such as those alluded to above (Slocombe 1993).

On the other hand, those who consider this to be a question of discussions without any practical implications simply ignore the matter and continue with their activities. This theoretical abstentionism is, from our point of view, a passive form of opposition that undermines the foundations of critical environmental education, which would construct better pedagogical answers to the multiple and diverse knots in the social fabric. This is because the freedom to recognize the existence of alternatives and decide among them implies risks (loss of security, of grounding, of essences) that individuals are not generally disposed to run. That is why many stakeholders prefer to pursue the search for technical solutions without much knowledge about the potential recipients of solutions, or to invoke external and comfortable attitudes of solidarity (African fauna or the children of Bosnia or Central America) that do not make us look at our own surroundings and revise our commitments.

For that reason, it is both important and noteworthy that the first issue of the *Canadian Journal of Environmental Education* began with the work of Lucie Sauvé (1996), who seeks to offer some basic coordinates so that environmental educators can identify their own positioning in relation to the environment, education, and sustainable development.

Setting aside our differences with Sauvé about her typology of educational paradigms—which would provide material for another study—we will focus our attention here on her taxonomy of concepts of sustainable development. The proposed concepts establish four distinct modes of classifying existing ideas about sustainable development, synthetically describe their principal characteristics, and relate them to environmental and educational paradigms.

Sauvé's account has the merit of bringing the discussion about sustainable development to a new level of discussion among environmental educators and of proposing a correlation between a concept of the environment and a pedagogical strategy. We recognize the importance of trying to offer coordinates against which educators can position their own work. Although Sauvé's classification of conceptions of the environment seems to us highly illuminating, her proposed typology of conceptions of sustainable development seems deficient in the light of the widespread debates about this theme which have taken place in recent years.[13]

The first two conceptions correspond to neoliberal technologist-economist optimism based on the consolidation of the global free market, though in the second a greater regulatory intervention is accorded to the top organizations. In reality there are not many differences when the structure of the top organizations is analyzed (for example, the United Nations Security Council, the World Trade Organization, the World Bank, etc.).

The third conception corresponds to the alternative worldview, with a marked emphasis on bioregionalism linked to deep ecology. We have serious doubts about the possibilities of linking deep ecology with the general principles of sustainable development, above all when it is advocated from fundamentalist positions. It should be pointed out that deep ecology has different positions within itself. The struggle for the recognition of living beings, and even of minerals, as possessing rights, displays significant variants, ranging from those that can hardly be distinguished from what has scornfully been called "shallow ecology with a weak anthropocentrism" (Sosa 1989), to more radical currents that promote the establishment of a "natural contract," whereby all of nature as a whole would be converted into an entity with rights.[14]

Table 1 A Typology of Concepts of Sustainable Development

Concepts of Sustainable Development	Principal Characteristics	Associated Concepts of the Environment	Associated Educational Paradigm
Continuous development because of technological innovation and free trade. Believes economic growth following neoliberal principles will solve social and environmental problems.	Productivity and competitiveness within a market-driven society; free trade on a world scale; scientific and technological innovation for economic growth; legislative control.	Environment as a resource to be developed and managed; rational use of resources for sustainable profit, and thus sustainable quality of life.	Rational paradigm: education as training, as an information transfer process (mainly of a scientific, technological, and legislative nature).
Development as dependent on a world order. Believes economic growth will solve social and environmental problems if a world order (from top organizations) regulates consumption, pollution, and the mechanism of distribution of wealth.	Free trade on a world scale; scientific and technological innovations for economic growth; restructuring of political, economic, and social organizations; world- or region-wide pacts, agreements, legislation, etc.	The whole biospheric environment, as a pool of resources to be globally managed by top organizations.	Rational paradigm: same approach as in previous concept of sustainable development, but acceptance of a certain critical approach of the failures of the neoliberal system.
Alternative development. Believes only a complete global shift in social values and choices will permit the development of sustainable communities.	Development of bioregional economy: distinguishing real needs from desires, reducing dependency, increasing autonomy, favoring renewable resources, stimulating democratic process, participation, and solidarity, etc.	Environment as a community project.	Inventive paradigm: a community-led process of critical investigation toward the transformation of social realities.
Autonomous development (indigenous development). Believes development is valued if it is rooted in cultural identity and if it preserves territorial integrity.	Collective subsistence economy based on solidarity; associated with one's territory and drawn from a distinct cosmology.	Environment as a territory (a place to live) and as a cultural community project.	Inventive paradigm: construction of contextually significant and useful knowledge, taking into account traditional values and know-how.

Source: Calgary Latin American Studies Group (1994) in Sauvé (1996).

The final conception, autonomous development, is linked with some of the varieties of sustainable development, because it must be recognized that many practices of indigenous societies do possess strong doses of sustainability. Nonetheless it is important to avoid a mythification of the cultural practices of indigenous ethnic groups at the present time. Even though their original cultural principles are rooted in a management of resources that differs substantially from that which has been promoted in a dominant form, it is also necessary to recognize that the insertion of these groups into markets renders them extremely fragile and vulnerable, since the processes of capitalist interchange are deployed in ways that are highly disadvantageous for indigenous regions. For example, ten of the fifty-six Mexican indigenous ethnic groups are today veritable cultural and linguistic relics.

Economic globalization is confronted with cultural fragmentation, but only in certain terms. Cultural fragmentation or tribalization has arisen as a process of resistance to the accelerated rhythms of loss of distinctive identity, which is manifested of course in violent urban and rural territorial struggles. The loss of identity, of a sense of belonging, as people are fused into the amorphous amalgam of globalization is fostering bloody defensive reactions.

Nonetheless, within the framework of this new intermeshing of conflict the defense of traditional knowledge about the management of natural resources normally takes a secondary place to political confrontation or economic interest. This will carry with it, in the case of the indigenous ethnic groups, the extinction of numerous and diversified forms of sociocultural relationships with the local environment, particularly in the helpful use of species, many of which have not yet been registered in the anthropological annals, cutting off real possibilities for the people who possess that knowledge.

For all the above reasons, we agree more with the pre–United Nations Conference on Environment and Development classification of Michael Colby (1990), who proposes five paradigms for the environmental management of development: frontier economics, environmental protection, resource management, eco-development and deep ecology. We nonetheless disagree with using the notion of paradigm in the typology, concurring more with Sauvé in the use of a less loaded term such as conception or approach.

Colby's work includes a greater number of elements within its typology than those advanced by Sauvé, although of course he makes no effort to link education, environment, and sustainable development. The

Table 2 A Typology of Paradigms of Sustainable Development

Paradigm Dimension	Frontier Economics	Environmental Protection	Resource Management	Eco-development	Deep Ecology
Dominant Imperative	"Progress" as infinite economic growth and prosperity	"Tradeoffs," as in ecology versus economic growth	"Sustainability" as necessary constraint for "green growth"	Co-developing humans and nature; redefine "security"	"Eco-topia": anti-growth "Constrained harmony with nature"
Human-Nature Relationship	Very strongly anthropocentric	Strongly anthropocentric	Modified anthropocentric	Ecocentric?	Biocentric
Dominant Threats	Hunger, poverty, disease, "Natural disasters"	Health impacts of pollution, endangered species	Resource degradation; poverty, population growth	Ecological uncertainty. Global change	Ecosystem collapse. "Unnatural" disasters
Main Themes	Open access/free goods Exploitation of infinite natural resources	Remedial/defensive "Legalize ecology" as economic externality	Global efficiency "Economize ecology" Interdependence	Generative restructuring "Ecologize social systems" Sophisticated symbiosis	Back to nature "Biospecies equality" Simple symbiosis
Prevalent Property Regimes	Privatization (neoclass.) or nationalization (Marx) of all property	Privatization dominant; some public parks set aside	Global Commons Law (GCL) for conservation of: oceans, atmosphere, climate, biodiversity?	GCL + local common and private property regimes for intra/intergenerational equity and stewardships	Private plus common property set aside for preservation
Who Pays?	Property owners (Public at large: esp. poor)	Taxpayers (public at large)	"Polluter pays" (producers and consumers) (poor)	"Pollution prevention pays" Income index, environmental taxes	Avoid costs by forgoing development
Responsibility for Development and Management	Property owners: individual or state	Fragmentation: development decentralized, Management centralized	Toward integration across multiple levels of gov't. (federal/state/local)	Private/Public Institutional innovation and redefinition of roles	Largely decentralized but integrated design & management

Table 2 Continued

Paradigm Dimension	Frontier Economics	Environmental Protection	Resource Management	Eco-development	Deep Ecology
Environmental Management Technologies and Strategies	Industrial agriculture: High inputs of energy, biocide, and water; monoculture, mechanized production; fossil fuel energy; pollution dispersal Unregulated waste disposal High population growth "Free markets"	"End-of-the-pipe" or "Business as usual plus a treatment plant." Clean-up. "Command and control." Market regulation: some prohibition or limits, repair, and set-asides. Focus on protection of human health, "Land doctoring" Envir. impact statements	Impact assessment and risk management, pollution reduction, energy efficiency, renewable resource/conservation strategies, restoration ecology, population stabilization and technology-enhanced carrying capacity; some structural adjustment	Uncertainty (resilience) management, industrial ecology/eco-technologies, e.g.: renewable energy, waste/resource cycling for throughput scale reduction, agro-forestry, low input agriculture, extractive forest reserves Population stabilization and enhanced capacity	Stability management Reduced scale of market economy (including trade) Low technology. Simple material needs. Non-dominating science. Indigenous tech. system. "Intrinsic values" Population reduction

Table 2 Continued

Paradigm Dimension	Frontier Economics	Environmental Protection	Resource Management	Eco-development	Deep Ecology
Analytic Modeling and Planning Methodologies	Neoclassical or Marxist closed economic systems: reversible equilibria, production limited by man-made factors, Natural Factors not accounted for. Net present value maximization. Cost-benefit analysis of tangible goods and services	Neoclassical plus: environmental impact Assessment after design; optimum pollution levels Equation of willingness to pay and compensation principles	Neoclassical plus: include natural capital, true (Hicksian) income maximization in UN system of national accounts; increased, reed trade; ecosystem and social health monitoring; linkages between population, poverty, and environment	Ecological economics: biophysical-economic open systems dynamics; socio-technical and eco-system process design; integration of social, economic, and ecological criteria for technology; trade and capital flow regulation based on community goals and mgmt. land tenure and income redistrib.; geophysiology?	Grassroots bioregional planning. Multiple cultural systems. Conservation of cultural and biological diversity, Autonomy
Fundamental Flaws	Creative but mechanistic; no awareness of reliance on ecological balance	Defined by F.E. in reaction to D.E.; lacks vision of abundance	Downplays social factors Subtly mechanistic; doesn't handle uncertainty	May generate false security Magnitude of changes require new consciousness	Defined in reaction to F.E.; Organic but not. Creative How reduce population?
	(F. E.)	(E. P.)	(R. M.)	(E. D.)	(D. E.)

most recent discussions have incorporated other themes that are not taken into account in his typology (Welford 1995; Cooper and Palmer 1995). Nonetheless, Colby cautions that the vision of the problem is rapidly changing and that the proposed "paradigms" are related among themselves, and also that within each one there exist disagreements and multiple schools of thought.

Educational Strategies

Certainly every conception of the environment and sustainable development tends toward one or more pedagogical strategies and proposals relating to the problem. We will analyze here the ones that are most obvious in the taxonomy of sustainable development proposed by Colby.

A) A pedagogy linked with the frontier economics paradigm would be based on promoting moderate use of resources that are scarce and others that could become scarce because of their rate of utilization. Obviously the cost factor would automatically exclude those without the means to access these resources. This is not a futuristic problem. It constitutes a painful daily reality for the enormous sectors of the population in developing countries who cannot consume animal protein or use clean water, to cite only two cases—resources that are not considered scarce by developed countries. The concept of scarcity is mediated mainly by the distribution of wealth.

From this point of view, the problem of excess production on a world level, which has become an economic and political force of global dimensions, cannot be managed. Likewise, its posture that "we are all responsible for deterioration"—which it also shares with the paradigm of environmental protection—has given rise to numerous biases in the development of educational programs, by failing to identify those specifically responsible for the different problems in their very distinct degrees and levels. Ultimately, "we are all responsible" necessarily ends up meaning that nobody is responsible.

Nature in this paradigm is understood in the framework of a static conception—a still life—placed there to be made use of. In the end, it corresponds to the cornucopian vision of endless resources, of the infinite dilution of emissions, etc. Essentially it is not that exhaustion of resources is not recognized, but that vastness is argued as a form of masking deterioration and, subsequently, declaring it an inevitable cost to be paid for "progress."

A perverse component of this paradigm is institutional change to reduce regulations that leads, for example, to a kind of hallowing of
deconcentration and decentralization of responsibility for safeguarding
resources. From this perspective, the deregulation demanded cannot take
place without a better public organization, one that favors a greater social
participation in the decisions that affect peoples' lives, in order to avoid
transferring the discretion of the public sector to the private. Similarly, the
control of the big corporations through juridically binding international
accords is an imperative.

B) As for the pedagogical strategies linked to the deep ecology paradigm,
despite the lack of theoretical unification this approach would emphasize
more spiritual, ethical, and social aspects on varying planes, according to
the radicalism of their positions. The decentering of the human species in
the cosmic order produces a sweeping change in relations with the environment, that questions many current scientific postulates. This would
produce a qualitative modification of the curriculum, not only with regard
to the selection and orientation of its contents, but also in the criteria of
its organization in the fields of knowledge. We do not know of an integrated pedagogical proposal that corresponds to the most extreme postu-
lations of deep ecology, perhaps because at bottom its positions would
tend to have recourse to a kind of preindustrial ruralized deschooling
(Illich 1971) which, given current conditions, could only be applied in
some developing countries or in some form such as the hippie com-
munes of the 1960s or as offshoots of Eastern philosophies. Nonetheless, traits of deep ecology exist in many environmental education projects
oriented toward conservation.

We do not entirely reject all the theses of deep ecology. Nonetheless,
we believe that the search for nature's rights should not blind our eyes to
the rights of people who have nothing, of those who suffer, of those who
have become dispensable. That would lead to a sophisticated form of
social exclusion based on green excuses.

All the same, we are convinced that the truth can and must be sought
in different ways, including spirituality, religion, and art, so that human
beings can attain fullness. We are convinced as well of the need to revise
our ethical limits with rigor, because science and technology have also
become instruments of domination, power, and death (Delors 1996). Thus,
in accord with the results of the Delors Commission, we recognize that
the tension among the spiritual and the material is a challenge to educators to encourage each and every one, acting in accordance with their

traditions and convictions and paying full respect to pluralism, to lift their minds and spirits to the plane of the universal and, in some measure, to transcend themselves. Thus, one of the four pillars is

> *learning to live together*, by developing an understanding of others and their history, traditions and spiritual values and, on this basis, creating a new spirit which, guided by recognition of our growing interdependence and a common analysis of the risk and challenges of the future, would induce people to implement common projects or to manage the inevitable conflicts in an intelligent and peaceful way. Utopia, some might think, but it is a necessary Utopia, indeed a vital one if we are to escape from a dangerous cycle sustained by cynicism or by resignation (Delors 1996, 18–22).

C) With respect to the pedagogical proposals that can be derived from the environmental protection paradigm, we may think they refer to a pedagogical approach that emphasizes correcting damage. The perspective of manifestation of impact, even though it contains a component of prevention, is usually a limited resource if it is not supported by strong institutions. This paradigm attempts to persuade us of that technological solution called the "end of the pipe." Its proposal to internalize externalities is weakened by its concept of the general public, since it pays no heed to the needs of those groups most vulnerable to the environmental impacts of productive processes. Moreover, because it is applied within the framework of a sectorial schema, its possible effects are neutralized by institutional policies and strategies that often are not oriented in the same direction.

Although the proposal contemplates strategies of social communication and participation, the restricted scope of the approach means that it is not always clear how to handle such strategies. For that reason, the pedagogical proposals of environmental protection normally do not go beyond the sectorial sphere within which the institutional management is carried out, and it does not enter into the schooling system, except for its repercussions in the higher education curriculum on careers linked to technology and engineering.

Lastly, the environmental protection paradigm has usually given rise to the appearance of the "green market," constituted by advertising directed to consumers about the marvels of certain products and processes, most frequently in the domain of industrialized foodstuffs. This phenomenon, which is not completely regulated in developing countries, in many cases turns out to be a propagandistic apparatus without foundations adequate to the task, but which in spite of everything has nonetheless contributed to promoting public participation by inhibiting or inducing patterns of consumption in upper-middle and upper class groups, whose income allows them to absorb the price differentials.

The natural areas protected in this paradigm are conceived as a function of the decision to conserve unaltered samples of the natural heritage for their aesthetic or representative characteristics. That is what underpins environmental interpretation programs.[15]

D) The resource management paradigm contains a more socially oriented approach than the two previous paradigms in virtue of giving importance to vulnerable groups, above all by incorporating the poverty element. That has significant repercussions for constructing pedagogical proposals, because better conditions pertain for defining the subjects of education with greater clarity. As Colby already cautioned, in this paradigm particularly one observes a range of diverse options that establish marked differences among themselves, from patrimonial accounts (an instrument used in economics to assign a price value to a natural resource—like air, water, natural forests—that doesn't have one in the conventional market) to the concept of current and potential services furnished by ecosystems. Hence the broad meaning given to the notion of a natural resource, which is considered to be more than merely a raw material; and protected natural areas are conceived of as a strategic reserve, which leads to community educational projects for the better management of shared resources.

This paradigm requires a sound mastery of information in order to treat it appropriately in educational projects. This is important above all in the light of evidence of the frequent lack of knowledge on the part of environmental educators about the problems they are addressing. This ultimately promotes emotional and intuitive reactions to them more frequently than affective and political commitments.

The matter of global environmental problems acquires a different dimension when a relational framework is established that permits a better comprehension of particular contributions to them. Similarly, the need for institutional reform is taken into account as a condition for heading toward sustainable development. Here is where the concept of "the polluter pays" comes in which, in pedagogical terms, obviously suffers in terms of its preventive focus and takes its place among the policies of dissuasion through economic sanctions. Moreover, the income derived in this fashion usually is not applied to strengthening the corresponding sector, which does not direct additional budget gains to environmental management.

The resource management paradigm, which is more on the side of primary than of secondary production, intervenes in the green market by reactivating productive processes in rural areas that employ a larger quantity of laborers and use organically based technological models with which they produce much less damage to the soil and water, among other characteristics—although it is clear that those who implement the resource management paradigm often see it more from the standpoint of market opportunity than in terms of it being an educational and cultural process.

E) Very much related to some forms of the resource management paradigm, the ecodevelopment paradigm is understood as an open system that emphasizes the conservation of natural capital and its productive capacity. The resulting pedagogical proposals are more complex and demand an action of greater commitment, insofar as we strive to rely on accurate and opportune information in order to know how to orient our intervention as subjects and also how to enter into the field of values and attitudes through a critical rethinking of the status quo.

Though they are not an exclusive feature of this paradigm, its multidisciplinary approaches are more accentuated and systematized. That also implies building partnerships among the different stakeholders and identifying common concerns from the angle of their own cultural perspectives, priorities, and values, which permits the emergence of authentic leadership.

The ecodevelopment paradigm has a primarily preventive focus. The slogan "prevention pays" bestows a different meaning on pedagogical action and participates in the development of a self-directed process as a function of one's own decisions, adopted in order to arrive at a new way of life, a new *ethos*. That also clarifies the importance of a global policy with its starting point, as we have already said, in the effort toward change, and links the diverse struggles undertaken in association with the protection of the environment: human rights, peace and disarmament, the rights of minorities and antipoverty work, among many others.[16] In other words, this paradigm cannot be separated from the struggle for conserving the nature of social justice.

In the matter of population growth, where the other paradigms are unclear ecodevelopment appeals to a familiar process of self-limiting family size, which has been labeled the demographic transition. In this process education plays a fundamental role in fostering consciousness raising and decisions that are truly free. Facts are not isolated from the domain of values; they are never strictly neutral and objective in the traditional sense.

This is particularly important in the development of environmental education about the theme of demographic growth—which has lent itself to all sorts of distortions, basing itself only on numerical increase quite apart from the ensemble of factors that determine it—as well as other problems associated with population distribution and urban hypertrophy. Critical thought must develop the capacity to interrogate those who claim the need to reduce the existing situation at all costs.

Some Conclusions

Sauvé's conceptions and Colby's paradigms show us the need to clarify the orientation of our work and how it relates to other orientations. It is not a question of closing the discursive circuits with essentialist taxonomies, but of contributing lines of discussion in an open system of analysis in order to define better our own postures toward the educational process and—this is the point—to air them more frankly in authentic exchanges.

It is not difficult to infer the presence of "paradigmatic cross breeding" in the current state of environmental education; it is not easy to detect the origins and amalgams of what we think, say, and do in relation to environmental education. This dearth of clear references has generated diverse pedagogical approximations that are beginning to produce adverse reactions to the field.[17] Although we may recognize that many attacks issue from the economic interests that have been affected by the growth of environmental consciousness, on a self-critical plane we should acknowledge that they also find their justification, in part, in those discourses of environmental education that truly constitute aporias.

We need, for example, to be able to identify those economic interests that, although they are at the center of environmental policy with conservationist disguises, pursue a contrary effect. Or to clarify the scope of that vast mass of well-intentioned projects that center on recycling actions without any further pedagogical reach, and that in reality actually help slow down consciousness of the necessity for radical changes. A better familiarity with the situation in which we are enmeshed could help us to know how much we are lending ourselves to the games of those who do not wish their own role in the process to be analyzed and who insist on presenting the problem as homogeneous, when it is a matter of a multi-faceted and polyphonic universe.

Arditi (1996), citing Derrida, mentions the concept of the contradictorily coherent, and proposes using the analysis of the structurality of the structure in order to be able to understand how we inscribe ourselves, each one of us, in relation to the center of the structure in which we move—why we do not want to admit that the center is part of the structure. The paradigms that have been presented here have their own forms of overcoming the constitutive conflict of sustainable development and the role played in it by education. Thus two problems can be raised about which we environmental educators should debate: Is it a question of beginning to overcome the conflict or only of postponing it?

Notes

1. Translated by Hoyt Rogers.

2. In 1991 Lester Brown pointed out that during the twenty years in which Earth Day had been celebrated since its establishment in 1970, the world had lost almost 200 million hectares of tree-covered surface, about the surface of the United States east of the Mississippi River, as well as some 480 billion tons of the upper vegetal layer, more or less equivalent to the quantity that covers the agricultural lands of India.

3. Capacity to adapt to impacts. Resilience is the process of return—or not—of an ecosystem to the conditions previous to its perturbation. It depends on multiple factors, such as the intensity and frequency of the perturbations, the present conditions of the areas, the diversity of species, and the complexity of the food chains, among others (Martins de Canalho 1994, 369).

4. For a recent study on predictable scenarios, see Jeffrey McNeely (1996).

5. For a discussion of the problem of poverty in México and in Latin America, see Plieck and Aguado (1995), Campos (1995), and Jusidman (1996).

6. The imposition of particular visions as universal criteria is a widespread practice among dominant groups. For example, it is possible to find this practice in projects directed toward standardizing professional profiles, the principal risk of which is that such standards can subsequently be used as parameters for legitimization, evaluation, and sanctions independently of the context out of which they were formulated (see Chapter 3).

7. This definition of sustainable development was disseminated in *Caring for the Earth: A Strategy for Sustainable Living* (IUCN/UNEP/WWF 1991).

8. It seems that agricultural society has been assigned to the developing world and urban society to the industrialized world. McNeely notes that Whittaker and Likens (1975)

   > have estimated that an agricultural world, in which most human beings are peasants, should be able to support 5,000 to 7,000 million people, probably more if the large agricultural population were supported by an industrial-promoting agricultural activity. In contrast, a reasonable population supported by an industrialized world society at the present North American material standard of living would be 1,000 million. At the more frugal European standard of living, 2,000 to 3,000 million would be possible. Some scientists contend that the highest quality of life would come with a human population of around 1.5 billion, about the same number of people as existed at the turn of the 20th century" (McNeely 1996, 10; see also Rapalus 1994, 176–77).

9. See Edgar González-Gaudiano (1997c).

10. For a discussion of current terms of information technology, see Nicholas Negroponte (1996).

11. Angel Maya notes that during the preparatory meetings of the UNCED (United Nations Conference of Environment and Development) of 1992, the delegation of the United States challenged the developing world with a phrase that established the terms of the negotiation: "The consumption pattern which the industrialized countries have reached is not under discussion. It is an acquired right" (1995, 40).

12. Patricia Cardona (1996) cites Steve Trent, information officer for the Environmental Investigation Agency and promoter of the document "Corporative Power, Corruption and Destruction of the Planetary Forests." Trent "points out that the U.S. company Boise Cascade produces 3.1 million tons of paper, 1.8 million cubic meters of wood and 180 million square meters of plywood each year. Its earnings for 1995 reached 5.4 billion dollars. Despite everything this company presents itself as a world leader in the sustainable management of forest resources" (14).

13. Sauvé (1996) proposes a typology of six conceptions of the environment in environmental education: environment as nature, as a resource, as a problem, as a place to live, as the biosphere, and as a community project. She mentions the type of relationship with each one, its principal characteristics and examples of teaching/learning strategies. In our view this makes an outstanding contribution.

14. This tradition is rooted in the early works of Aldo Leopold in the United States, continuing through Hans Jonas in Germany to Michel Serres in France and California.

15. See: Ballantyne and Uzzell, 1993.

16. The world spends more than 1,150 billion US dollars per year on armaments—a quantity that was supposed to decrease following the East-West détente.

17. See: *The Environmental Advocate*, the newsletter of the National Environmental Education Advancement Project, Fall 1996.

Chapter 3

The Professionalization of Environmental Educators: Critical Points for a Curricular Proposal[1]

A story is a plot which interrelates man, the world, and the gods. . . . To put a story into practice is to live in such a way that the story becomes true . . . it is to strive to make it turn into reality.

—Ismael, in Quinn (1995, 49)

Traits

The field of environmental education has a number of traits. We will summarize these briefly, in a telescopic glance, in order to embark upon our theme of professionalization.

First, environmental education is a field that has taken root very rapidly in comparison with other emerging fields of education. If we summarize its early formulations—without ignoring the polemics surrounding its appearance on the scene—we have to recognize that environmental education has grown up within a time span of just thirty years.[2] This buildup has not been exempt from conceptual divergences. Some of these have been discarded in the process, such as mesological education, which was proposed by the United Nations Educational, Social and Cultural Organization (UNESCO) in 1971 within the framework of the Man and the Biosphere Program (MAB). Others, such as conservation education, have given rise to environmental interpretations of a more specific character. All the same, polemics persist in relation to the education-pedagogy dyad, on the one hand, and the environment-ecology dyad on the other, the different combinations of which have produced signifiers with blurred demarcations. The most conspicuous example is the insistence by some

Spanish educators on distinguishing between environmental education and environmental pedagogy.[3]

Second, the evolution of the various theoretical approaches is noteworthy. While this evolution has proceeded in tandem with the development of international environmental policy, it has undergone its own transformation through the influence of different traditions of pedagogical thought. Studies of the diverse approaches to environmental education point to an increasing theoretical sophistication (Smyth 1995; Pardo-Díaz 1995; Sauvé 1996; González-Gaudiano 1997b). The scope and range of an environmental education, whether focusing on ecology or as a multidisciplinary subject, to mention only two approaches, have been advanced repeatedly. The evolution has not, of course, been linear. It has acquired its own particular characteristics in different professional and geographic spaces, although it has been marked by the coexistence of approaches that are often expressed in an eclecticism that amalgamates the intuitive and the empirical. This coexistence of approaches, which occasionally appears as a trait of the plurality of the field, has produced a sort of "classical" conception of environmental education.[4]

Although it might appear self-contradictory to speak of a classical conception within a field that we acknowledge as emerging, one certainly exists as a result of the swiftness and radicalness of the transitions experienced by environmental education during its thirty-year history. This classical conception refers to the particular pedagogical proposal that has assumed the status of the hegemonic perspective within the field of environmental education.

To explain: Linguists, at least from Saussure onward, maintain that no sign possesses an intrinsic meaning. For them the relationship between signifier and signified is arbitrary and can be modified continually. The determination of the meaning of a sign—which they label the "value" of the sign—depends on the relations it contracts with other signs. In line with this reasoning, let us accept for a moment that a basic characteristic of the social sphere—and environmental education is no exception here— is the continual transformation of the sense or value we assign to ideas, methods, or propositions. Let us accept also that some ideas, methods, and so forth succeed in domesticating or colonizing a field of knowledge during a certain time span. The latter aspect is important in order to understand the earlier point about a hegemonic perspective. It indicates that there are sedimented ideas, methods, or propositions; that is to say, ones which institute themselves as the objective perspective within a discipline. Ernesto Laclau describes this as follows:

In the measure to which an act of institution has been successful, a "forgetting of the origins" tends to occur; the system of alternative possibilities tends to vanish and the traces of the originative contingency tend to efface themselves. In this way what has been instituted tends to assume the form of a mere objective presence. This is the moment of sedimentation. It is important to see that this effacement implies a concealment. If objectivity is founded on exclusion, the traces of this exclusion will always be present in one way or another. What happens is that the sedimentation may be so complete, the privilege of one of the dichotomous poles so fully achieved, that the contingent character of this privilege, its *originative* dimension of power, does not immediately make itself visible. That is how objectivity constitutes itself as mere presence (1993b, 51)

This is precisely what happened in the field of environmental education when the developed countries and the international organizations—through the International Environmental Education Program (IEEP)—officially pushed forward a certain way of conceiving the goals, scope, and methodological approaches of environmental education. This sedimentation imposed the preeminence of schooling—realized through educational technology—and of approaches centered on conservation per se, which served to conceal the asymmetrical distribution and consumption of planetary resources, and consequently, the political substratum of educational projects.[5]

Third, and linked with the above, the consolidation of the field of environmental education as a consistent social practice still leaves a lot to be desired. It is a process that runs up against institutional resistances of various kinds, which on many occasions turn out to be justified. We could mention a range of difficulties, but for the purposes of this chapter we are more interested in highlighting the composition of the body of educators who make up the field itself.

Elsewhere (González-Gaudiano, 1993) it has been observed that the guild of environmental educators comprises an enormous diversity of proponents. They include professionals of highly varied training and experience. Although this might also represent advantages, the lack of systemization and of a better-defined orientation of pedagogical action have hampered the task of formulating integrated projects. Professional variety is not the only element to be considered. It must also be mentioned that these professionals, generally speaking, have gravitated to the field of environmental education on the basis of an empirical practice very close to trial and error. Only recently has the rise of training programs for environmental educators sparked new readings of its foundation disciplines, in order to try to articulate them from the perspective of environmental education—not always with very good results. In addition, we must include in this contingent those who have gravitated to environmental education without possessing any professional training. Interested citizens, men and women of the most disparate backgrounds, circulate as volunteers among groups and communities, often bringing with them only their good intentions. This has notably restricted their possibilities of developing educational projects within programs of greater scope. On the whole they have been content to promote specific actions of a remedial nature that have contributed to a progressive erosion of the credibility of pedagogical intervention, above all when it is carried out under conditions of extreme hardship, as happens with many of our organizations that work with the rural population or the urban poor.[6]

As we can see, the field of environmental education is neither homogeneous nor one-dimensional. Nor would we claim it to be so, because the reality we face is not homogeneous or one-dimensional either. Even those of like mind with regard to our profession as environmental educators come up with different readings of the same problems. It is a matter of readings that are inscribed in differing spaces of politics and labor, to cite just two spheres, and that allow us to observe the absence of a unified reference as to the field of environmental education and the values that are promoted within it.

The lack of unified references produces insecurity and uncertainty among those who are inclined toward stable foundations and one-dimensional objectives and identities. In Latin America this has given rise to the appearance of a *caudillismo* or dictatorial stance that pontificates about "maximalist" versions although, fortunately, not so much in the field of environmental education as in the heterogeneous world of environmentalism. According to García-Canclini (1995), this *caudillismo* appeals to a Macondo-like fundamentalism that freezes the Latin American world into a sanctuary for premodern nature. Regrettably, this epic-folkloric vision is deeply rooted among some environmental educators. In the same manner, the search for unified references manifests itself in other parts of the world as well, although in each instance with characteristics of its own. Such is the case of the work deployed by the North American Association of Environmental Education (NAAEE) in the formulation of national standards.[7]

However, Latin American environmental educators not only lack arguments to take issue with that usurped representation; often they do not even notice that this fundamentalism makes its plea to us on an emotional level, almost like a hymn to some "essence" unto itself, based on the notion of a hyper-mystified environment and on a Promethean discourse. It is a notion that does not correspond to the obvious needs of our peoples. Worse still, it makes them more vulnerable in the face of the spread of fragmented and transnational symbolic forms, which invade our cultural sphere with greater frequency as a result of globalization processes. By the same token, we are not in any condition to present counterarguments to "standardizing" and prepackaged proposals, which are also liable to be turned into criteria of certification and normalization, given the trend that can already be observed within some professions in México, as an offshoot of the commercial accords with the United States and Canada.[8]

The Fissures

As we can readily perceive, environmental education does not constitute a monolithic and closed field. On the contrary, it is a field made up of different conceptions with regard to both education and the environment, where it is possible to identify sedimented discourses that are beginning to be called into question as well as alternative discourses that seek to rearticulate the field of environmental education. Thus the structure of the field is found to be fractured, its diverse fissures reflect varying positions vis-à-vis the play of forces between the necessity and the contingency of the environmental quandary. In the light of this heterogeneity, it becomes obvious that environmental education is not completely dominated by that conventional "classical" position to which we alluded earlier.[9]

In other words, no definitive suture has been produced that is capable of suppressing other forms of pedagogical intervention with respect to the environmental conflict. On the contrary, at least in the Latin American context, the conventional position not only coexists with other forms of conceiving the problem and acting in regard to it, but also finds itself increasingly beset by emerging discourses such as popular environmental education and approaches detached from critical pedagogy. Hence our constitution as subjects—as pedagogical subjects—is overdetermined by our empowerment vis-à-vis the environmental conflict and by the positioning we assume in the educational task to be effected within the social framework.[10]

That is why these fissures in the field of environmental education are an expression of the multiple possibilities that open up for the educational enterprise. The fissures are in fact positive. They represent alternatives in building up the field, as opposed to the search for the primordial *identity* of environmental education. This type of quest, undertaken on the basis of the traditional propositions, strives to formulate in some definitive manner the meaning of the conflicts that are produced among the social, economic, and ecological spheres. The productive dimension of these fissures resides in their capacity for rearticulation, for generating alternatives within the field of environmental education.

How is this? In the first place, it is because the fissures are derived from social participation in environmental education projects that displays different levels of commitment and intermittences. These levels correspond to intersubjective factors linked with the double global/local dimension of the problems that move people to act. More specifically they refer to the distinct form in which the environmental conflict affects the individual, since this shapes his or her differing responses to it.

Benjamin Arditi's work (1993a; 1993b) can help us interpret such fissures. Arditi points out that strong and stable commitments to institutions have weakened. This in turn has eroded participation. Arditi adds that there has been a parallel process of the multiplication of commitments, which "diversifies people's interests, expands associationism and multiplies the networks of belonging." These ideas help us explain why numerous environmental educators in the region find themselves involved in networks and organizations of different types and aims (democracy, peace, human rights, the physically challenged, gender, development, etc.). This will have to be recognized as a constitutive element of their stances toward the environmental problem; such recognition will serve to help develop strategies that allow for building bridges among their varied interests and harnessing the fluctuation that occurs among their diverse commitments. That is, rather than dissolving commitments to environmental education, the diversification of interests produces new interstices in the porosity of the social sphere in order to mesh with environmental concerns, thus enriching its strategies and widening its scope.

Second, it is also possible to identify fissures generated by belonging to an extremely diffuse guild in which often we do not succeed in identifying either the principal tasks or the key concepts and messages. We do not know how to account for ourselves as environmental educators even to ourselves.[11] Neither can we rely for that purpose on a project, or else we merely constitute ourselves by means of numerous immediate, remedial, and dispersed activities which enjoy—for the moment—social approval (although one can observe an increasing distrust, above all in the better-informed sectors, with regard to the middle- and long-range viability and importance of many such proposals).

Nevertheless, the opacity that exists in the recognition of our identities also opens up new lodes that we can mine for our constructs, by virtue of making manifest the presence of distinct flows within the field. These flows express themselves in differing forms and at different moments. Occasionally, as when forces are mobilized that have been called together for landmark events (Rio + 5, for example), they turn into torrents that provoke rapid but transitory advances in areas that had stagnated (financing, technological transfer, etc.). In the absence of these exceptional episodes, educational and cultural processes acquire the form of a laminar flow which shifts slowly and superficially on the social surface. This flow does not succeed in permeating the different layers of the population—since it is easily obstructed by multiple factors (habits, customs, interest groups, economic and political crises, etc.). It nonetheless has a greater permanence, and gradually occupies socio-cultural interstices from which it is not easily dislodged. These interstices, initially found along the edges, gradually turn into definite folds within the social fabric, into new centers of strength. In order to harness these processes we need to be able to identify with greater clarity the differing interests and commitments within the field, so as to be capable of organizing the different realms of action. Obviously, not all environmental educators wish to work in conservation projects, nor do all want to be researchers, to mention only two among many types of intervention.

Faced with this, how can we strive to rise above our deficiencies through environmental education discourses, when some of them are so sedimented and others are so eroded? How can we take better advantage of these fissures that constitute the field? Here as well we may refer to some of Arditi's ideas (1993a) in order to outline an answer.

Arditi argues that although the determining factors of class, race, gender, ethnicity, nation, or religion have not disappeared, a long-range weakening of stable identities has been apparent in recent decades, along with a weakened sense of strongly belonging to a group, a party, an ideological perspective, a theoretical line, or a cultural tradition. There is a to-and-fro in belonging, a certain nomadism that characterizes the contemporary individual and leads him or her to roam through differing spaces. This reflects "the shifting mosaic of the multiple cultural worlds in which contemporary existence finds itself immersed" (Arditi 1993a, 1).

In the light of these assertions we can understand why a critical social practice—such as environmental education claims to be—must develop the capacity to transform its discourses in a timely fashion. That is the ineluctable condition for being able to keep up with the rapid turns and numerous contingencies that constitute the processes in question at the present moment.

Taking up the problem again from the perspective of the subject, Adriana Puiggrós (1990, 41) remarks that "all pedagogy defines its subject. Each pedagogy determines the elements and the norms which order it as a meaningful ensemble whose function is to mediate among the political and social subjects acting in society." Puiggrós subsequently adds that modern pedagogical subjects are imperfect: They not only receive the commands passively, but also reorganize and transform them, straining the established order—especially in the public schools, the institutional form that dominates the pedagogical link. At this point we should ask: Who are the subjects of environmental education in our region? How do they express their adherence to the field? These questions are highly significant. From their answers we can derive possibilities for analyzing professionalization.

Professionalization

MacDonald (1997) remarks that the concept of profession (from the Latin *profiteri*, whose original meaning—"to profess"—was linked to the religious orders) was secularized between 1700 and 1800, absorbing the liberal professions such as medicine, law, military service, education, and natural sciences. Around 1900 this concept comprised the attributes and traits that separated the professions from other occupations, justifying discriminatory practices toward those of different race, gender, and class. Professionals accounted for themselves more by what they were not than by what they were, assuming themselves to be experts in some vital and hermetic (initiatory) field of knowledge. At this stage they formalized the certification processes and specified the codes of conduct. By midcentury, professionalization in terms of attributes gave way to a characterization based on processes.

In this evolution, education has been considered a weak *profession* (dependent and with a limited autonomy) because of its relation with the state and its lack of hermetic knowledge, although strong in its professional *associations*. Hence, with particular reference to environmental education, MacDonald wonders whether, in order to acquire social power and status, we want a professionalization that implies the following:

a) Establishing a unified body of general and systematized knowledge

b) Demanding a long period of university training with certification and a license to practice
c) Clarifying its unique social contribution, particularly its intellectual practice
d) Standardizing income control and exclusion from the field, applying a code of ethics, and verifying the necessary level of autonomy

We can see that the analysis of the professionalization of the environmental educator is beginning to strengthen. Already some approaches have framed the problem in dichotomous terms, opposing the profile of the specialist to that of the generalist (Gómez-Gutiérrez and Ramos Álvarez, 1989, 38). Others have described it as a field that is still in gestation (MacDonald 1997), where all sorts of profiles converge, from experts to amateurs. From our perspective, the problem cannot be framed in these terms: at least, not without making a number of caveats. Ideas advanced by Popkewitz lend support to this view. According to Popkewitz:

> Belonging to scientific communities presupposes a participation in certain premises and lines of reasoning which make knowledge valid. Each scientific area has at its disposal a particular ensemble of questions, methods, and procedures. These ensembles furnished the world of working, and of verifying the studies of others. Training an individual with a view toward his or her integration into a scientific community demands something more than merely conveying the contents of the corresponding discipline. The student must also learn to consider, to think, and to act in the world in a certain manner (1988, 31).

Popkewitz points out also that the conflicts that underlie scientific work are constitutive of science. The coexistence of rival perspectives makes the different groups direct their attention toward different problems and offer differing answers, based on the different fundamental assumptions as to the nature of the world with which they are working.

Although Popkewitz's ideas were advanced for the purpose of analyzing academic production, they can be appropriated for discussing the professionalization of environmental education. While acknowledging the debate about professionalization itself and the wide range of positions being set forth, we do not take as our point of departure the concept of professionalization as necessarily being understood from the perspective of university training. Our stance does not center on the formal element, since we do not restrict the problem of professionalization to the express recognition an academic institution bestows on one's fitness to practice a specific professional activity.[12] The academic criterion is valid for those who graduate from programs on environmental education, but not for everyone in general—and not even for all the graduates themselves.

In México, for example, the academic programs linked with environmental education were initiated around 1993, initially in the form of lower diplomas and then through some master's degrees.[13] The rapprochement among some branches of the Autonomous National University of México and other national institutions of higher education in order to promote a doctoral program is very recent, and has become possible thanks to the existence of an increasing number of graduates of doctoral rank with a specialization in the field.[14]

Nevertheless, we must point out the lack of a consensus not only on theoretical and methodological approaches, but even on the academic weight accorded to the degrees. In part this is due to the composition of whichever discipline is promoting the diploma in question (biology. chemistry, humanities, etc.). But it also reflects the absence of academic-administrative regulation of this educational modality. This absence is already being addressed within some institutions.[15] However, a comparative evaluation of the results obtained since 1993 that goes beyond the numerical data on the graduates has yet to be undertaken. Even so, we can safely assert that some marked formative differences exist. That would not be a negative consideration if there existed some explicit agreement to attend to the numerous socio-professional needs of the field mentioned above. The problem is that these formative differences correspond to the existing sedimentations that are attributable to the promoting area, and that stamp a particular bias or orientation on each curricular proposal. Hence, being a graduate of an academic program in environmental education does not always appropriately qualify one to perform in this field.

On the other hand, there is information about the experiences of nongovernmental organizations that have fostered the training of their personnel via practical modalities linked to the resolution of specific problems—though often their focus is not on the environment, but rather on the satisfaction of basic needs. In fact, some of the best-established projects in environmental education are those amalgamated with community development programs. These experiences are most frequently carried out in rural areas and at times are not even put forward as environmental education projects, since the educational ingredient is mixed in with other socio-cultural, productive, and juridical elements that make up a project of greater scope. Along these lines, from an environmental perspective, the "Agenda for the Education of Adults" by Esteva and Reyes affirms:

The education of adults must emphasize the indissoluble relation between development and environment, considering the latter a space for possibilities and satisfactions. . . . [Likewise] it must favor the collective training of autonomous subjects, who critically analyze the naturalness of their reality and are able to call the instituted normativeness into question. In turn, this would imply the creation of an institutionality whose internalization does not limit but rather widens people's capacity to become subjects who are critical of that very institutionality (1997, 39).

The practical training that can be obtained through direct activity with people is evident in a broad range of possibilities. But one must be aware of the distortion which "empiricism"—a mode of "learning on the job" and learning by doing without any close attention to underlying and supporting theory—can introduce into the experience. All practical activity requires moments of critical evaluation, of honest analysis of the results, of forward-directed reflection in order to incorporate the necessary corrective measures in a timely fashion. The self-complacency into which we fall when we continue to work on the basis of tasks which seem to have gotten off to a successful start—a frequent situation in environmental education—usually produces mirages about their middle- and long-range possibilities. And when working with people in change work, mirages may prove very costly.

Another type of practical modality for training may be observed in the organizational record of the regional networks of environmental educators (mainly those of the southwestern and central regions). The idea is to take advantage of their periodic meetings in order to offer workshops to the participants so that they can become better equipped to integrate themselves into the network. Nevertheless, this training modality would need to be thought through with an intention to professionalize the trainees, which would imply precisely defining its aims and contents with that orientation in mind. For the moment this modality presents itself more as a potential than as a reality on the move.[16]

Both modalities, the academic and the practical, operate as professionalization strategies in the sense set out earlier. In other words, if environmental education has as its mission to contribute to the shaping of new horizons of knowledge, values, and competence concerning the relation between our societies and the world of which we form a part, as well as concerning the internal relations of those societies within themselves, then an environmental education professional can be understood as someone who develops that social practice in the framework of a possible pedagogical project, whatever it may be, and who pursues the project with a definite sense of purpose, whether manifest or not.

There is no need to make propositions about whether professionalization might become the criterion of exclusion or inclusion of those who make up the field. The field is composed of a multiplicity of practices, some of them dispersed and specific, others organized and directed. Their re-cognition is necessary in order to deconstruct their different contributions and scopes, and to enable us to be in a better position to produce our part of the web of discourses that constitute us and our differing forms of perceiving the world.[17]

Gee, Hull, and Lankshear (1996, 10)—following Bourdieu and Foucault—argue that a Discourse creates social positions (or perspectives) among those people who are "recruited" to speak, listen, act, read and write, think, feel, believe, and appraise in certain characteristic, historically recognizable forms, in combination with their own style and individual creativity. They also point out that every Discourse embodies complex relations of complicity, tension, and opposition with other Discourses.[18]

Where does this lead? Let us accept that environmental education is invested with different types of Discourses that constitute different categories of environmental educators, with differing perspectives and commitments. Given this, it will be necessary to identify the principal Discourses that traverse the field of environmental education, as well as the conflicts among them, in order to be able to think about the conditions of possibility that will give definite meanings to the processes of the professionalization of environmental educators. If we do not take this into account, we run a double risk. First, it might be thought that the only *professionalizing* discourse is the academic Discourse of environmental education which, to that extent, can legitimate itself and thereby exclude Discourses constructed through nonacademic practices. Second, we might believe we can construct an environmental education Discourse appropriate for the reality of our peoples, but without recognizing its true impacts on our bodies and minds.[19]

Where to Look for It

We cannot think about a professionalization project in environmental education without a pedagogical vision and imaginative pedagogy that allows us to reactivate educational practice, opening up discursive alternatives which "desediment" the environmental education Discourse of fixed meanings, of all-embracing metanarratives of nature, of representations that appeal to an impossibly idyllic relationship between society and environment.[20]

What, then, might our pedagogical vision/imaginative pedagogy of professionalization of environmental education be like? We do not know with any certainty, but are convinced that we have to think about an open system that makes room for the differing profiles required by the different settings of pedagogical intervention, although with a certain discursive unity which allows us to articulate the various activities around a political project in continuous construction.[21] We have striven to develop a pedagogy of environmental politics capable of opening new avenues of social participation based on understanding and espousing the rights and obligations of one and all. In the same manner, we must lay the groundwork for building an environmental education politics that redefines the role to be performed by pedagogical processes, within the framework of an environmental management that goes beyond declaring good intentions within accords which become nothing more than documentary references.

We need an imaginative pedagogy that does not partition off the defense of nature from the struggle for the rights of people. Of all people. Even though we are aware that social inequality is inevitable, we can contribute in different ways to modifying the terms and the planes of conflict by means of environmental education.

Advances have indeed been made. But environmental educators have been very self-indulgent in judging the stages of the constitution of their field. We do not deny that a qualitative change has occurred. Environmental educators have moved from the pedagogical conception expressed by the first books published by the IEEP, whose focus was the ecological study of nature, to the complex conception linked to sustainable development. But we are not yet entitled to affirm that over these three decades our path has been as linear and harmonious as some reports portray it (González-Muñoz 1996; Sterling and Cooper 1992). Nor can we admit that the accomplishments achieved in each decade constitute a phase superior to the preceding one, sidestepping our own deficiencies (Novo 1986).[22]

At various meetings, although mainly at Eco-Ed Toronto (1992), the participants decried the lack of a qualitative assessment of the true scope and range of environmental education on a worldwide level—above all because the educative effort pursued for twenty-five years in the developed countries has yielded such flimsy results.[23] We have to probe deeper and more honestly in order to defend a pedagogical field that has already acquired its operating license—even though we are constantly having to get it renewed—as well as to contribute genuinely to the fulfillment of our part in the processes of environmental management.

We raise this because it would seem that the critical and somewhat subversive Discourse of environmental education formulated in Chosica (1976) and Bogotá (1985) has been strongly distorted by the immune system of the status quo.[24] As a result, the Discourse of environmental education has invested more effort in insisting on the "transversality" (cross-curricular nature) of environmental education in the school curriculum when faced with attempts to reduce it to a course than in analyzing how environmental education articulates within the critical corpus of contemporary social theory.[25] Although it is still in its early stages, this is certainly a topic that is commanding a stronger presence among some environmental educators in the developed world, although it is not discussed as part of the problem of professionalization.[26]

Professionalization can be seen as closely linked with the possibilities for consolidating research processes in the field of environmental education.[27] There is general agreement within the sector about the importance of fostering research—above all because we are faced with an almost total absence of appropriate exemplars that are in tune with the socio-cultural and economic characteristics of the populations toward which the educational projects are directed. To put it in a nutshell: Without research there is no field, and without a field there is no possibility of professionalizing.

In the same fashion, academic professionalization is also associated with curriculum development. Some of the traits and fissures that characterize the field of environmental education, exemplified by the situation that pertains among the programs offered by institutions of higher learning in México, have already been mentioned. Curriculum development in this field is no less a problem. In addition to the interdisciplinary complexity of its contents, there is the difficulty, already pointed out, of the different approaches and stances toward the problem and the varying range of the pedagogical projects.[28] These aspects must mesh in turn with the conception of environmental education that prevails among the different agents involved in shaping and implementing curriculum (de Alba 1991). As if this were not enough, the operation of programs in environmental education is severely limited by the rigid academic-administrative structures of our school systems on their different educational levels.[29]

By way of conclusion, we propose four interrelated vertical axes for the study plan of an environmental educator (see González-Gaudiano 1997a, 270–71) as follows:

1. *The epistemological-theoretical training axis.* This axis tries to develop a capacity to construct one's own explanations of reality, using as its point of departure the study of various schools of philosophical thought and their logics of the construction of knowledge, as well as an understanding of theoretical categories derived from diverse intellectual traditions in respect to the environmental and educational spheres. This constitutes the sustaining axis of a study plan for environmental education.

2. *The critical–social training axis.* This axis tries to enhance understanding of the complexity of environmental problems, using as its point of departure the specific historical, social, economic, political, and cultural frameworks that shape the local, regional, and global reality of social subjects. The idea is to construct appropriate referential frameworks in order for us to place ourselves in a concrete time and space, as well as to identify avenues of intervention when faced with problems. This constitutes the problematization axis.

3. *The ecologico-environmental training axis.* This axis aims to discuss the bases and general principles for understanding the dynamics of the phenomena of nature, in order to equip us to gauge problems from the perspective of the vital processes in which the human species itself is inscribed. This constitutes the contextualization axis.

4. *The pedagogical training axis.* This axis seeks to encourage the construction of a new language in environmental education, in order to apprehend the field theoretically as well as to intervene critically in educational practices and processes. This will be a language that promotes the capacity to analyze environmental reality in order to respond to it with educational proposals within prevailing structures of power, but a language in which the subjects of education acquire the capacity to determine and not only to be determined. This constitutes the pedagogical intervention axis.

The professionalization of environmental educators can become a task of greater social and political importance than we may recognize at first glance. The challenges are not simple. We must foster a process of professionalization in a context where professionalizing is typically characterized by an academicist stamp that has been imposed on other forms of acquiring abilities, knowledge, and values. This is a stamp marked by the disappearance of social accords, to make way for exclusive visions whereby an ensemble of monopolistic practices is imposed on us. Professionalization is a challenge. It is also, however, an opportunity to become better equipped to construct the Discourses we want. The time has come to strengthen our shared efforts in that direction.[30]

Notes

1. Translated by Hoyt Rogers.

2. Some authors (Sureda and Colom 1989; the chapter contributors to Caride 1991; Giolitto 1984) identify roots and antecedents for environmental education in the pedagogical formulations that arose in the sixteenth century, with J. J. Rousseau as a notable exponent in the eighteenth century. These proposals originated a movement in which the natural surroundings are preeminent for educational processes—hence it is known as pedagogical naturalism—and which has had differing expressions subsequently. Nevertheless, the use of nature as a didactic resource, as a means of instruction, and as the content of teaching, even though it is related to what is designated today as environmental education, cannot be acknowledged as its foundation. Environmental education is a problematic contemporary pedagogical field that arises mainly from our concern about the high rates of deterioration in the natural world and their repercussions on the quality of life, a phenomenon of increased intensity in the second half of the twentieth century. That concern also generated the environmental movement and the institutional development regarding this subject on a worldwide scale.

3. In this respect, Sureda and Colom (1989, 49) consider environmental pedagogy "a specific type of pedagogy interested in knowing about the influence of the environment on educative processes, thereby undoubtedly opening out on a technology which, by controlling and becoming familiar with such influences, might go on to modify and influence those processes in accord with preestablished patterns and objective. . . . By contrast, environmental education is a formative proposition which . . . is based fundamentally on the protection and regeneration of the environment." Novo remarks that

   > Environmental Education conceives of the individual from an ecological perspective, as a being integral to ecosystems. In this sense it tends to abandon the traditional anthropocentrism which has sustained the forms whereby man has maintained a "dominant" relation towards Nature, in order to promote a type of relation between man and the environment which is based on symbiosis and respect for natural cycles. . . . But the conception of this relationship between man and the environment goes beyond the theoretical presuppositions of socialization. Also espousing as its ultimate education objective the development of the critical and creative capacity of its students, Environmental Pedagogy advocates that a new form of relationship between human groups and their surroundings is only possible precisely through the empowerment of the individual capacity of each human being to question his or her own lifestyle and to develop an open attitude towards the future which will permit him or her to think out new solutions to problems (1986, 98).

   Ultimately, the recent appearance of signifiers constructed with the prefix eco-, such as ecoeducation and ecopedagogy, has only served to distract the attention we need to devote to important matters.

4. Gutiérrez-Pérez puts it this way:

    > The theoretical approaches to the topic have been wide and varied: ranging
    > from a strictly pedagogistic perspective which viewed our surroundings as a
    > mere resource in the service of education, to radically opposed positions
    > which champion the protection of natural endowments and place educa-
    > tion at the service of a cause whose ends are not in the recipients of that
    > education themselves but in the improvement of the environment; to exces-
    > sively psychologistic versions which are exclusively concerned with compre-
    > hending and explaining in depth the patterns of perception of our sur-
    > roundings. In order to be able thereby to impinge upon them and modify
    > them; to more current perspectives like the critical approach of education
    > for development, where environmental quandaries are filtered through the
    > questioning of socio-economic and political structures on a local or
    > transnational level (1995, 137–38).

5. A work close in spirit to environmental educators is that of Daniel Quinn, quoted
    in the epigraph to this essay. In describing a story, Ismael, the main character of
    the work, says:

    > There's no need to hear it. No need to name it or analyze it: each one of
    > you has known it by heart since you were six or seven years old. White and
    > black, man and woman, rich and poor, Christian and Jew, American and
    > Russian, Norwegian and Chinese, you've all heard it. And you hear it non-
    > stop because every propaganda medium and every educational medium
    > pour it out non-stop. And by hearing it non-stop, you don't hear it. No need
    > to hear it. It's always present as a murmur in the background. So there's no
    > need to pay any attention to it. . . . Given a story that must be put into
    > practice and that will place you in harmony with the world, you'll live in
    > harmony with the world; but given a story to put into practice which will
    > place you in discord with the world, such as yours does, you'll live in dis-
    > cord with the world. Given a story to put into practice in which you are the
    > masters of the world, you'll act like the masters of the world. And given a
    > story to put into practice in which the world is an enemy that has to be
    > conquered, you'll conquer it like an enemy; and one day, inevitably, your
    > enemy will lie bleeding at your feet, just like what's happening to the world
    > right now (1995, 43, 44, 94).

6. Esteva (1997, 44), citing Bengoa (1988, 7) in relation to popular education (PE),
    points out that

    > the "movement" character of PE has hindered popular educators from at-
    > taining a precise theoretical conceptualization of their aspirations. In a real-
    > ity as vast and complex as Latin America, the expressions of PE have been
    > determined by the requirements and the specific nature of social move-
    > ments in the national and even local spheres in each country. . . . Because
    > of its cultural character and its "movement" aspect, PE has lacked a corpus
    > of well-defined ideas or doctrines on a precise theoretical level. Rather, it is
    > related to an ensemble of deschooled, practical educational activities and
    > options revolving around the defense and autonomy of the popular world
    > (1997, 44).

In support of these ideas and particularly in the case of Spain, it has also been asserted that "an analysis of the current state of PE obliges us to detect the episodic and spontaneous character of the majority of the actions undertaken in this field, which is made manifest by the non-elucidation of a didactic model" (MMA 1996, 230).

7. On this matter see the provisional report "Environmental Education Guidelines for Excellence: What School-age Learners Should Know and Be Able to Do," and "Environmental Education Materials: Guidelines for Excellence," sponsored by the National Project for Excellence in Environmental Education with support from the United States Environmental Protection Agency (EPA). The last of these reports, about to be undertaken, is entitled "Environmental Education Guidelines for Excellence: Teacher Education and Professional Development," and this is the one most relevant to the theme of this chapter. An extensive discussion of the pros and cons of the standardization project that is being carried out in the United States may be found in the *Canadian Journal of Environmental Education* volume 2 (1997). See especially the article by Arjen Wals and Tore van der Leij. In relation to this discussion, it is important to avoid the possible confusion between the concept of professionalization that is being studied in this chapter and that of standardization.

8. In relation to this matter, Arditi (1989, 96) remarks:

    Special fields of knowledge or demarcated rationalities operate as nets which we cast again and again over the fluidity of life, seeking certainties, determinations of meaning, collective referents which make communication and action possible. For it is obvious that a rationalization process in one segment of social material promotes the formation and development of regularities, without which it is not possible to submit the practices or range of phenomena of a given sphere to criteria of calculation and predictability, and consequently, to modalities of control. . . . The gestation of such regularities (habits, routines, etc.) alludes to a veritable process of domestication of the social material by means of norms, a normalization through which the phenomena and the practices and the acting subjects become governable categories.

9. Some recent stances such as that of Huckle and Sterling (1996) indicate that there exists a crucial contradiction between the "weak" sustainability championed by the liberal reformers and social democrats and the "strong" sustainability advocated by the green socialists and radical utopians. Citing Ken Webster, they mention that in this framework postmodernity is eroding the bases of modern schooling and that teachers who are preparing themselves to promote a critical consciousness can now really contribute to new educational arrangements that are more consonant with ecological principles, better developed, and more plural and open.

10. Barnes (1996, 43), citing Driver (1992) and referring to geographers, emphatically affirms that their professional development "should reflect critically upon the origins of their own discipline and the very power relations which are inherent to their subject of inquiry."

11. It is common to observe that in environmental education we educators assume our role in differing forms, in diverse spaces, and by means of different proposi- tions: for example, some in the curriculum through ecological contents, others in open areas through naturalist and ludic activities. Frequently we are recognizable in reforestation, in the classification of waste, in the conservation of species, or in different forms of prohibition: don't smoke, don't waste water, etc.—although only with difficulty are we recognizable as environmental educators in function of the theoretical and political positions we assume vis-à-vis our work.

12. Gutiérrez-Pérez and others set forth a "research agenda for the future" and iden- tify five points that concern the members of the guild. The first of these—which alludes directly to our topic—is the professional development of the agents or environmental educators. Gutiérrez-Pérez and his colleagues note that they do not take up in their study "the specific questions relative to the professional profile of good environmental educators, nor to the formative institutions which must address these themes. The central content of this debate has been tilted toward formative strategies, and especially self-training strategies spearheaded by the active agents" (1997, 6).

13. According to the database of the Center for Education and Training in Sustain- able Development of the Ministry of the Environment, Natural Resources and Fishing, at the present time México offers nine diplomas, two specializations, and five master's degrees. Four diplomas are institutionally linked to the area of biol- ogy, three to chemistry with an orientation toward engineering, and two to the humanities; the majority of the master's degrees (four) and the two specializations are linked to pedagogy, particularly to teacher training. The master's degree of the University of Guadalajara is the only program which operates under the mo- dality of long-distance education, and it is linked to the area of biological, agricul- tural, and husbandry sciences.

14. Spanish environmental educators have joined in with these initial aims: They are interested in promoting an interinstitutional and international doctorate that would harness the existing capabilities.

15. The absences evoked here refer to the problem that until recently there did not exist an administrative-normative framework that determined the academic weight of the diplomas. Accordingly we found that some diplomas were offered for a duration of forty hours of intensive work during a single week, and others for a duration of 200 hours of coursework over a period of five months of weekend courses. At the present time, institutions such as the Autonomous National Uni- versity of México (UNAM) and the Ibero-American University, among others, have established requirements for academic coursework that fluctuate between 200 and 220 hours. Thus the modality of the diploma is comparable to what in Spain is designated as a master, given that in neither country is it acknowledged as a graduate level of study; rather, it is generally placed among the programs in continuing education.

16. In Spain the Ongoing Seminars on Environmental Education, promoted jointly by the Administration and by environmental educators since 1987, have been an

interesting experience. See Susana Calvo in José Gutiérrez-Pérez and others (1997, 11–19). A report about two programs of professional development in environmental education carried out in the United States and Australia, based on a strategy using mentors, can be consulted in Fortino (1997).

17.   Arditi remarks:

As opposed to the founding totalities of the essentialist model, unity can no longer be *constitutive*, it must be *constituted* or instituted as the result of an effort to structure the phenomenal diversity of the world, stamping it with a form or specific unity. To put it more precisely, unity is constituted and *only then* does it go on to be constitutive. Once a type of fixation has been instituted in the differential magma, whether it be called theocratic society or bourgeois subject, it is undeniable that objects, values, fields of knowledge, hierarchies, and routines will arise which are marked by that form of the institution of order (1992, 112–13).

In a footnote he elucidates: "It should be remembered that we are referring to a purely analytical distinction; in practice, the processes of the institution of order and the constitution of phenomena intertwine and modify each other reciprocally (113).

18.   The authors write "Discourse" with a capital "D" in order to distinguish it from "discourse" which means "a stretch of spoken or written language" or "language in use." "A Discourse is composed of ways of talking, listening, reading, writing, acting, interacting, believing, valuing, and using tools and objects, in particular ways and at specific times, so as to display or to recognize a particular social identity" (Gee, Hull, and Lankshear 1996, 10). Laclau (1993a, 104), points out that "if we maintain the relational character of all identity, and if, at the same time, we renounce the fixation of those identities in a system . . . the social dimension must be identified with the infinite play of differences, that is, with what we may call discourse in the strictest sense of the term—on the condition, of course, that we free the concept of discourse from a meaning which restricts it to speaking and writing." Affirming the above—and paraphrasing Foucault—Ball (1994, 6) remarks: "Words and concepts change their meaning and effects according to the discourses in which they are developed. Discourses limit the possibilities of thought. They order and combine words in specific forms and exclude or displace other combinations. Nevertheless, to the extent that discourses are constructed by exclusions and inclusions, by what must not be said as much as by what may indeed be said, they maintain antagonistic relationships with other discourses, other possibilities of meaning, other pleas, rights, and postures."

19.   McLaren (1994) reflects upon the importance of the body in the framework of postmodern social theory, in the sense of "body/subject" as the "sphere of the flesh where meaning inscribes, constructs, and reconstitutes itself," that is, "as the place of incorporated or 'incarnated' subjectivity which also reflects the ideological sedimentations of the social structure inscribed in it" (87).

20.   Giroux, Lankshear, McLaren, and Peters (1996) offer us an excellent discussion about counternarratives, from two perspectives: on the one hand, in relation to

the "grand," "master," or "meta"-narratives, issuing from the culture of the Enlightenment, set forth in the framework of the philosophies of history that accompany the Rights of Man, Truth, Justice, and Beauty and that represent Western culture and "the United States" as the ultimate projection of European ideals, as the apex of an unswerving and evolutionary development of 2,000 years of civilization; and on the other, in relation to the "official" and "hegemonic" narratives of everyday life, that is, those legitimizing stories that are propagated with specific political purposes in order to manipulate public awareness by proclaiming an ensemble of national ideals held in common.

21   Rorty remarks on the importance of

> a global turning away from theory and toward narrative. That turning may be a symbol of our renouncement of the attempt to gather all the aspects of our life into a single vision, to rediscover ourselves by means of a single lexicon. It may be tantamount to an acknowledgment [of] what . . . I call "the contingency of language": the fact that there is no way of emerging from the diverse lexicons we have employed, of finding a meta-lexicon which somehow would take into account *all* the possible lexicons, all the possible forms of judging and feeling. A historicist and nominalist culture such as I conceive would, by contrast, be satisfied with narrations which connect the present with the past, on the one hand, and with future utopias on the other. And, what is even more important, it would consider the achievement of utopias, and the elaboration of subsequent utopias, to be an unending process, like the ceaseless achievement of Freedom, and not a convergence toward an already existing Truth (1991, 17–19).

22.   Some criticisms of modernity advanced by Vattimo (1996, 74–78) are directed precisely against this conception of history, seen as a unitary and progressive process that implies the existence of a center around which events are gathered and ordered. He points out, citing Walter Benjamin, that "history as a unitary course is a depiction of the past constructed by the dominant social groups and classes." In opposition to this unitary conception, Vattimo proposes the idea that there are many histories and notes that "the crisis of the idea of history entails that of the idea of progress: if there is no unitary course of human vicissitudes it cannot be maintained, either, that these are advancing towards an end, that they are effecting a rational plan of improvements, education, and emancipation."

23.   The state of the evaluation of environmental education in the region is particularly critical. A report on this aspect may be found in González-Gaudiano and de Alba (1997).

24.   Previous to the Intergovernmental Conference on Environmental Education of Tbilisi, the Subregional Workshop on Environmental Education was held in Chosica in March of 1976, and the First Seminar on the University and Environmental Education in Latin America and the Caribbean took place in Santafé de Bogotá in 1985. In the authors' opinions, these were two of the regional meetings that contributed the most to building an alternative approach to environmental education.

25. Theoretical training does not imply "teaching theories" but, rather, developing in the environmental educator an attitude that empowers him or her intellectually to find his or her own explanations (González-Gaudiano 1997a). In the words of Henry Giroux (1996, 184), the educator must become an agent creating theory, in what he calls a pedagogy of theorization, which has as its object—following the ideas of Joseph Harris—that "the students should theorize about how they, as subjects, are simultaneously produced, situated, and contained within the lecture hall . . . [turning into] something more than an affirmation of the student's voice . . . into a form of critical insurgency, a space for the possible where one is called to intellectual responsibility so that one must continually clarify questions of conscience, desire, and personal and social identity."

26. See, for example, the *Canadian Journal of Environmental Education*, or the *Australian Journal of Environmental Education*. Examples of authors include Lucie Sauvé, Noel Gough, Ian Robottom, Paul Hart, Bob Jickling, and Arjen Wals, among others. Paradoxically, some of the most lucid and committed theoreticians of critical pedagogy (such as Henry Giroux, Michael Apple, Peter McLaren, and Stanley Aronowitz, to mention a few) have not incorporated the environmental dimension into their formulations about the educational sphere. Only Colin Lankshear has accorded importance to this matter, perhaps because of his greater personal immersion in the Latin American context.

27. This is true not only in relation to the experiences of professional training linked with research projects (Papadimitriou 1995, 85–97), but also because of the need for specialized personnel with an academic focus, required in order to strengthen this facet of the field that has been neglected in the region, and particularly in Latin America and the Caribbean. An interesting discussion about the situation of research in the field of environmental education may be found in Mrazek (1996).

28. Smyth (1995) remarks that the objectives of environmental education can be seen as stages. *Environmental consciousness-raising*, understood as the process of alerting people about the numerous factors that influence their environment, represents the first step in a systematic path of thought. *Environmental literacy* is built on that awareness by means of the acquisition of a clearer knowledge and better understanding of the components of the system, the liaison between those components and the dynamics of the system. *Environmental responsibility* acknowledges the special role of humanity in the determination and orientation of change, as well as in the capacity to evaluate the differing options. *Environmental aptitude* implies a degree of mastery of the system, not only in order to understand and assess, but also in order to contribute effectively to its better functioning. And *environmental citizenship* denotes a concept of participatory membership in the system. Smyth exhorts us to leave behind our emphasis on environmental consciousness-raising in order to aspire to the other stages. Despite our reservations with conceiving educational processes as sequential stages, we have salvaged Smyth's assertions in order to confirm the demand that is continually being formulated about the scope and range of our projects in environmental education.

29. Apparently this is a fairly common problem, even in the industrialized regions of the world. By way of example, see Giolitto (1997). In this report about the European Union, to be sure, there is no mention of the problem of the professionalization of environmental educators. All that is presented is a quick inventory of the measures adopted in those countries for the training of basic education teachers.

30. See González-Gaudiano (1997a) for an account of ideas about a curriculum for training environmental educators.

Chapter 4

Postmodern Science in Aotearoa/ New Zealand? Conservation, Cosmology, and Critique

How did it feel to the Whanau-a-Apanui people of Te Ika a Maui watching the great white ship of James Cook ghosting grandly around Orete Point into Whangaparaoa Bay, so-called White Island smoking like a spent cannon at the 'Bay of Plenty' horizon, the beach crowded with fervent festive people, and the headland too where they stood intently shaking gourds and rattles? Down by the sea the empowered tohunga were summoning whales to the beach . . . calling to the panake to come and ground their vast meat and bone upon the sands—chanting, maximum power.

Ian Wedde, *Symmes Hole*

He came riding through the sea, our sea god Kahutia Te Rangi, astride his tipua, and he brought with him the mauri, the life-giving forces which would enable us to live in close communication with the world. The mauri that he brought came from the Houses of Learning called Te Whakaeroero, Te Rawheoro, Rangitane, and Tapere Nui a Whatonga. They were the gifts of those houses in Hawaiki to the new land. They were very special because among other things, they gave instructions on how man might korero with the beasts and creatures of the sea so that all could live in helpful partnership. They taught *oneness*.

Witi Ihimaera, *The Whale Rider*

. . . [W]hether Leviathan can long endure so wide a chase, and so remorseless a havoc; whether he must not at last be exterminated from the waters, and the last whale, like the last man, smoke his last pipe, and then himself evaporate in the final puff.

Herman Melville, *Moby-Dick*

Natural science does not simply describe and explain, it is part of the interplay between nature and ourselves.

Werner Heisenberg, *Physics and Philosophy*

Introduction: History, Science, and Conservation

Some years ago a news item on National Radio in New Zealand prompted our reflection on the dramatic value reversal that has occurred in the Pakeha (the Maori term for European) perception of the natural world since the early days of contact and first settlement in Aotearoa/New Zealand. The news item concerned a story about 100 or so pilot whales that had become stranded inside Parengarenga Harbour in Taitokerau. According to the report, about forty Conservation Department staff and volunteers attempted to keep the survivors alive by hosing them down and preventing them from crushing each other. The whales were to be refloated in the next high water.

The news item highlighted the contrast between the contemporary conservation of the whale with the beginnings of the whaling industry in Aotearoa/New Zealand in the late eighteenth century. Today's organized state commitment to the scientific monitoring of endangered species, to the restoration of natural ecosystems, to conservation management strategies, and to the implementation of legal protection and the like appear to be set in strong contrast with the accounts of whaling in the Pacific during earlier times: the huge commitment of men, capital, and resources devoted to hunting down and slaughtering entire generations and species of whales. By one account (Baker 1990, 14), the peak year for deep-sea whaling was 1849, which saw 760 North American whaling ships in the Pacific. During the mid-nineteenth century some 200 ships a year of British, French, and North American origin called at New Zealand ports. In the early 1840s there were roughly 100 shore stations in New Zealand accounting for the slaughter of over 4,000 whales per season.

We begin this chapter with a brief account of the value reversal of our perception of whales. This will serve three main purposes. First, it demonstrates the inextricable link of science with history: science in the service of the whaling industry beginning in the late eighteenth century and science in the service of conservation today. Interestingly, the basic scientific monitoring and regulation of whaling began in the late 1930s. Governments agreed to regulate whaling in the Antarctic after it became obvious that the stock of blue whales was declining. Such regulation and conservation grew out of questions of sustainability of the industry rather than any real ethic of conservation. It should not surprise us altogether that the whaling industry addressed the question of sustainability; in 1930 alone the industry produced over 600,000 tons of Antarctic oil from some 40,000 slaughtered whales (Matthews 1968, 165). Five countries

(Japan, Norway, the USSR, Great Britain, and the Netherlands) supporting some 260 vessels were still killing whales in the early 1960s and
although New Zealand stopped whaling in 1964 there were still 97 vessels from three countries operating in 1968 (Berzin 1972, 311).

That science was in the service of the whaling industry is beyond any
dispute. Some early evidence is provided in the account given by the Rev.
Henry Cheever on the homeward cruise of the *Commodore Preble*, entitled *The Whaleman's Adventures in the Southern Ocean* (1850). This
is an extraordinary book. It combines a chapter called "The Whale's Physiology and Natural History" and descriptions of its habits and cruising
grounds, with accounts of the pursuit, harpooning, eventual capture and
piece-by-piece severing of the body. The so-called process of cutting-in of
a whale, although it is rather gruesome, demonstrates the convenient
marriage of modern science and industry:

> First came one of the huge lips, which, after they had nearly severed close to the
> creature's eye, was hooked into what they call a "blubber hook," stripped off, and
> hoisted on board by the windlass. It was very compact and dense, and covered
> with barnacles. Next came one of the fore-fins; after that the other lip, and then
> the upper jaw, along with all that peculiar substance called whalebone, through
> which the animal strains his food. It is all fringed with coarse hair that detains the
> little shrimps and small fry on which the creature feeds (37).

Cheever's narrative combines elements of science—physiology and
natural history—with religion ("A Plea on Behalf of the Sabbath for
Whalemen"), enterprise, history, and practical advice. It is a curious mixture of Christian faith, science, adventure, and British racism. The whale
in biblical times was referred to as Leviathan, which not only meant the
name of some aquatic animal (real or imaginary) of enormous size, but
also the great enemy of God, Satan. Whaling science, it seems, was an
integral part of Western enterprise and the science and enterprise of
whaling was justified by Christianity.

Surgeons who sailed in whaling vessels published accounts of the natural history of the sperm whale and the observations of whaling captains
became material for scientific chartings of whale distributions. Early classifications of whales and descriptions of their physiology helped the industry to process these giant mammals. Accounts of their life cycle, breeding grounds, and migration patterns were crucial to the exploitation of
the whale. Marine laboratories were often sponsored by the whaling industry and set up close to whaling stations charged with biological work
on food chains and the analysis of sea water samples (Matthews 1968).

Today, by contrast, scientific research focuses on monitoring, on studying and explaining individual and herd strandings, on devising new management regimes, and on determining the effects of boats, planes, and people on whales in order to assess whether the new whale-watch tourist industry can support more permit holders. Science in this case is clearly related to conservation values. There was a time, less than thirty years ago, when New Zealand "most blatantly used scientific whaling to boost its whaling industry" (Cherfas 1989, 178). In other words, just as Japan in the last few years has killed hundreds of whales annually for "scientific" purposes in order to escape the International Whaling Commission's (IWC) ban on commercial whaling, New Zealand in the early 1960s used scientific permits to go after sperm whales.

Second, although whaling demonstrates the inextricability of science with history, it is a *particular* and *local* history—one, in fact, which predates the signing of the Treaty of Waitangi and organized colonized settlement by the New Zealand Company. It is a history, further, that includes some of the earliest of contacts between Maori and European peoples, and, therefore, between the traditional knowledge systems of the Maori (their folk taxonomies) and modern European science. (Maori is the name for the indigenous people of Aotearoa/New Zealand.) The excerpt from Ian Wedde's postmodern novel is used as a preface for this chapter because he explores these themes so well. As Keehua Roa, a purported social anthropologist (and fictional character created by Wedde), explains in an introduction to *Symmes Hole* (1986), the early whalers depended on the local Maori people for food. Maori made up the boat crews and became expert whalers (in the European style), although whale hunting was never part of Maori culture. Whalers married into local tribes. Together they formed what Edward Gibbon Wakefield called "a new people" but he did not like them for they represented "an unwelcome interruption to the model history proposed" by "Wakefieldian ideals" and their history "was to go underground before the advancing wave of organized colonization" (Roa, in Wedde 1986, 8). Roa suggests that this "amounted to a submersion of proletarian history under capitalist glosses; disenfranchisement of a people who had been the labour of the disenfranchising economic system" (8).

Third, the value reversal indicates a symbolic break between modern and postmodern science: between one view of science that emphasizes an ahistorical account of knowledge based on a series of dichotomies such as the theory/observation, fact/value, and schema/content distinctions and a view that stresses the primacy of history for understanding the scientific endeavor and recognizes the sciences not as unified logical systems but rather as "forms of life," communities made up of agreed-upon practices and guided by sets of values. This view juxtaposes a mechanical, reductive, and unified science based on a single method against a holistic, organicist, and pluralist notion of science that uses a variety of methods. It also accepts a major difference in terms of both the scope of scientific inquiry and the concept of scientific progress. Stephen Toulmin argues the case in the following terms:

> The emergence of post-modern science has several implications for scientific activity, for our concepts of scientific progress, and therefore, for science policy. One is that the old positivist idea that all the sciences have to be based on a single set of methods is no longer viable. Another is that since the scientist-as-spectator option is no longer open to us, neither is the assumption that science is value-free or that scientists bear no responsibility for the social consequences of their work. Post-modern science must be increasingly bound up with social, political, and ethical considerations (1985, 29).

Toulmin pinpoints a view of science that may go some way toward explaining the value reversal from exploitation to conservation. The Enlightenment view of science that prevailed in the nineteenth century tended to regard science in ahistorical and universal terms. Scientists based their work on a single method which equated with rationality itself. Science was, therefore, seen as value free and quite separate from political or ethical questions. The question of the whale's physiology and natural history was divorced from the whale's exploitation and possible extinction. Such a view of science received fresh emphasis and orientation with the formation of the Vienna School and the emergence of the logical empiricists in the 1920s. This view, known popularly as positivism, held sway in one form or another until the efforts of Popper, Kuhn, Feyerabend, Quine, and others began to dismantle it in the 1950s.

These contrasting views might be teased out further in terms of their respective stated goals of science, theories of reality, methods, criteria of theory evaluation, and so on. Before discussing these issues further this chapter will return briefly to the notion of the postmodern, concentrating on the notion of postmodern science. Finally, the chapter suggests an account of postmodern science that might serve as a framework within the local context to take account of the voices and values of Maori people and conservationists.

The Postmodern Yet Again

The standard definition of the postmodern, in the context of architecture and literature, focuses on two elements. The first element of definition uses postmodern as a periodizing concept, that is, the post-modern is supposed to be subsequent to or later than, what is modern. This element captures, for instance, Linda Hutcheon's (1988) account of postmodernism as a style that takes up the past in a way that neither simply reiterates it (classicism) nor rejects it (modernism). This definition also captures most sociological accounts of the postmodern as the "postindustrial age" or the "information society" or the "global information economy." Yet this aspect of the postmodern is a rather contentious one in that a number of theorists specifically use the notion in a nonperiodizing sense to characterize an attitude, an ethos, or a style. For Jean-François Lyotard (1984), the postmodern is not a different historical epoch but rather a critical attitude or mode of thought about time and history. Lyotard defines modernism also as a mode of thought about time (rather than a period) which rests on two features: time as succession and an atemporal subject. As Bill Readings explains:

> The discourse of history is thus structured as a narrative sequence around an "I" dedicated to the possession and control of both nature and itself through the organization of time as a sequential series of phrases (1991, 161).

Without becoming too technical, the point that Lyotard makes is that the postmodern is a critical way of thinking about a conception of time, history, and, indeed, the very urge to periodize that is characteristic of modernism. This critical approach could be construed as a reevaluation of the modernist notion of time as an ordered, sequential, temporal succession of events synthesized in an atemporal subject and, therefore, as an attack on the modernist notion of history as the continuous chronology of reason. More simply, postmodernism (in Lyotard's terms) is a fundamental questioning of the idea of history as the progress of reason. Dmitry Khanin asks a rhetorical question: "What is at stake after all in the current controversy over postmodernism if not the idea of progress?" He prefaces his remark with the following comment:

> Modernism can be formulated as simply this: it is the conviction that what is new is better than what is old just because it is a product of a later stage of development. What underlies this view is a particular conception of history as an evolving process whose further phases necessarily supersede the previous ones in every possible respect, using them as a platform for new breakthroughs. The debate of the ancients and the moderns in seventeenth-century France . . . might be taken as a watershed between the medieval type of consciousness which rested on the maxim the older the better (the older being closer to the sacred truths of revelation), and the modern one, assured of the superiority of the present as more sophisticated and refined than what came before (1991, 246).

Postmodernism, then, is a questioning of the modern assumption that what is new is better; it is a questioning of the past as an ordered, linear, and cumulative development that represents Western civilization as the apex of this process of cultural evolution. Leonard Meyer directly addresses this notion in talking about developments in Western art. Art since the First World War has brought to an end the preceding 500 years of ordered, sequential change. We have now entered

a period of stylistic stasis, a period characterized not by a linear, cumulative development of a single style, but the co-existence of a multiplicity of quite different styles in a fluctuating and dynamic steady state (1967, 98).

The second element of the dictionary definition refers to postmodernism, specifically in the arts and especially in architecture, as a movement against modernism (see the Introduction). Taking the example of postmodern American fiction, one critic with mock seriousness lists November 22, 1963 (the day John F. Kennedy died), as the day postmodernism was officially inaugurated—"since that day was the day that symbolically signaled the end of a certain kind of optimism and naiveté in our collective consciousness, the end of certain verities and assurances that had helped shape our notion of what fiction should be" (McCaffery 1986, xii). McCaffery shapes up postmodernism in the works of Thomas Pynchon, John Barth, Vladimir Nabokov, Robert Coover, William Gass, and Richard Brautigan as a movement against modernist realistic fiction, a form that he links with the epistemological assurance and optimism of Western empiricism and rationalism. American postmodern fiction, by contrast, experiments with subjectivity, turned inward to the world of language and dream, to challenge the realist convention of a unified subject living in a world of stable essences. These experiments shared

a general sense that fiction needed to acknowledge its own artificial, constructed nature, to focus the reader's attention on how the work was being articulated rather than merely on what was happening. Distrustful of all claims to truth and hypersensitive to the view that reality and objectivity were not givens but social or linguistic constructs, postmodern writers tended to lay bare the artifice of their work, to comment on the processes involved, to refuse to create the realist illusion that the work mimics operations outside itself (McCaffery 1986, xxi).

The architect and critic Charles Jencks, in 1987, offered the observation that modernism had ended on 15 July 1972 at 3:32 p.m., the exact moment of the demolition of modernist Minouru Yamasaki's Pruitt-Igoe housing project. He describes as "tragic" the connection between modernist architecture and modernization and writes:

The Post-Modern Movement was then, and remains today, a wider social protest against modernization, against the destruction of local culture by the combined forces of rationalization, bureaucracy, large-scale development and, it is true, the Modern International Style (Jencks 1987, 29).

The opposition between modernism and postmodernism architecture for Paolo Portoghesi is characterized in terms of a break with the hegemony of Euclidean geometry; for Victorio Grigotti, another Italian architect, it is characterized by the fact that there is no longer any relationship between the architectural project and socio-historical progress toward human emancipation on the larger scale. As Lyotard describes Grigotti's view:

Postmodern architecture is condemned to generate a multiplicity of small transformations in the space it inherits, and to give up the project of a last rebuilding of the whole space occupied by humanity. . . . [T]here is no longer a horizon of universalization, of general emancipation before the eyes . . . of the postmodern architect. The disappearance of this idea of progress within rationality and freedom would explain a certain tone, style or modus which are specific to postmodern architecture (1989, 7).

Kenneth Frampton (1987) agrees with aspects of what both Jencks and Lyotard have to say and proposes a critical culture of architecture that, while not entirely rejecting the thrust of modernization, at least resists being totally consumed by it. Frampton calls this culture a "critical regionalism" and characterizes it in terms of six points of resistance: culture and civilization, in order "to become modern and yet to return to sources"; the transformation of the avant-garde, emphasizing the possibility for what he calls "an anti-phallocentric, anti-Eurocentric reflective culture"; development versus place forms, that is, the creation of local, public places to set against the "increasingly privatized universal reality of the megalopolis"; culture versus nature, "inscribing the built work into the ground," "the regional inflection of buildings" in terms of climate, light etc.; and the mediation of the visual by the tactile (Frampton 1987, 16–30).

Perhaps the most comprehensive assessment of postmodern architecture is that offered by Heinrich Klotz, who lists the following defining characteristics:

- *Regionalism* has replaced internationalism.
- *Fictional representation* . . . has supplanted geometric abstraction.

- The tendency toward fictional representation has led away from the late-modern tendency to view a building exclusively in terms of function, and toward seeing it as a *work of art of building* that belongs in the realm of the illusory.
- Postmodernism relies not on the symbolic value of the machine and of construction as defining progress in architecture, but on a *multiplicity of meanings*.
- *Poetry* has supplanted technological utopianism. Postmodernism draws from the world of the imagination rather than from the "brave new world" mentality in which velocity is equated with progress.
- Postmodernism opposes the sterile faith in the continuous improvement of instruments and construction with *improvisation* and *spontaneity*. Instead of striving for untouchable perfection, it favors the disturbed and the imperfect, which are now seen as signs of life.
- Whereas modernism sought to free itself from history and made architecture purely a thing of the present, with postmodernism we have regained *memory*. And rather than exploit history for "interesting" effects, we can now entrust ourselves to the spirit of irony.
- Rather than view a building as an autonomous, universally valid geometric form, we can now allow it to be *relativized* by its historical, regional, and topological conditions, and can appreciate the *palpable individuality* of the particular solution. Heroism gives way to compromise, to equitable treatment of old and new, and to respect for the given environment.
- Instead of a dominant style, with its tendency to become dogma, a broad *range of vocabularies and stylistic languages* exist alongside one another. Postmodernism denies the self-referential inventiveness of the Modern Movement and pays tribute to the pluralism of referential allusions.
- Rather than identify architecture with life, postmodernism establishes anew the *aesthetic distance* from life. Fiction as well as function! (see Klotz 1988, 421).

In the New Zealand context, Richard Killeen's images, Ronald Hugh Morrieson's "post-provincial" novels—Keri Hulme's *The Bone People*, Roger Donaldson's *Smash Palace*, Greg McGee's *Foreskin's Lament*, Janet Frame's *Living in the Maniototo*, C. K. Stead's *All Visitors Ashore*, and the short stories of Russell Haley and Michael Morrissey—have been talked of and discussed in postmodernist terms although with important local differences. One could add Mike Johnson's *Lear* and *Anti-Body Positive*. In addition, the exhibition of over 100 works by nine New Zealand photographers entitled *Imposing Narratives: Beyond the Documentary in New Zealand Photography* (Wellington City Art Gallery, 26 November–22 January 1990) clearly and self-consciously fits itself into the postmodern. The photographs themselves were interspersed with texts that proclaim an allegiance to an international postmodern ethos under the headings of Narratives; Signs, Metaphors, and Symbols; and Context.

Narratives

"We expect a story to be coherent: to have a beginning, a middle and an end. If parts are not connected coherently they seem to make no sense. Only in dreams and surrealistic contexts have we learned to accept and tolerate inconsistency. Confronted with seemingly isolated parts we immediately start to create meaning by establishing connections and continuity" (from explanatory texts, Wellington City Art Gallery, 26 November–22 January 1990).

Signs, Metaphors, and Symbols

"We have learned that objects, gestures, poses, colors, etc. stand for something else and we read them accordingly. Some, like the heart, are very familiar and easy to decode; others need some more training and experience" (from explanatory texts, Wellington City Art Gallery, 26 November–22 January 1990).

Context

"Our perception—the viewer's and the photographer's—is conditioned by gender, psychological, social and cultural factors, and by the multitude of pictures from our mass culture" (from explanatory texts, Wellington City Art Gallery, 26 November–22 January 1990).

Krishan Kumar's *Prophecy and Progress* (1978) list, which draws attention to the sociological literature, indicates that the attempt to postulate the postmodern is not limited to architecture and the arts. In fact, Kumar's list and summary can be added to substantially: not only the varieties of postindustrial society, post-bourgeois society, post-scarcity society, information society, the society of the spectacle, media-saturated society and so on but also post-Impressionism, post-analytic philosophy, post-positivism, poststructuralism. What these labels demonstrate is the attempt by thinkers in quite diverse subjects and fields to typify a change not only with the so-called modern era but also with various traditionally modern ways of viewing the world. Toynbee, the British historian, used the term postmodern to delineate a fourth stage of Western history following the Dark Ages, the Middle Ages and the Modern Era, beginning in about 1875. In Toynbee's thought postmodern suggests anarchy, irrationality, indeterminacy and the end of Western cultural dominance. Peter Drucker's *Landmarks of Tomorrow* (1959, ix), subtitled "A Report on the New Post-Modern World," indicated that we had shifted from the modern Cartesian worldview to a "new universe of pattern, purpose, and process" characterized by education and knowledge and the new technologies they gave rise to. His description was roughly what, after the writings of Daniel Bell and Alain Touraine, we would call postindustrial society or the information society or the global information economy.

For both Bell and Touraine, who wrote in the 1960s and early 1970s, the West had moved irretrievably into a postindustrial society, a concept coined to emphasize the centrality of theoretical knowledge as the axis around which new technology, economic growth, and the stratification of society will be organized. Bell (1974) introduces the notion to identify a change in social structure that he describes in terms of a shift from manufacturing to services in the economic sector, the centrality of the new science-based industries in technology, and the rise of new technical elites and the advent of a new principle of social stratification. He charts the rise of new axial principles that are said to structure institutions in postindustrial society. In particular, he identifies theoretical knowledge as central, replacing private property. Whereas the main endeavor in industrial society was the accumulation of capital (the creation of savings and their conversion into investment), in postindustrial society the chief endeavor is the organization of science around the university and the research institute. The chief policy issues are the nature and scope of state support for science, the politicization of science, and the problems of the organization of work by science teams.

The idea of postindustrialism was used and developed by sociologists and economists from the early 1960s, an era of optimism when it was thought that there were no limits to growth or to the increasing affluence of the "long boom." By the mid-1970s this optimism and the idea of continuous economic growth on which it depended began to seem both misplaced and naive. After the oil shocks of the mid-1970s and the bite of worldwide recession, increasingly the mood and discourse shifted to one of crisis that emphasized doubts about the prospects for continuous economic growth. During this period when ecological arguments and green politics began to find their mark and when Western governments began to struggle with issues of deindustrialization and economic decline, visions of a postindustrial society appeared distant and even irresponsible.

Yet during that time new forms of postindustrial theory were being developed, based around the introduction and effects of the new information technologies. They have come to fruition in the late 1980s and early 1990s and now dominate contemporary debates. The new theories are, perhaps, more cautious than their 1960s counterparts but they are equally optimistic. Although they do not see the future unproblematically, they still cling to the idea that the most developed societies are witnessing a series of interrelated changes as significant as those that accompanied the shift from agrarian to industrial society.

The most recent policies focus on science and technology in the service of economic development. Restructured and fully rationalized according to the familiar principles of contestability, flexibility, user-pays services and cost effectiveness, public good science has been commercialized and commodified in the name of increasing national competitive advantage. These policies emphasize profound changes in information technology use and, in particular, the shift from stand-alone equipment and applications to computer-based networking and new information services. Information networking is seen as the basis of new services for the economy and for a strategic response to changes in the market environment. In addition, networking is seen as underpinning the trend toward the globalization of all economic activities, as well as having significant implications for both the location and structure of industries and the future international division of labor.

Postmodern Science

Consider Bruno Latour's (1987) account of the politics of scientific practice, involving a research scientist and her boss in a leading Californian laboratory. The scientist sees herself as pursuing pure science—research on a new substance called pandorin—unencumbered by wider social or political concerns. By contrast, her boss, the head of the laboratory, is involved in political activity most of the time. For instance, during a typical week he negotiates with a major pharmaceutical company over possible patents; he meets with the French Ministry of Health to discuss the opening of a new laboratory; he meets with the National Academy of Sciences to argue for the recognition of a new scientific subsection; he attends a board meeting of the journal *Endocrinology* to urge that more space be devoted to his area; he visits the local meatworks to talk about a new way of decapitating sheep without damaging the hypothalamus; he attends a curriculum meeting at the university to advocate more molecular biology and computer science; he discusses with a visiting scientist Swedish advances in the instruments used for detecting peptides; and he delivers an address to the Diabetic Association.

Some time later the effects of the boss's decisions, meetings, and advocacy begin to impact upon the laboratory scientist. Alan Chalmers recounts Latour's story:

> We find that she has been able to employ a new technician, made possible by a grant from the Diabetic Association, and she has two new graduate students, who have entered the field by way of the new courses designed by her boss. Her research has benefited from the cleaner samples she is receiving from the slaughterhouse and a new, highly sensitive, instrument recently acquired from Sweden which increases her capacity to detect minute traces of pandorin in the brain. Her preliminary results are published in a new section of Endocrinology. She is contemplating a position offered to her by the French government involving the setting up of a laboratory in France (Chalmers 1990, 120–21).

As Chalmers points out, the laboratory scientist is mistaken in her view that she is engaged in pure science uncontaminated by broader social and political matters. Indeed, the material conditions necessary for the pursuit of her research are obtained only through the political activity of her boss. Clearly, scientific practice cannot be separated from other practices serving other interests. Furthermore, by extension, it is possible to argue for the social character of all scientific practice.

We take this to be the main argument, with suitable refinements, of both the historicist and sociological turns in contemporary accounts of science, after Thomas Kuhn's (1962) *The Structure of Scientific Revolutions*. Indeed, in the Postscript written in 1969, Kuhn highlights the social character of scientific practice by strongly emphasizing the notion of scientific community—a notion he believes underlies his earlier work. A scientific community consists of practitioners who have undergone similar educations and professional initiations. These practitioners have absorbed the same technical literature and, although there are competing schools, in general they pursue a set of shared goals. Membership is established through advanced degrees, professional societies, journals read, and so on (Kuhn 1970). Kuhn's account has been taken up and elaborated by scholars like Marjorie Grene (1985), who has developed a "new" philosophy of science in contrast to what may be seen as the "old." Her account has been called ecological realism and emphasizes a biological approach to knowing and observing (see Reed 1992). Both Kuhn and

Grene have made their contributions to understanding what we will call postmodern science. There are at least two accounts of postmodern sci ence: One emphasizes the return to cosmology, the reintegration of science with philosophy; the other functions as a critique of contemporary science, stressing the bureaucratic rationalization of science and the way in which science as a reason of state has been put in the service of economic development. Both accounts seek to understand science historically as part of a set of social practices belonging to a culture. Making use of this general insight, they picture science as a changing enterprise or institution, to some extent reflecting changing historical conditions. Both accounts can thus be construed as sympathetic to the claims of those who have been excluded from science or suffered as a result of it.

The Return to Cosmology

Stephen Toulmin wrote a book in 1982 called *The Return to Cosmology: Postmodern Science and the Theology of Nature* in which he explicitly addresses the theme of postmodern science as a return to cosmology. At one point he writes:

> The "modern" world is now a thing of the past. Our own natural science today is no longer "modern" science. Instead . . . it is rapidly engaged in becoming "postmodern" science: the science of the "postmodern" world, of "postnationalist" politics and "postindustrial" society—the world that has not yet discovered how to define itself in terms of what it is, but only in terms of what it has just-now-ceased to be. In due course, the change from modern to postmodern science will evidently be matched by corresponding changes in philosophy and theology also; in particular, the "postmodern" positions and methods that natural scientists are now working out will have implications, also, for a possible reunion of natural science with natural theology (1982, 254).

Toulmin uses the term "postmodern" after the theologian Frederick Ferré (1976), who devotes his efforts to projecting a new set of values and institutions for a postmodern world. Toulmin's argument is straightforward enough: He argues that science and natural theology separated in the nineteenth and early twentieth centuries as a result of the professionalization of science and its consequent specialization. Under this increasing division of labor, the broader concerns of traditional cosmology disappeared. At the same time the role of the scientist came to be seen as that of a pure spectator who was expected to report "objectively" on the world of nature. The spectator view of knowledge carried with it a belief in the "value neutrality" of science such that it was seen as no longer able to throw light on moral, practical, and religious questions. In particular, Descartes' celebration of geometry as the model, which exemplified the essence of rationality, established a hierarchy of knowledge and elevated the sciences that dealt with general phenomena and downgraded those areas of study that dealt with particular events. Further, and perhaps more importantly:

> Cartesian dualism made canonical a split in our vision of the world, which had the effect of setting rational thinking humanity over against causal, unthinking nature, and so enthroned the human intellect within a separate world of "mental substance" (Toulmin 1982, 238).

Traditional cosmology, before its transition to modern science in the seventeenth century under the influence of Galileo, Kepler, Newton, Bacon, and Descartes, performed many and varied functions, at one and the same time practical, theoretical, symbolic and expressive. The return to cosmology symbolized in postmodern science seeks to reinsert humanity into the world of nature. Toulmin mentions late classical antiquity, the period dominated by Stoicism, as the last period in Western history when humanity and nature were thought of as complementary elements within a single scheme or cosmos. He sees green philosophy as a (nonacademic) contemporary counterpart of Stoicism, based as it is on a responsibility to deepen an understanding of the interdependence that binds humanity to nature and combining as it does both scientific and philosophical or ethical elements. In a later publication, Toulmin (1985) emphasizes pluralism and responsibility as hallmarks of postmodern science, through which the scientist-as-participant is encouraged to see herself as part of the natural processes she seeks to study. To the extent that scientists recognize their roles as participants, Toulmin argues, they will help to develop a worldview that is less mechanistic, reductionistic, and deterministic. Most recently, Toulmin (1990) returns to the seventeenth century to rediscover the ideal of society as Cosmopolis, a society as rationally ordered as the Newtonian view of nature. Such a view was reflected, for instance, in Hobbes's Leviathan, which elaborated a conception of society based on the scientific method as it was then understood. Toulmin reexamines the standard account of modernity and its defects, arguing against foundationalist accounts of knowledge that characterize the appeal to scientific rationalism. Science that still upholds or legitimates itself by referring to the seventeenth century view of rationality must be humanized and replaced by a notion of science along lines advocated by Paul Feyerabend. This would be a science that makes itself subordinate to the needs of citizens and communities, and that reappropriates the aims and values of practical philosophy implicit in Renaissance humanism

Other scholars have talked in similar terms as Toulmin: David Bohm (1980, 1985), Rupert Sheldrake (1991), Charles Birch (1988), Ilya Prigogine and Isabelle Stengers (1985), David Griffin (1988c), Bonadventura de Sousa Santos (1992), and Pauline Rosenau (1992). Rosenau, for example, develops a conception of "affirmative" postmodernism that she pits against a "skeptical" postmodernism. Affirmative postmod-ernism is the kind of notion that is unpacked by Toulmin, and that is developed further in Griffin's work as "constructive" or "revisionary" postmodernism. According to Griffin, constructive or revisionary postmodernism

> involves a new unity of scientific, ethical, aesthetic, and religious institutions. It rejects not science as such but only that scientism in which the data of the modern natural sciences are alone allowed to contribute to the construction of our worldview (1988a, x).

Griffin makes an explicit appeal to Toulmin in calling for a reenchantment of science based on a postmodern organicism. Both he and Rosenau contrast this view with a "skeptical" or "deconstructive" postmodernism inspired by Nietzsche, Wittgenstein, and Heidegger. It is this version, focusing on the politics of knowledge, that has been developed by French poststructuralist thinkers.

Science as a Reason of State: The New Zealand Example

Michael Ryan (1988) has stressed the relationship between liberal Reason and liberal politics, between "how knowledge is conceived and described by liberal philosophers and how liberal political, juridical, social and economic institutions are constituted" (154). Ryan follows Thomas Spragens in describing liberal Reason as consisting of the following eleven propositions:

- The assumptions and methods of the previously dominant Aristotelian-Scholastic tradition are mistaken and must be fundamentally revised or supplanted before genuine "natural philosophy" can be possible.
- Human understanding, guided by the "natural light" of reason, can and should be autonomous. Moreover, it constitutes the norm and the means against which all else is to be measured.

- It is possible and necessary to begin the search for knowledge with a clean slate.
- It is possible and necessary to base knowledge claims on a clear and distinct, indubitable, self-evident foundation.
- This foundation is to be composed of simple, unambiguous ideas or perceptions.
- The appropriate formal standards for all human knowledge are those of the mathematical modes of inquiry.
- The key to the progress of human knowledge is the development of explicit rules of method.
- The entire body of valid human knowledge is a unity, both in method and in substance.
- Therefore, human knowledge may be made almost wholly accessible to all men, provided only that they not be defective in their basic faculties.
- Genuine knowledge is in some sense certain, verifiable, and capable of being made wholly explicit.
- Knowledge is power, and the increase of knowledge therefore holds the key to human progress.

Ryan uses deconstructive philosophy to question liberal Reason: "the normativization of the logos"; the possibility of knowledge absolutely free of presuppositions; the possibility of self-evident foundations; "the absolute certainty of the mathematical model"; the unity of knowledge; and "the possibility of absolute certainty or determinacy" (153). Deconstructionist theory, he argues, offers a post-liberal description of Reason as fallibilist and historical, implying that post-liberal institutions are more democratic, egalitarian, and cooperative.

Science has become a reason of state (Nandy 1988). More closely linked than ever before to the modern notion of development and its connotations of progress, competition, and nationalism, science as a reason of state has been subjected to a new rationalization designed to optimize its contribution to the system's performance. Science, as Lyotard (1984) argues, has increasingly fallen under the sway of another game, that of technology. The game of technology follows the principle of optimal performance (maximizing output, minimizing input). Its goal or criterion is efficiency rather than truth or justice.

That science has become a reason of state tied to the politics of national development is not a recent phenomenon: The relation of science to development was cemented during and immediately after World War II and played a focal role in the politics of the Cold War. Arguably, modern science was conceived of as a reason of state: certainly Francis Bacon conceived of science as power over both nature and humanity in the service of the king. Increasingly since World War II, science and technology have been recognized as playing fundamental and determining roles in relation to socio-economic development. A number of factors have reinforced and highlighted this recognition: the relation between new forms of multidisciplinary basic science and emerging generic technologies (for example, electronics, information and communications, advanced materials and biotechnology); the role of these generic technologies in driving a new Kondratiev "long wave" of economic development; the consequent need for countries to fund future-oriented programs of basic mission-oriented or strategic research; and the changed external "boundary conditions" under which the scientific research system must now operate given that science has entered a "steady state" (Ziman 1994) in which demands for public accountability and "value for money" necessarily imply greater selectivity in the allocation of funds and more systematic approaches to planning.

These kinds of developments can be seen clearly in the restructuring of the New Zealand science policy regime. A number of reviews of science policy from the early 1980s onward made the case for the national importance of science and technology and the need for a coherent policy and strategic planning. In 1984 the government attempted to improve the equity of research funding largely through a user-pay policy that focused on funding cuts and the encouragement of greater contributions from the direct beneficiaries. Of course, this kind of reform, based on a very crude policy instrument, reflected the early days of a commitment to the market under the so-called New Right. A more comprehensive set of reforms was instituted by the National Government in 1990. The reforms were based on a number of principles that originated in public choice theory and served as a basis for the restructuring of the public sector as a whole (Scott et al. 1990; Boston 1991). These principles emphasize: the clear separation of policy advice from the allocation of public funding and the conduct of research and development; the contestability of policy advice and funding; the prioritizing of science for the production of public good science outputs; the government purchase of research and development services (on contract) necessary to achieve its stated outcomes; and the commercialization, corporatization, and competitive neutrality of public research agencies (Shaw 1990; Scobie and Jacobsen 1991).

To a large extent these principles, which have served as a basis for the restructuring of science, reflect what Christopher Hood (1991) and others have called New Public Management (NPM). NPM is characterized by a series of shifts: from policy development to management; from aggregation to disaggregation in public service organization (disaggregated budgets, internal markets, and rivalry); from planning and public service welfarism to a stress on cost cutting and labor discipline; from process to output controls and accountability mechanisms (performance measurement); and from permanent public bureau production to term contracts and private sector delivery (Hood and Jackson 1991, 178). NPM combines "new institutional economics" (public choice theory, principal agency theory, and transaction cost theory) built around ideas of contestability, user choice, transparency, and incentive structures, with elements of the fashionable "corporate culture" doctrines of the 1980s. It represents a development of the scientific management of Frederick Taylor and has become a vehicle for New Right ideology that emphasizes an avoidance of direct state management and a corresponding favoring of market-like arrangements for the allocation of scarce public resources. Further, Hood (1991, 3) notes that NPM is associated with attempts to slow down or reverse government growth in terms of public spending and staffing; the shift toward privatization and quasi-privatization and away from core government institutions; and the development of automation, particularly in information technology, in the production and distribution of public services.

Clearly, science policy restructuring has occurred in line with a new philosophy of administration, the principles of which reflect a distinct political ideology. Science, accordingly, will come to be practiced within a particular set of ideological parameters. Can the practice of science be separated from questions concerning the funding of public good science? Can the practice of science be separated from the policy context that articulates strategic goals concerning the overall direction of research and emphasizes its contribution to economic performance, particularly research in economic sectors which already have a competitive advantage or can add value? Will the practice of science in the future take place independently of national priority research themes? The answers to these questions are quite plain.

To be sure, criticisms have been raised in Aotearoa/New Zealand about the restructuring process and the new science policy regime. There have been criticisms of the cuts in government spending since the early 1980s, of the Department of Scientific and Industrial Research (DSIR) redundancies, and the loss of some 200 scientists in the three years before 1992. There have been criticisms of the ideological parameters within which science must now take place: Some worry that the new system will promote short-term research at the market end of the spectrum rather than longer-term, basic research. This fear is reinforced by the commercial orientation of the Crown Research Institutes (CRIs), in which private sector priorities and values are strongly represented. There have been criticisms of the bureaucratic nature of the new system which is seen as being both more centralized and less flexible than the old one. With ten CRIs, a ministry, and a foundation, in addition to high setting-up costs, it seems highly probable that more is being spent on administration and less on science than under the previous system.

More provocatively, we might comment on the new science funding system and the Public Good Science Fund in relation to two issues: conservation values and Maori interests. *Investing in Science for Our Future* (October 1992) presents an early snapshot of the New Zealand government's statement of science priorities in the 1990s. It is abundantly clear that a certain instrumental view of knowledge underlies the document. The overall strategic direction for New Zealand science is to foster a sustainable, technologically advanced society which innovates and adds value, especially to our strong base of biological production (24).

New Zealand's conception of state-funded science is not greatly different from those that underlie science policy regimes elsewhere in the West. Science is valued primarily for its capacity to "add value," and support "innovation, enterprise and exporting" so that New Zealand can "attain the growth in incomes and employment needed for an improved quality of life" (1). Strategic goals emphasize a partnership with the private sector, a concentration of resources in those research areas in which results can be readily exploited for economic gain, and a concentration of effort on research in economic sectors that already have a competitive advantage. In essence, this view represents a market model of knowledge; science has become commodified.

This, of course, is not surprising for it simply reflects dominant neoliberal values and ideology. How does it relate to conservation values? The word "sustainable" appears in the strategic direction outlined above, and which refers to the importance of New Zealand's physical environment "not only in terms of the 'clean green' image it projects in the marketplace but also for its contribution to our productive base and quality of life" (1). The questions remains: How compatible is the notion of sustainability with an emphasis on science for economic growth?

It could be argued that sustainability should be defined widely as a broad concept of social and economic progress that enables the needs of the present generation to be met without compromising the ability of future generations to meet their needs. This definition, codified in New Zealand's Resource Management Act (1992), is clearly compatible with a science that emphasizes economic growth and a notion of progress. Yet this interpretation might be said to ignore or show little "understanding of the New Zealand environment or environmental process sufficient even to know upon what criteria sustainable management should be based" (Glasby 1991, 74). One scientist, reviewing research produced within the last decade on environmental problems, concludes that in spite of the myth of clean-green New Zealand the environment has steadily deteriorated "due to increased development, poor planning and inadequate resources for environmental understanding and management." He notes that although such a deterioration may not be noticeable in terms of years, it will be significant over decades. He maintains that "the prospects for the environment in New Zealand over the next 50–100 years do not look promising" and concludes that achieving sustainable management will be a costly exercise that will require compulsory reallocation of land and a large investment in compensation to landowners (Glasby 1991, 74, 76).

Against this kind of assessment we should note that the statement of science priorities generated in the early 1990s (MoRST 1992a) emphasized science as a way to add value to the country's agricultural industries and its strong base of biological production. In funding terms this meant relative increases to research concerned with the processing of meat, dairy products, textiles, wood and paper. Overall those science output categories concerning ecological concerns have received less funding or, at best, a very small increase. The point here is that given the funding pattern and the lack of official recognition of the extent of environmental problems (Glasby 1991), the chances of achieving sustainability look slim.

The fact is that the notion of sustainability simply does not sit well with the market system, because the market fails to consider ecological constraints and the conditions necessary for sustainability. The market system does not cope well with problems related to externalities and tends to overexploit collective goods such as the atmosphere, the seas, fisheries and so forth. Furthermore, the devolution of resource management to regional governments involves all sorts of goal conflicts (Meister and Weber, 1991). There are also considerable barriers to sustainable development in natural resource–based economies in which the pressures to maximize output levels in the short term will compromise environmental protection and resource management strategies designed for longer-term development purposes. Using Australia as a case study, Peter Daniels argues that external debt pressures and a struggling trade sector based on primary sector exports undergoing extensive terms of trade deterioration could well induce an insidious and protracted period of simultaneous economic decline and degradation or depletion of natural capital stocks. This situation would represent a fundamental constraint upon the attainment of sustainable development proposals (1992, 247).

The conditions Daniels describes in general terms for natural resource-based economies clearly applies to New Zealand as well as to a number of other countries.

To what extent does the statement of science priorities advanced in 1992 (MoRST 1992a) cater for Maori interests? The *Strategic Goals for New Zealand Science: Annex A* (in MoRST 1992a) do not refer to Maori interests directly at all. The goals do not even mention social or cultural development or differences. Maori interests are mentioned in the priority research themes. Under the heading of "generic themes across outputs" we find reference to "Implications for Maori cultural and economic development in appropriate output classes." The government's specified outcomes identified economic development and especially the improvement of export performance as of primary importance. Maori cultural, economic and social development, however, does not figure in the priorities (MoRST 1992a, Annex A).

When one analyzes the 1992 document, it is clear that of twenty-three explicitly stated outcomes only one referred directly to Maori interests. Certainly, this early statement of science priorities did not bode well for Maori interests. Wider questions of scientific priorities vis-à-vis Maori must be addressed than the question of equitable access to research funds. For example, to what extent are Maori involved in science and technology at and beyond the school level? What are Maori views of Western science and technology and their potential involvement with them? How do Maori get recognition for matauranga Maori (Maori knowledge) within the present science policy regime? What are appropriate consultation procedures for Maori? Why out of ten CRIs is there not a single Maori research authority? These questions provided the basis for a recent hui (meeting) with the Ministry of Research, Science, and Technology. That it took until the early 1990s for such questions to be addressed is highly revealing.

The fact is that science, like all other monocultural institutions, has systematically excluded Maori interests. Historically, science has defined itself against other forms of knowledge and, particularly, against traditional knowledge systems. Western science has typically been seen in universal and ahistorical terms. It has been clearly separated from questions of time and place and contrasted with traditional knowledge and authority. For instance, as Anne Salmond has argued, European evaluations of Maori knowledge in Aotearoa characteristically have been ideological and preformed by evolutionary ideas and political interest. In particular, European evaluations of Maori knowledge, built on assumptions of Western cognitive superiority, characterized traditional Maori knowledge as "pre-logical," "pre-philosophical," less abstract, more mystical (1985, 256). In contrast to Western science, "Maori were said to have no knowledge, only superstition and myth; and their thought was held to be inferior to European reason—by men who could not speak Maori, and knew nothing at all of Maori knowledge and thought." Salmond concludes on a prophetic note:

> Western thought is often closed by premises of intellectual superiority to radical cross-cultural reflection and thorough-going inquiry, and the process of opening Western knowledge to traditional rationalities has hardly yet begun (1985, 260).

It *has* begun. Let us mention briefly three examples. First, the report of a ministerial task group charged with reviewing science and technology education (MoRST 1992b) charts an alternative, emerging view to the prevalent idea that science has little to learn from indigenous peoples. The report acknowledges that "an enormous body of knowledge would be lost if indigenous peoples lose or are deprived of their culture and heritage," and argues for including such knowledge within the school curriculum (48). An invited group of Maori representatives requested that the task group acknowledge the existence of a Maori body of scientific knowledge, Maori learning and teaching styles, and Maori assessment and evaluation procedures. Furthermore, the task group gave some consideration to the development of Maori input into science and technology education.

Ngahuia Te Awekotuku (1991) has prepared a discussion paper for Manatu Maori: "He Tikanga Whakaaro: Research Ethics in the Maori Community." It begins with a description of customary concepts of knowledge, research and scholarship in the ancient world, then focuses on contemporary realities, noting that because research is the gathering of knowledge for use within a variety of different applications, it is necessarily about control, resource allocation, information and equity. Te Awekotuku writes:

> To avoid the cultural imperialism of past research practices and researchers, research itself should be responsive to expressed Maori needs; needs expressed

from within the community, and not needs perceived by those outside it—a mis-
judgment often made by political agencies. It is also vital that the knowledge
gained from research benefits the community; this may be a sensitive area in
academic undertakings, but in policy directed research, the activity itself should
have value and relevance to the people studied. The collective interest subsumes
the individual's; in policy directed activity, the community's interest should have
the highest priority; the collective interest should subsume the agency's (1991,
14).

This philosophy is the basis for a set of principles articulated to guide
researchers in the Maori community. It provides, in essence, an ethic of
community responsibility that can recognize that accountability has both
internal and external lines of communication—to the scientific community
and to the community at large, to present and future generations, to
people *and* the environment they help comprise. It is an ethic that unfortunately does not fit well into today's context of neoliberal individualism.

Second, Aroha Mead (1992) has described the cultural and intellectual
property rights of Maori people as a history of denial based on exploitation. She talks of this exploitation in terms of both the denial of the
validity of matauranga Maori, of Maori scientific knowledge, and the Pakeha
attempt to assume ownership of the intellectual property rights of Maori,
defined in terms of folklore and crafts, biodiversity, and indigenous knowledge. According to the United Nations, the biodiversity of traditional territories of indigenous peoples is part of intellectual knowledge, together
with indigenous knowledge of the use and development of species of
indigenous flora and fauna.

Finally, at a UNESCO symposium, "Science and the Boundaries of
Knowledge: The Prologue of Our Cultural Past," held in Venice in 1986,
participants concluded by noting that we are witnessing a new worldview
brought about in basic science by developments in physics and biology.
The second point of agreement expressed in the Venice Declaration emphasizes a theme of this chapter:

> Scientific knowledge, on its own impetus, has reached the point where it can
> begin a dialogue with other forms of knowledge. In this sense, and while recog-
> nizing the fundamental differences between Science and Tradition, we see them
> as complementary rather than in contradiction. This new and mutually enriching
> exchange between science and the different traditions of the world opens the
> door to a new vision of humanity, and even to a new rationalism, which could
> lead to a new metaphysical perspective (cited in Peet 1992, 255–56).

The declaration recognizes the need for transdisciplinary research
"through a dynamic exchange between the natural sciences, the social

sciences, art and tradition" (255) and stresses that the challenges of our times throw a new light on the social responsibilities of the scientific community. We might call the new worldview to which these scientists collectively refer "the postmodern." As a shorthand cipher, or code word, the postmodern captures the breakdown in the boundaries between the disciplines and different forms of knowledge and signals a new pluralism in which no one single method or science establishes hegemony as the paradigm.

The Shift to The Knowledge Society and the Discourse of Futurology

The science policy regime in New Zealand has undergone a number of changes since the early 1990s. In particular there has been a shift from strategic planning to scenario-building and science foresight built around the concept of "the knowledge society," a term recently adopted by the Ministry of Research, Science and Technology (MoRST). The concept is embedded in a discourse of futurology and the MoRST Foresight Project which is a future-oriented public discussion exercise designed to encourage a consensus among various sector groups in New Zealand about a "desirable future." The exercise is based on the notion of foresight, which is neither a form of prediction nor of planning but rather an analysis of global trends, how they will affect New Zealand, and, given national resources, how the country might take advantage of them. The project links government investment with New Zealand's development toward a "knowledge society" on the understanding that the government's strategic investment in public good science and technology must be used effectively to underpin New Zealand's development as a knowledge society if New Zealand is to compete successfully in the global economy.

In the period leading up to the new millennium, a comprehensive review of the priorities for public good science and technology was to be carried out under the umbrella of the Foresight Project, which would have four phases, including an overview designed to establish a context for thinking about the future; the development of sector strategies, which involves developing a widely shared and compelling understanding of what is important for New Zealand; the identification of the priorities for public good science and technology; and, finally, implementation of new priorities and investment processes from July 2000.

MoRST claims that although the future is not entirely predictable, trends are presently unfolding that must be included in the foresight process.

The project specifies seven such trends, including the knowledge revolution; globalization; global science and technology trends; changing consumer behaviors and preferences; industry convergence; environmental issues; and social organization. This discussion will focus upon the knowledge revolution. We are informed that the knowledge revolution constitutes a significant global paradigm shift that is changing the structure of New Zealand's economy and society. Knowledge is the key to the future because it, rather than capital or labor, drives productivity and economic growth and, unlike either capital or labor, it cannot lose its value, which may even increase with future applications. Knowledge, we are informed, "includes information in any form, but also includes know-how and know-why, and involves the way we interact as individuals and as a community" (MoRST 1998, http://www.morst.govt.nz/foresight/front.html).

Knowledge economies are directly based on the production, distribution, and use of knowledge and information. This is reflected in the trend toward growth in high-technology investments, high-technology industries, more highly skilled labor and the associated productivity gains. Knowledge, as embodied in people ("human capital") and in technology, has always been central to economic development. But it is only over the last few years that its relative importance has been recognized. MoRST's description of the "knowledge revolution" is sprinkled with references to such authors as Alvin Toffler, Peter Drucker, Nicholas Negroponte, Charles Handy, Kevin Kelly, Hazel Henderson, and Paul Hawken.

The framework, the philosophy, and the process of planning for the future in the knowledge age that MoRST adopts is a form of management theory called *scenario-building* born out of the dissatisfaction with strategic planning during the 1980s. Advocates of scenario-building theory believe it overcomes conceptual limitations of strategic planning, including its elitism and lack of engagement with sector representatives and its lack of vision and orientation to the future (Wallace and Packer 1998). Wallace and Packer note that the concept of scenario originates in film practice as a kind of scaffolding or framework for the production of a movie and they describe its popularization in the corporate world by Royal Dutch Shell and its subsequent adoption as a tool of business management (see Schwartz 1991).

MoRST sees hindsight as a useful way of seeing the paradigm shifts that have occurred in New Zealand. It offers the following description of the past and the future as a series of Kuhnian paradigm shifts: from the regulation, protectionism, public ownership, welfarism, and egalitarianism of the 1970s to deregulation, open markets, privatization, self-responsibility, and the emphasis on self-achievement in the 1990s. The big question for MoRST futurologists is to guess what will be the paradigm for 2010.

The Foresight Project uses scenario-building to develop an awareness of irrevocable events while reviewing priorities for public good science and technology. On this basis the project develops possible strategic responses to these scenarios. The Foresight Project identifies three possible scenarios for New Zealand:

Possum in the Glare. New Zealand is caught like a possum in the glare of the headlights of the oncoming future. But possums are hardy creatures, and New Zealand muddles along by finding new markets for traditional agricultural products and combating falling prices with new production technologies.

Shark Roaming Alone. After a period of economic difficulty, New Zealand adapts quickly to keep up with the changes of the early twenty-first century. Rapid uptake of new technology and the Internet and the success of the entrepreneurial approach make us a highly individualized society of sharks.

Nga Kahikatea. There is much interest in the social change that has occurred in New Zealand over the first decade of the twenty-first century. What marks New Zealand out from other countries is a strong and widely shared sense of purpose, a national intent. New Zealand has become a nation of kahikatea (a species of pine tree) standing together.

On the basis of this scenario-building exercise and after consultation with the different sector groups, in early 1999 a set of seventeen target outcome descriptions were arrived at that outline a series of desirable outcomes for the future of New Zealand that can be significantly advanced by research, science, and technology activity. These are as follows:

- A culture of innovation
- Anticipation and creation of new markets
- Distinctive and positive cultural identity
- Empowered individuals and communities
- Globally connected New Zealand
- Healthy, diverse, resilient ecosystems
- High health status
- Infrastructure for a knowledge society
- Knowledge and learning networks
- Maori development
- New health care possibilities
- People integrated with their physical environments
- Security in hazardous environments
- Self-determination and ethical principles
- Sustainable ecosystem use
- Wealth from Biological & Physical Resources
- Wealth from new knowledge-based businesses

We can clearly see that environmental conservation values inform the list of target outcomes, as does Maori development. Maori development is defined as "a dynamic, ongoing process through which Maori achieve cultural affirmation, social well-being, economic self sufficiency and mutually beneficial partnerships" (MoRST 1998, http://www.morst.govt.nz/fore-sight/front.html).

The officials, of course, would argue that considerable progress has been made and because both Maori and environmental/conversation values have made the target outcomes list. Yet some critical questions remain concerning both the notion of the knowledge society and the process of scenario-building.

First, is this really scenario-building? Are these equally valid or possible options? Is there any hard data to support these three possible scenarios? How does one test the viability of one scenario over another? Do all three scenarios really constitute desirable futures?

Second, if strategic planning has its problems, so too does scenario-planning. The focus on investment-driven science and on technology policy makes some simplistic assumptions about the concept of knowledge and the "knowledge revolution."

For one thing, the Foresight Project does not make the standard philosophical distinction between "knowledge" and "information." The traditional account of knowledge, which goes back to Plato, relies on "truth" to ground justification. The following conditions are seen as necessary and jointly sufficient for knowledge in the traditional account. For A (a knower) to know *that p* (where "p" is a proposition or statement): A must believe that *p*; *p* must be true; and, A must be justified in believing that *p*. In other words, there is a belief condition, a truth condition, and a justification condition, all of which must be met for something to count as knowledge. For data to qualify as information, none of these conditions must be met: For information to count as information there is no belief condition, no truth condition, no justification condition. All that has to occur is for data to be sent from a sender to a receiver. As we all know, forms of disinformation, infomercials, edutainment and so on clearly do not count as knowledge. The Foresight Project conflates knowledge with information, collapsing the two, and thereby also perpetrates flawed accounts of both the production and consumption processes of knowledge and of knowledge institutions.

The Foresight Project does not consider the history of the notion of the knowledge society or the information society or associated concepts such as the global information society. These are not uncontested terms. They are value-laden and theory-laden concepts that have been part of social and cultural theory for over thirty years. There is no innocent approach to these terms or to their unproblematic use that can be separated from the accumulation of theory, especially the sociology of postindustrialism and post-Fordism, to which they belong. MoRST officials have an obligation to acknowledge these theory contexts and to present them clearly as part of the overall discussion.

Finally, the Foresight Project is grounded in the corporatist management theory of scenario-building. Although such a theory includes sector interests and less elitist than its predecessor, strategic planning, it still carries with it the ethos of the corporation and reflects the interests of business rather than the interests of the wider society or nation. Wallace and Packer (1998) ask of MoRST's Foresight Project's scenarios "Who is telling the story, and therefore whose perspective is at least implicitly being privileged?" and they suggest that scenarios, normally used as a business tool for controlling the future of a company, tend to assimilate the nation to the status of a corporation. They comment that the almost exclusive focus of the scenarios is on the relation between technology and the economy (and, in particular, economic growth and productivity). Not only are social and cultural issues consigned to economic ends insofar as they are mentioned at all but the technological forces that are allegedly responsible for propelling us into the future are acultural and asocial; they exist somehow apart from culture and society and impact upon it.

Chapter 5

Postmodern Perspectives on the Curriculum: A Poststructuralist Critique[1]

Introduction

Curriculum theorists have begun the task of reexamining the curriculum in terms of "postmodern" perspectives based on an appeal to new developments in science, ecology, theology, and metaphysics. In *Understanding the Curriculum*, William Pinar and his colleagues, for instance, suggest "contemporary advances in ethics, cosmology, liberation theology, and hermeneutics . . . all contribute to this legitimation of the theological in contemporary discourse" (1995, 637). They quote Patrick Slattery with approval: "The reconceptualisation of curriculum and theology is a process of concientization and liberation; it is an autobiographical journey and a spiritual *phronesis*" (cited in Pinar et al., 1995, 643). As a further example, William Doll (1993) takes as his starting point the work of Stephen Toulmin (e.g., 1982, 1990) and David Griffin (1988c) who, to him, indicate the signs of a new "megaparadigm." (For an account of "postmodern science," drawing on Toulmin's work, see Chapter 4). For Doll, the "modernist" curriculum built upon a "linear, sequential, easily quantifiable ordering system" should give way to "a more complex, pluralistic, unpredictable system or network" that he takes as characteristic of postmodernism (Doll 1993, 3). Indeed, Doll champions the process thought of Dewey and Whitehead as the basis for a new curriculum model. As he argues:

> A network in process is a transformative network, continually emerging—one moving beyond stability to tap the creative powers inherent in instability. In such a transformative network, prediction and control, key elements within the modernist curriculum model, become less "ordered" and more "fuzzy." Really

what happens is that a whole new sense of order emerges: not the symmetrical, simple, sequential order classical science borrowed from medieval thought, but an asymmetrical, chaotic, fractal order we are now beginning to discover in the post-modern sciences (Doll 1993, 3).

These current examples indicate something important in new theorizing about the curriculum: First, that new perspectives on the curriculum are legitimated on the basis of appeals to accounts of "postmodern science" and, in particular, "cosmological" readings that attempt to integrate theology and ecology with science; second, that these cosmological readings of postmodern science tend to rest upon both apolitical constructions and self-consciously elide poststructuralism or poststructuralist accounts of postmodern science. This tendency is, perhaps, most pronounced in the following statement by Doll when he writes: "I will follow the lead of David Griffin and Stephen Toulmin and draw mostly on scientific-theological-ecological trends, not on aesthetic-literary-political ones" (Doll 1993, 12). While Doll acknowledges the latter, he depends for his account of the postmodern curriculum on the former, suggesting that the choice for him is one of preference because he knows the disciplines of science and mathematics better than he does those of art, architecture, and literary criticism. Yet he also advances two further reasons for his choice: First, as he says, the American school curriculum has been shaped by its modernist view of science more than any other factor, and second, "it will be a new version of science—more complex, indeterminate, and interactive than the classical version—that will dominate and be generative in this new paradigm" (Doll 1993, 12). For Doll then "Modernism as an all-encompassing intellectual movement has outlived its usefulness, yet it lives on as a, if not the, force in curriculum practice" (Doll 1993, 11). For him the curriculum is best organized in terms of four directions which he uses to characterize the postmodern perspective: Piaget and the "open vision" of living systems; Prigogine and the concept of chaotic order; Bruner and the "new epistemology"; and, the process thought of Dewey and Whitehead. These four directions provide what he calls "a foundational framework for curricularists interested in studying the postmodern vision" (Doll 1989, 251).

There are many questions that can be posed here, and especially in reference to Doll's account. What is the meaning of "postmodern" in theorizing the curriculum? What is the meaning of the "modern" (and, therefore, of science) against which such a "scientific" postmodern curriculum might be established? Was there really ever a "modernist model" of the curriculum in any self-conscious sense or is this label rather more a rational historical reconstruction made possible by hindsight? Can the term "modernism" be applied to science? By modernist science Doll seems to mean nothing more than the mechanistic worldview advocated by Descartes and brought to fruition by Newton, and by postmodern science he seems to be referring to science that is essentially Einsteinian. If this is the case, then why all the fuss? Einstein, and for that matter Whitehead and Dewey, were first active in the early decades of the twentieth century: After almost eighty years of what he calls "postmodern" scientific developments, why hasn't the new megaparadigm already changed the organization of the curriculum and why might we expect it to do so *now*?

We might also ask: why, indeed, appeal to postmodern science rather than, more generally, to the postmodern condition (Lyotard, 1984)? Why should we accept perspectives on the curriculum that are shaped primarily by science? Given the controversy in American higher education over notions of what counts as a discipline or canon and the rise of black, feminist, and gay studies within universities, approaches based on appeals to Doll's characterization of postmodern science seem unnecessarily reductionist, apolitical, and blind to the wider challenges Western sciences face in the postmodern condition (see, e.g., Harding 1991, 1993; Petitjean et al. 1992; Markley 1999). Certainly, a characterization of postmodern science solely in terms of its internal developments distracts us from viewing science as part of an evolving cultural formation—that is, as a set of institutions based on certain forms of inherited cultural practices. Accounts of criteria based on histories internal to science implicitly insulate the curriculum from challenges to cultural authority that have been systematically mounted by social movements and cultural forces outside the academy. Perhaps, most significantly, one of the central features of accounts of postmodern science, especially by French theorists such as Lyotard, Bruno Latour, and Michel Serres, is to provide *cultural* readings or to emphasize the importance of regarding science as a cultural institution, and certainly not as an ahistorical formation separate from the rest of culture and thought.

By focusing entirely upon internal developments to sciences that are seen to buttress a new cosmological worldview, some versions of postmodern science, such as Doll's, have no explanatory force when it comes to questions of the politics of knowledge and the "knowledge economy" or philosophical questions concerning the relationship between the curriculum and processes of identity formation. Perhaps, most important, such accounts do not sufficiently ground themselves in the new emerging economy of neoliberal globalization in which science, and, increasingly, global information industries, become instruments of state in the game of international competition and enterprise.

This chapter develops the notion of a crisis of cultural authority to argue for the untenability of these cosmological accounts of postmodernism, especially when they are used to legitimate postmodern scientific approaches to the curriculum that integrate theology and ecology, for we would argue that it is difficult to understand radical ecological/environmental or contemporary theological movements without understanding something about the politics of new social movements and their combined resistance against forms of cultural homogenization accompanying neoliberal globalization that many see as threats to the life-world. We might simply suggest that these versions represent new forms of holism or the development of new unifying metanarratives.

By contrast, this chapter develops three lines of inquiry that bear upon the curriculum that might be said to spring out of a strand of contemporary French philosophy often called poststructuralism: first, the siting of the curriculum within what we call, after Foucault (1979), neo-liberal forms of governmentality; second, an understanding of curriculum in terms of the emerging postindustrial society in the West structured by the so-called new information economy; third, a challenge to the modern curriculum according to the "crisis of cultural authority" of the West—a crisis that can be explained in part by a logic of increasing internal differentiation (the proliferation of subcultures and lifestyles) and an increasing multiculturalism characterized by the revitalization of indigenous cultures, philosophies of decolonization, and strong international labor mobility, immigration, and the flow of refugees.

A number of preliminary observations must be made concerning "cosmological" versions of the postmodern before indicating the direction of these three lines of inquiry. First, we firmly reject the distinction between two kinds of postmodernism drawn in terms of an uncompromising binary opposition as wrong-headed and inimical to the spirit of postmodernism for all the reasons that have been advanced against such dualisms. David Griffin (1988a, x), for instance, draws a distinction between a "deconstructive or eliminative postmodernism" and a "constructive or revisionary postmodernism." William Doll (1993) follows Griffin in this regard. Pauline Rosenau (1992) also makes the distinction between "skeptical" and "affirmative" postmodernism. This strategy that accompanies some cosmological versions of postmodernism is wrong-headed because, like the stereotypical distinction between analytic and Continental philosophy, it confuses rather than clarifies the issues at stake. Let us give one clear example: Lyotard, often taken falsely as the ultimate skeptical postmodernist, is not anti-modernist, nor does he interpret postmodernism in an anti-modern sense. He writes: "postmodernism

. . . is not modernism at its end but in its nascent state and this state is constant" (Lyotard 1984, 79).

We would add that neither Nietzsche nor Wittgenstein (figures who are often referred to as the grandfathers of postmodernism) is against science per se, but only certain conceptions of it—for example, Cartesianism and logical empiricism. Indeed, both thinkers, more so than most contemporary thinkers, emphasize the importance of ethics in relation to science. Certainly, Nietzsche should not be taken as *advocating* a kind of nihilism, nor does his philosophy (or Wittgenstein's) lead to nihilism; a claim often made by those who wish to make the distinction referred to above between "skeptical" (read "nihilistic") and "affirmative" postmodernism (see Peters and Marshall 1999). Nietzsche suggests that when "all transcendent claims for a meaning to life have been reduced to mere values" and the human, all-too-human, origin of our values have been exposed, then "our reactive response—that is to say, our Christian response—is to declare that existence is meaningless" (Critchley 1997, 357). It is this Christian declaration of meaninglessness that Nietzsche identifies as nihilistic and it is this discovery that drives him to demand a revaluation of all values.

Second, it is important to recognize that poststructuralist thinkers themselves theorize and draw upon recent developments in science but in a way that acknowledges the importance of culture and technology. Lyotard (1984), for example, draws upon a range of new scientific developments in terms of undecidability, uncertainty, fracta, catastrophe and complexity theory, local determinism, and the like, as theoretical principles underwriting a movement against universalism and totality (see Peters 1995b). Foucault writes histories of the human sciences. The assertion, therefore, that there are two kinds of postmodernism—one predominantly scientific and affirmative and one predominantly aesthetic and skeptical (where poststructuralism is consigned to the latter)—is conceptually misleading and historically false. Indeed, if one examines the intellectual forces that have helped shape poststructuralism, then it is clear that studies of science and epistemology by Jean Cavailles (e.g., 1943/1987), Gaston Bachelard (e.g., 1984), and Georges Canguilhem (e.g., 1977) have been central and have pre-dated the sorts of conclusions reached by historians of science such as Thomas Kuhn.

Third, there is something logically circuitous in the move to abstract principles of curriculum drawn from one subject area (i.e., science) as a means for legislating all other subjects that comprise the curriculum. A curriculum constructed upon postmodern scientific principles is open to the criticism of scientism: that is, it grants a spurious validity and truth to such principles. When postmodern science is run together with theology and radical ecology, and used to underwrite a new cosmology, it takes on an all-embracing worldview and synthesis of hegemonic proportions.

Fourth and finally, it is the so-called skeptical or (falsely named) nihilistic postmodernism, inspired by Nietzsche, Wittgenstein, and Heidegger, that has been developed by French thinkers such as Jacques Derrida, Michel Foucault, and Jean-François Lyotard, among others, that takes questions of the politics of knowledge seriously to function, in part, as a critique of contemporary Western science as it is practiced in liberal capitalist "knowledge economies." The views articulated by these thinkers challenge the standard liberal epistemological interpretation of science based on the understanding that all interactions between knowledge and power are external. This point needs a brief explanation.

Toward a Political Philosophy of Science

The standard liberal epistemological interpretation of science is based on the received view of the relationship between knowledge and power. We can summarize this relationship by saying that all interactions between knowledge and power are external, meaning that while power can influence what we believe, considerations of power are completely irrelevant to which of our beliefs are true and what justifies their status as knowledge. In other words, as Rouse (1987, 13) succinctly expresses it: "Knowledge acquires its epistemological status independent of the operations of power." According to this general account, knowledge can be applied in order to achieve power, or power may be used to prevent the acquisition of knowledge, or knowledge might liberate us from the effects of power, but power *cannot* contribute constructively to the achievement of knowledge. This standard view rests on three features ascribed to the notion of power: that it is possessed and exercised by specific agents; that it operates on our representations but not on the world represented; and that it is primarily repressive (Rouse 1987, 15). Only the second point needs explanation: Our beliefs about the world may be changed or imposed by the exercise of power over us, but the exercise of power cannot guarantee the truth of our beliefs or change how the world is.

The received view of the relations between knowledge and power has been seriously challenged. For instance, pragmatism challenges the claim that power is external to knowledge by arguing that truth is the product of consensus of a scientific community and that there are no identifiable criteria of truth apart from what we arrive at through the practice of inquiry. In this view, if truth criteria themselves are a product of inquiry, then a consideration of power is integral to epistemology and the traditional epistemological problem of distinguishing true from false beliefs is transformed into "the political problem of distinguishing free inquiry from inquiry constrained and distorted by the exercise of power" (Rouse 1987, 19). Such a view has forcefully been argued for by Jürgen Habermas, the leading present-day representative of the Frankfurt School. Habermas (1972) develops the thesis that all knowledge is political, by which he means that knowledge is always constituted on the basis of human interests that have developed in and been shaped by social and historical circumstances. He classifies three main types of "knowledge-constitutive interests": the technical interest characteristic of the natural sciences produces instrumental (means-end) knowledge aimed at prediction and control; the practical interest of the human sciences produces knowledge governed by the interpretation and understanding of meaning; and the emancipatory interest of the critical social sciences is premised on the values of freedom and rational autonomy. Further, the new empiricists (Putnam, Laudan, Hesse) challenge a range of distinctions which supported the received (liberal) account of the relationship between knowledge and power: fact/value, theory/practice, pure/applied, scheme/content. They also reject representational or realist interpretations of scientific theories. In their terms, successful theories have nothing to do with the accuracy of their representations of the world. Successful theories are those which improve our ability to cope with the world, to control it technically, and "technical control, the power to intervene in and manipulate natural events, is not the application of antecedent knowledge but the form scientific knowledge now predominantly takes" (Rouse 1987, 20).

In one very influential account we are now to talk of "power/knowledge" as an indissoluble unity (Foucault 1980). Michel Foucault rethinks the nature of modern power, tracing its development in the birth of the human sciences and associated liberal institutions of the clinic, the prison, and the school. New mechanisms of modern power go hand in hand with the birth of the human sciences. Modern power is "productive" rather than simply repressive; it is "capillary" in that it operates in everyday social practices rather than through beliefs; and it is both local and continuous. Truth, knowledge, and belief are a product of the "politics of the discursive regime." A plurality of incommensurable discursive regimes succeed each other historically. Power/knowledge is a discursive regime comprised of a matrix of practices which defines its own distinctive objects of inquiry, truth criteria, institutional sanctions, etc. The term "power/knowledge," as Nancy Fraser (1981, 274) notes:

covers in a single concept everything that falls under the two distinct Kuhnian concepts of paradigm and disciplinary matrix but, unlike Kuhn, Foucault gives this complex a political character. Both the use of the term "power" and, more subtly, that of the term "regime" convey this political coloration (1981, 274).

Discursive regimes function on the basis of social practices which involve forms of constraint: the valorization of some statement forms over others; "the institutional licensing of some persons as being entitled to offer knowledge-claims and the concomitant exclusion of others; coercive forms of extracting information from and about certain persons and groups of persons; and so on" (Fraser 1981, 274). While Foucault did not apply his insights directly to the natural sciences, others have done so. For example, Rouse uses Foucault to develop a political philosophy of science. He writes:

> Power relations permeate the most ordinary activities in scientific research. Scientific knowledge arises out of these power relations rather than in opposition to them. Knowledge is power, and power knowledge. Knowledge is embedded in our research practices rather than being fully abstractable in representational theories. Theories are to be understood in their uses, not in their static correspondence . . . with the world. Power as it is produced in science is not the possession of particular agents and does not necessarily serve particular interests. Power relations constitute the world in which we find agents and interests (1987, 24).

This kind of view of the relations between knowledge and power underlies Jean-François Lyotard's account of the postmodern condition. Lyotard's single point of departure in attempting to describe and chart the transition in Western societies to the postindustrial age is scientific knowledge. He argues that the leading sciences and technologies—cybernetics, telematics, informatics, and the growth of computer languages— are all significantly language based, and together they have transformed the two principal functions of knowledge: research and the transmission of acquired learning.

Knowledge is changed or redefined within this context of general transformation. Anything in the constituted body of knowledge which is not translatable into quantities of information will be abandoned. Knowledge, in other words, loses its "use-value." The technical transformation wrought by a continued miniaturization and commercialization of knowledge machines will further change the way in which learning is acquired and classified. Knowledge is exteriorized with respect to the knower, and the status of the learner and the teacher is transformed into a commodity relationship of "supplier" and "user." As Lyotard (1984, 4) argues: "Knowledge is and will be produced in order to be sold, it is and will be consumed in order to be valorized in a new production: in both cases, the goal is exchange." Already knowledge has become the principal force of production, severely altering the composition of the work force in the most developed countries. The mercantilization of knowledge will further widen the gap between developed and developing countries. It will disrupt the traditional view that learning falls within the purview of the state and raise new legal and ethical questions for the relationship between the state and "information-rich" transnational corporations. This scenario, Lyotard admits, is not original or even necessarily true, but it does have *strategic value* in allowing us to see the effects of the transformation of knowledge on public power and civil institutions, and it raises afresh the central problem of legitimation. Who decides what is "true" or what is to be regarded as "scientific," as belonging to the discourse of a scientific community? In postmodern society, where knowledge and power are to be regarded as simply two sides of the same question, the problem of legitimation of knowledge necessarily comes to the fore: "In the computer age, the question of knowledge is now more than ever a question of *government*" (our emphasis; ibid., 9).

A Poststructuralist Critique: Three Lines of Inquiry

1. Neoliberal Governmentality: Economy, Society, and Curriculum

It is the argument of this chapter that any account of the curriculum must be situated within the wider global and policy context, and that changes in the curriculum reflect profound changes in advanced liberal states as they attempt to come to terms with changes in the global economy. Contemporary Western states have been dominated by neoliberalism, which, operating on the basis of a revival of *homo economicus*, based on assumptions of rationality, individuality, and self-interest, has restructured economy and society. Such reform has included the restructuring of science and technology policy, so as to harness them and press them into service of the economy.

It was during the decade of the 1980s that forms of American neoliberalism, inspired by Friedrich Hayek's (e.g., 1944, 1949a, 1960) political and economic philosophy, were used by Thatcher and Reagan to legitimate the attack on "big government" and the bureaucratic welfare state with a policy mix based on "free" trade and the establishment of the "open" economy. By American neoliberalism we mean in particular the Chicago School (see e.g., Friedman 1962), public choice theory (see e.g., Buchanan and Tullock 1962), and human capital theory (e.g., Becker 1964). We can describe this policy mix in the following terms: as economic liberalization or rationalization characterized by abolishing subsidies and tariffs; floating the exchange rate; freeing up controls on foreign investment; restructuring the state sector, including corporatization and privatization of state trading departments and other assets; "downsizing"; attacking unions and abolishing wage bargaining in favor of employment contracts; and, finally, the dismantling of the welfare state through commercialization, "contracting out," "targetting" services, and individual "responsibilization" for health, welfare, and education. In this view there is nothing distinctive or special about education or health; they are services and products to be traded in the marketplace like any other.

These policies, sometimes referred to as the Washington Consensus, were designed to "restructure" or adjust national economies to the dramatic changes to the world economy that have occurred in the last twenty years: the growing competition among nations for world markets; the emergence of world trading blocs and new "free trade" agreements; an increasing globalization of economic and cultural activities; the decline of the postwar Keynesian welfare state settlement in Western countries; the collapse of actually existing communism and the "opening up" of the Eastern bloc; and the accelerated worldwide adoption and development of the new information and communications technologies.

Structural adjustment has been associated with the correction of imbalances in foreign accounts and domestic consumption. It has also been associated with the deregulation and privatization of the economy. Such policies are to be identified with a fiscal austerity program designed to shrink the public sector, and in some countries, with growing poverty and the unequal distribution of income. Yet, as Martin Carnoy observes, the practice of structural adjustment followed by the high-income OECD countries and the newly industrializaing countries (NICs) of Asia does not conform to this picture. He suggests that the focus in these countries has been on

> increased exports, reduced domestic demand, various constraints on government spending and some privatization; with a few notable exceptions, it has not entailed policies that greatly increase inequality or poverty. Rather, many of the richer economies have focused on "self-adjusting" mechanisms to rationalize production and the public infrastructure that serves productive and social functions. Their educational systems have not suffered and, in general, their education professionals have made income gains. In the best of cases, education has improved and teachers have participated in making that improvement happen (Carnoy, 1995, 654).

Drawing upon this difference in practice, Carnoy surmises that there are several categories of structural adjustment and that in the case of the richer nations the term stands for a *set of policies* which originated in the United States during the 1970s as the dominant view of how economies in crisis, typically those of developing countries characterized by high indebtedness, should reorganize to achieve growth. Such policies called for cuts in public expenditure on services, including education, precisely at the point when a shift to a global information economy required massive public investment in an information infrastructure—with an attendant emphasis on mass education—necessary to take advantage of changes in the nature of the world economy.

Carnoy attributes the emergence of the dominant view to two factors: The richer nations of the OECD already enjoyed favorable conditions which allowed them to self-adjust and to respond positively to rapidly changing technology; and the paradigm shift from Keynesianism to neoliberal monetarism led to "a dramatic increase in real interest rates to reduce inflationary tendencies . . . and to sharp cuts in foreign loans" (655). The neoliberal monetarist paradigm also became the dominant view at the international level, shaping the outlook of world institutions such as the International Monetary Fund (IMF) and the World Bank (WB), which imposed structural adjustment policies (SAPs) on developing countries as a response to their continuing and exacerbating debt problems.

Neoliberalism has been associated most in the popular imagination with policies of privatization. Indeed, it is privatization that has provided the basis for strategies to reduce the size of the state (while, paradoxically, often strengthening its constitutional powers), to reduce the accumulated national debt, at the same time encouraging foreign investment and, advocates claim, inaugurating the age of popular capitalism. Privatization can be a complex phenomenon. Le Grand and Robinson comment, "any privatization proposal involves the rolling back of the activities of the state" (1984, 3). Privatization thus involves three main kinds of activity which parallel the three main types of state intervention: a reduction in state subsidy; a reduction in state provision; and a reduction in state regulation. Privatization can take many forms: Schemes differ not only in the type of state intervention whose reduction or elimination they require but also in what is proposed in its stead—the replacement of the state by the market, by another form of state activity, or by non-profit-making organizations such as charities or voluntary organizations that are neither private firms nor state enterprises (Le Grand and Robinson 1984, 6).

A number of commentators have pointed out that privatization takes the form not only of the sale of state-owned assets and enterprises: Other parallel forms include contracting out, deregulation, user fees, voucher systems, and load-shedding. Others (e.g., Heing et al. 1988) have concluded on the basis of comparing recent experience in Britain, France, and the United States that privatization is more of a political strategy than an economic and fiscal technique. While the case for privatization is based on well-known theories, the drive for privatization is more complex and often involves political factors such as reducing public sector borrowing or reducing government financial risk. Pitelis and Clarke (1993, 6) note that the case for privatization policies is often strong in a priori theorizing and weak in empirical confirmation.

This section, drawing upon our work in Chapter 1, explores and develops Foucault's notion of governmentality in relation to an understanding of neoliberalism and the notion of an enterprise society. Much of the argument for understanding the changes that we have referred to above under the description of neoliberalism, especially the changes of governance as they affect education and the construction of the curriculum, have already been advanced in some detail in Chapter 1. We will summarize aspects of that understanding here briefly.

Foucault uses the term "governmentality" to signal the emergence of a distinctive kind of rule that became the basis for modern liberal politics. As we mentioned in Chapter 1, he (Foucault 1991) begins to examine the problematic of government by analyzing the *series*—security, population, government—and he examines the discourses on the "art of government" that began in the sixteenth century. During the early seventeenth century the art of government develops around the notion of "reason of state" based upon rational principles involving, in particular, the first entry of "economy" into political practice (Foucault 1991a, 92). So governmentality is to be defined in terms of a specific form of government power based on the "science" of political economy, involving, for example, "state-istics" or as we know the term "statistics," a science of state and a form of governmental knowledge or *savoir* essential for governing a territory. Focuault is not interested in theorizing this history or in explaining the doctrine—he is more interested in the question of *how* power is exercised and this interest makes his analysis applicable to contemporary affairs.

In Chapter 1, we also examined both Foucault's notion of governmentality and the recent work undertaken by scholars who seek to advance an understanding of new forms of governance that have developed in association with neoliberalism. In Figure 1, we provided what we called "Elements of Neoliberal Governmentality." In outlining these main features of neoliberalism it is important to bear in mind that there are both affinities, continuities, and overlapping concepts as well as differences and theoretical innovations with classical liberalism. So, for instance, neoliberalism shares with classical liberalism an emphasis on the limits of reason and the state's right to know.

As we argued in Chapter 1, neoliberalism (which is also known as a form of economic liberalism or economic rationalism), like liberalism, is concerned to limit government in relation to the market. To this end, neoliberalism constructs the notion of the minimalist state through the legal, institutional, and cultural conditions that enable the competitive game of entrepreneurial conduct to be played to best effect. Neoliberalism promotes enterprise culture through the development of quasi-economic models. Under neoliberalism there is an enterprise form that is generalized to include all forms of conduct, especially through the promotion of enterprise culture and the enterprise curriculum (Burchell 1993, 276). This is, perhaps, one of the most significant differences between classical liberalism and, particularly, the liberalism of Friedrich von Hayek and forms of neoliberalism: a difference between *natural* versus *contrived* forms of the market. Hayek's notion of natural laws based on spontaneously ordered institutions in the physical (crystals, galaxies) and social (morality, language, market) worlds has been replaced with an emphasis on the market as an artifact or culturally derived form and (growing out of the "callaxy" approach) a *constitutional* perspective that focuses on the judicio-legal rules governing the framework within the game of enterprise is played (see Buchanan 1991). Further, the politics-as-exchange innovation of public choice theory, which involves the marketization of the state, extends Hayek's spontaneous order conception (callactics) of the institution of the market beyond simple exchange to complex exchange and finally to *all processes of voluntary agreement* among persons (see Buchanan and Tullock 1962).

With neoliberalism there also exists a new relationship between government and self-government. Liberalism as a doctrine positively requires that individuals be free in order to be governed, which is what we understand by government as the community of free, autonomous, self-regulating individuals. The neoliberal revival of *homo economicus*, based on assumptions of individuality, rationality, and self-interest, is developed as an all-embracing re-description of the social as a form of the economic and individuals are "responsibilized" as moral agents. Sometimes this new relation between government and self-government is understood in terms of the new managerialism involving a shift from *policy* and *administration to management*, the emulation of private sector management styles, an emphasis on "freedom to manage" and the promotion of "self-managing" (i.e., quasi-autonomous) individuals and institutions. This "degovernmentalization" of the state (considered as a positive technique of government) is encouraged by a process of government through and by the market, including promotion of consumer-driven forms of social provision (health, education, welfare), "contracting out, and, ultimately, privatization. In this context we can talk of the decentralization, "devolution," and delegation of power/authority/responsibility from the center to the region, the local institution, or the "community"—what we might also term the replacement of "community" for "the social." Some scholars who refer to social policy in terms of decentralization and devolution—effected through a form of contract mechanism—talk of the emergence of the shadow state in which the development of an informal voluntary sector (and an autonomous civil society) is encouraged as an alternative source of welfare. The development of an enterprise society, along with the privatization of the public sector and the development of quasi-markets, rests increasingly upon a curriculum of competition and enterprise.

One way in which neoliberalism creates a rationale for restructuring education can be seen in the promotion of the notion of enterprise. Enterprise contains two elements that need to be bonded together through education. The major structural changes to the state, and later, education, were couched primarily in the language of neoliberalism with its appeals to the efficiencies of the market, the liberty of individuals, and the minimalist state. In terms of governmentality, "this programme has increasingly also come to be represented in cultural terms, as concerned with attitudes, values and forms of self-understanding embedded in both individual and institutional activities" (Keat 1991, 1). The more positive attributes of cultural engineering are also called for in the project of constructing the enterprise culture. Under enterprise education there is a deliberate effort to rid the self of so-called dependent and passive attributes. A new sovereign, enterprising self is to be constructed—and it is in this sense that the control of education (and, therefore, of science) is vital.

The point of the Foucauldian analysis of neoliberal governmentality is to indicate how various forms of market relations have been substituted for the state, how the state now governs "through" the market, so to speak, and how this has led to notions of the enterprise society and to forms of the enterprise curriculum, both demanding a specification of the subject as "enterprise individuals." To offer such an analysis, of course, is not to condone or support such developments but rather to develop an understanding that shows how the construction of the curriculum is closely related to new forms of market governance in advanced liberal societies.

2. The Information Economy

We are entering the nirvana of the Age of Information—information is the catchword and the catch cry of bands of enthusiastic "progressives" and reformers in education in the last decade of the twentieth century. Indeed, most curricula in Western schools are being restructured by what can be called the informational economy. But the *form* that this "new" education should take in this new age of electronic communication is seldom discussed, or even problematized. Essentially it seems to be seen as a continuation and *extension* of traditional print literacy, and the move from the printed word to electronic language is not philosophically problematized in the educational literature (see Peters 1996b; Peters and Lankshear 1996; Peters and Marshall, 1995).

Given the power effects of discourses, in the manner to which Foucault has drawn our attention, Doll's approach to the curriculum is severely limited in not being able to account for the effects of the moves in educational "thinking" from knowledge to information and skills, and from knowing some *thing* (content) to processes and activities. Such limitations are serious, given that the informational economy is a major force restructuring the curriculum, our social and cultural relations, established notions of rights, power and authority, and our notions of subjectivity.

Fundamental questions about the nature of knowledge and pedagogy are generally not discussed in the core philosophy underpinning official curriculum proposals for schools (for the New Zealand case, see Ministry of Education 1993). This is a philosophical "silence." However, we believe that central to curriculum considerations are questions about what counts as knowledge, how it is defined and controlled, and whose knowledge is selected for inclusion—who decides and on what basis? What counts as important knowledge also defines what is seen *as not worth knowing* and, consequently, the interests of different gender, class, and ethnic groups may be unequally represented in what is included and excluded in the curriculum offered.

Knowledge, in the sense of knowing *that* something is the case, has been replaced by knowing *how*, with the explicit emphasis on getting skilled, while learning as process has replaced knowing some thing in the notion of learning areas, in getting skilled, and in the area of attitudes and values, where it is an attitude toward learning (as a process) that is valued and not an attitude toward knowledge (as something known). It is the processes—the ever ongoing learning and reskilling processes—that are seen as having paramount importance. There are parallels here with the support for approaches to the curriculum which can broadly be called "constructivist." What is important pedagogically is the process of construction, and not the object constructed, especially in radical versions of constructivism.

In part this is because the outcome is no longer knowledge but *information*. And in part it is because information has to be continuously "relearned," readjusted, and restructured to meet the demands of the consumer in the service information industry. It is the consumer who determines quality (truth?) in the information industry (Barker 1993). Hence the necessity to value "learning" and "lifelong" learning.

There are a number of related issues here—access to information, the fragility of social networks, the breakdown of traditional authority structures associated with oral and written communication, new ways of exercising power relationships through these different forms of knowledge, and new ways of constituting the self.

Consider the form of face-to-face social networks associated with oral communication and compare it with the written word where the authority of the speaker, *who* that person is, is different from the authority of the *author*, and contrast both of these with the information encoded in the pixels on the electronic screen. The social networks associated with oral and written communication can become very fragile in electronic communication because of the introduction of a virus, say, which may bring about a breakdown, or require the complete shutdown of the network. The information encoded by an emitter can be transformed on receipt by the recipient. Unwanted information can appear on the screen and may be irrelevant, contradictory, intemperate, abusive, or even obscene.

It is not just that the social networks are tender but that the roles of speaker or author are instantly reversible and not subject to the same social conventions that govern oral and written communication. Further, authority structures become tenuous. These concern not merely the authority that accompanied oral communication—that of *who* the speaker is—or that of written communication—where the notions of truth, evidence, and of being *an* authority are important—but also the authority of controlling what is said. If unwanted communication cannot be controlled, traditional notions of being *in* authority become very tenuous. Of course a "solution" to this is to control emitters and emittees so that they are passive senders and receivers.

The notion of the free autonomous chooser is a notion of the self that underlies the reform literatures in which information is a key building block. According to Foucault, the Enlightenment notion of personal autonomy did not provide freedom. But nor will neoliberal autonomous choosers be free either, because what can be called busnocratic rationality and busnopower (Marshall 1995) will shape them as particular kinds of subjects, so that they will choose in certain general ways. Furthermore Foucault's bio-power (Foucault 1980),with its emphasis on the body, does not seem very appropriate in relation to electronic communication. Education, embedded in the frameworks of busnopower and busnocratic rationality, is the first step in this literature toward the new individualizing and totalizing functions of busnopower, and the production of the autonomous chooser within a total enterprise culture.

In the Age of Information, and in relation to identity, the new self will be decentered and dispersed, as in poststructuralist theory, without spatiotemporal and bodily constraints. But if the physical body has *nothing* to do with identity in electronic communication, it is almost as though the embodied self has become invisible. It is not just that the self can "transport" itself spatio-temporally: It is almost that there is no self other than the self-reflexive signs of electronic communication—the pixels on the screen. But as the emitter's information can be obliterated almost immediately by the changing of the pixels in the process of receiving and transmitting information, then so too can the self be obliterated because of the self-reflexive character of language in this new mode of information. At best the self is in continuous instability as pixels change in the flow of information between emitter and emittee, who are also in constant "reversal" of roles. It seems as if the self becomes obliterated or unidentifiable in the flux, maze, and buzz of information. But because there is nothing other than the flux, the self cannot be obliterated, since in order for that to happen the self had to first exist, which is not possible in the flux of information. But if the self is not identifiable, in principle, this poses additional problems for traditional authority structures and governance.

Mark Poster recognizes the importance of a study of electronic languages that does not merely look at technologies, machines, and the new efficiencies brought about in communication (see e.g., Poster 1993, 1995). According to Poster "an adequate account of electronic communications requires a theory that is able to decode the linguistic dimension of the new forms of social interaction" (Poster 1993, 5). He argues, correctly in our view, that traditional critical theory is inadequate for the task.

As a step in that direction, Poster advocates the concept of the mode of information that provides both a historical category that divides and periodizes the past and a metaphor for how certain activities are privileged. This parallels Marx's account of the mode of production—especially as presented in *The German Ideology*—which similarly served these dual ends. Poster (1993, 6) defines the mode of information thus:

By mode of information we similarly suggest that history can be periodized by variations in the structure in this case of symbolic exchange, but also that the current culture gives a certain fetishistic importance to "information."

With this definition in place, Poster identifies three important periodizations of forms of symbolic exchange: first, face-to-face and orally mediated exchange; second, written exchanges mediated by print; third, electronically mediated exchanges. These are not to be seen as progressions or improvements. But is the third stage just an extension of the second and, thereby, just another form of printed exchange? Poster's major claim is that it is not.

Poster argues further that these matters and their restraints or enhancements can govern with striking force the shape that societies take. For him technicist approaches do not reach the heart of the matter, "the configuration of information exchange," or, as he calls it, "the wrapping of language." He argues that the configuration of language is an analytically autonomous realm of experience. This is especially apparent with the rapidly changing modes of electronic communication that do not merely alter but *restructure* networks of social relations and constitute subjects in very different ways than the personally autonomous agent of the second stage and any representational view of language. Changes in the wrapping of language, then, alter the way meanings are derived, restructure social relations, constitute the subject in different ways, and alter the relations between subject and the world.

The message sounded loud and clear by Foucault, among others, is that language has an important capacity for our constitution as subjects. By distancing emitter and emittee, electronic communication disturbs our normal conceptions of relations between speaker and hearer, or between writer and reader, thereby reconstituting both subjects and their relations to symbols. Indeed, for a subject in electronic communications, there seems no longer to be a material world as normally represented by language, but just a flow of electronic language. Instead of a real world behind the language we have, instead, a simulated world, with simulacra and no real objects.

The Age of Information requires a broader view of critical theory, which permits the new linguistic dimension of social interaction to be decoded and become part of any theoretical reconstruction and description of social and cultural life. For education it is especially important that a critical theory be able to decode the new linguistic dimensions of electronic communication. This becomes important on account of the epistemological shifts from knowledge to information and from content to process, the problems of reference of signs in electronic writing, problems of identity and how the self is constituted, and new problems relating to authority and governance.

Doll simply does not account for these issues. His approach to the curriculum pays scant attention to the importance of the linguistic dimension. Indeed, his version of postmodern theory seems unable to deal with this dimension in any of the modes of information identified by Poster. The philosophical import of electronic communication cannot surface within Doll's problematic.

3. The Crisis of Cultural Authority

One of the phenomena characteristically associated with the postmodern and its analysis is the discovery of the Other, described variously as "the discovery of the plurality of cultures" (Ricoeur 1965, 276), "post-colonialism," the philosophy of decolonization, the development and proliferation of postwar youth subcultures, and the rise of the "new social movements." In an influential article called "The Discourse of Others: Feminists and Postmodernism" Craig Owens begins his account with the following statement:

> Decentered, allegorical, schizophrenic . . . however we choose to diagnose its symptoms, postmodernism is usually treated, by its protagonists and antagonists alike, as a crisis of cultural authority, specifically of the authority vested in Western European culture and its institutions. That the hegemony of European civilisation is drawing to a close is hardly a new perception; since the mid-1950s, at least, we have recognised the necessity of encountering different cultures by means other than the shock of domination and conquest (1987, 57).

Owens cites the historian Arnold Toynbee as among the first to indicate the beginning of a new postmodern age characterized by the coexistence of different cultures, and locates Claude Levi-Strauss's critique of Western ethnocentrism and Jacques Derrida's critique of Levi-Strauss within the same context. What is at stake, says Owens, is "not only the hegemony of Western culture, but also (our sense of) our identity as a culture" (59). Owens's specific concern is to explore the intersection between the feminist critique of patriarchy and the postmodern critique of representation, with the understanding that the representation of women as subjects (rather than as objects) has been denied all legitimacy.

More recently, Stephen White (1991) defines the postmodern problematic in terms of four phenomena: an increasing incredulity toward metanarratives; a new awareness of the dangers of societal rationalization; the new informational technologies; and the emergence of "new social movements." Drawing on Habermas's analysis, White argues that the new social movements are associated with the emergence of new values in Western industrialized societies. For these new social groups politics is no longer a matter of compensations that the welfare state can provide: that is, a matter of distribution of scarce public resources. Rather, politics now comprises conflicts ignited over questions concerning the forms of life and the state's colonization of the life-world. He asserts:

> The women's movement, antinuclear movement, radical ecology, ethnic movements, homosexuals, and countercultural groups in general all share, at least to some degree, this new status, even if they differ in many substantive ways. They all have a somewhat defensive character, as well as a focus on struggling to gain the ability to construct socially their own collective identity, characteristics that make them rather anomalous in relation to the standard rules for interest group behavior in the modern state. (White 1991, 10).

Peters (1991) has argued for a close theoretical relationship between the rise of the new social movements and the poststructuralist critique of reason. Neither classical Marxism nor contemporary neoliberalism can account for this new social phenomenon. Peters interprets what Habermas (1982) has called the new social movements—by which he means "subinstitutional, extra-parliamentary forms of protest"—as the historical means by which Marxism as the master discourse of liberation has been stripped of the overtly rationalistic and scientistic elements it inherited from the Enlightenment. Peters also argues that poststructuralism has taught us that all *outsider groups*—those based on ethnicity, gender, and class, along with Nature as an excluded Other, the incarcerated, the deviant, and the institutionalized—question the active construction and social reproduction of human beings as "individuals." They question the basic working assumption of individualism as it underlies both capitalism and liberalism.

Postmodernism as the "culture" of advanced industrial society or late consumer capitalism is an exploration of the margins, the borders and limits of high modernism. It is, above all, a central questioning of the absolutist and ahistorical categories and values, sustained and propagated through the symbolic power of the grand narratives by which "Man," "Reason," "History," and "Culture" were first projected in universalist European terms. Yet postmodernism is more than an internal critique of modernism and its interpretation of classical reason. It not only challenges the overly rationalist and elitist pretensions of modernism and modernity by exposing the gender, ethnic, class, and sexual biases written into its founding legitimating myths or metanarratives, but also seeks an entirely new problematic for understanding the social construction and self-constitution of individuals as collective or social subjects.

This problematic, in its theoretical infancy, can be seen in the fact that the "philosophy of consciousness"—the tradition of subject-centered reason which inaugurated modern Western philosophy, prefigured in Descartes' *cogito* and brought to fruition by Kant—is exhausted. This rich seam of European philosophy which in one way or another provided the foundations in epistemology, in the human sciences, and in many of the institutions and practices that pervade contemporary Western culture, has been worked out. This has been argued not only by poststructuralists like Derrida, Foucault, Deleuze and Lyotard, but also by their arch-opponent Habermas (1987), and by the leading American "postmodern" pragmatist Richard Rorty (1979). In his introduction to Habermas's appraisal of poststructuralism, Thomas McCarthy (1987) writes:

> In sum, then, Habermas agrees with the radical critics of the Enlightenment that the paradigm of consciousness is exhausted. Like them, he views reason as inescapably situated, as concretized in history, society, body and language. Unlike them, however, he holds that the defects of the Enlightenment can only be made good by further enlightenment. The totalized critique of reason undercuts the capacity of reason to be critical (xvii).

The new problematics, the emergent outlines of which can be discerned in a variety of methodologies and approaches across the disciplines, operates on the basis of a radical decentering that denies an epistemic or historical privilege to both the traditional Cartesian notion of a centered, transparent, individual subjectivity and the humanist ideal of a rational, autonomous, and responsible self. These developments are clearly related to shifts in the centrality of both notions of language and culture in social science theorizing in recent years.

In sociology, for example, Mike Featherstone (1989, 148) has noted the way in which an interest in culture up until the mid-1970s was considered eccentric and marginal. He charts the huge rise of journals in the English-speaking world concerned with theorizations of culture and indicates how feminism, Marxism, structuralism, poststructuralism, semiology, critical theory, and psychoanalysis raised the profile of cultural questions.

More precisely, Eisenstadt has detected a shift in the notion of culture within recent sociological analysis. This is a shift away from culture conceived as "fully structured according to clear principles, embedded in the very nature of the human mind, which, through the medium of a series of codes, regulate human behaviour," and toward a view which emphasizes, in a hermeneutical manner, the symbolic and expressive dimensions (1989, 6). Both the structuralist-functionist and the symbolic-expressive conceptions are motivated by underlying theories of language, giving the cultural a greater importance in social theory than was previously the case. The shift itself from strictly structuralist accounts (based, historically, on the work of Saussure and others) to interpretivist, symbolic, and hermeneutical models is directly related to developments in the theory of language and, in particular, those developments attributable to the work of Saussure, Heidegger, Gadamer, and Wittgenstein, among others.

Most recently, the growth of interest in poststructuralism, deconstruction, and postmodernism, also motivated by changing conceptions and theories of language, have helped to push questions of cultural (and aesthetic) interest to center stage. It is clear that these developments across a range of disciplines immediately focus on the interrelated concepts of language and culture. Certain views in the philosophy of language, dating historically from different traditions—those of Nietzsche, Heidegger, Wittgenstein, and Saussure—have provided an orientation toward a more anthropologically differentiated notion of culture in the first instance which emphasizes at one and the same time its "linguisticality," its historicity, its dependence on a "politics of representation" and its role in socially constituting new "intersubjectivities" (Featherstone 1989, 150).

Surveying a collection of essays devoted to examining the politics of postmodernism, Andrew Ross (1988, vii) notes that, for some theorists, a politics of difference and a politics of the local and particular "are not only symptoms of, but also essential strategies for coping with a postmodernist culture that advertises itself as decentered, transnational, and pluralistic." He sees postmodernism as "a belated response to the vanguardist innovations of high modernism . . . the continuation of modernism by other means" (ix).

Similarly, in describing the reformulation of the socialist project attempted in an earlier work, Chantal Mouffe (1988) indicates how such a project demands a non-essentialist epistemological perspective. This reformulation, while acknowledging the role that the epistemological perspective of the Enlightenment played in the emergence of democracy, now sees it as an obstacle in understanding the new form of politics which is characteristic of our times. An appropriate understanding, we are told, is to be gained from using "the theoretical tools established by different currents of what can be called *the postmodern in philosophy* and of appropriating their critique of rationalism and subjectivism" (our emphasis; Mouffe 1988, 33). By "the postmodern in philosophy," Mouffe clearly means poststructuralism, the philosophy of language of the later Wittgenstein, and post-Heideggerian hermeneutics. She writes:

> To be capable of thinking politics today, and understanding the nature of these new struggles and the diversity of social relations that the democratic revolution has yet to encompass, it is indispensable to develop a theory of the subject as a decentered, detotalized agent, a subject constructed at the point of intersection of a multiplicity of subject-positions between which there exists no a priori or necessary relation. (Mouffe 1988, 35).

Conclusion

What can we conclude from this brief analysis?

First, characterizations of postmodern science in terms of recent internal developments distract us from viewing science as part of an evolving Western cultural formation. In ignoring science as a cultural formation, that is, as a set of institutions based upon certain forms of inherited cultural practices, a conception of the curriculum is insulated from the challenges to such cultural authority that have been mounted by outsider groups. We have in mind here the feminist and Third World critiques of Western science.

Second, characterizations of the curriculum in terms of cosmological readings of postmodern science are unable to respond to questions concerning the politics of the gendered or mono-cultural nature of curricula or knowledges. This is a glaring problem given the controversy in American higher education over notions of what counts as a "discipline" or a "canon" and the rise of black, feminist, and gay studies within universities.

Third, clearly the "crisis of cultural authority" also points out the untenability of the distinction between two types of postmodernism, especially when it comes to questions of (radical) ecology or theology, for it seems impossible to understanding the ecological movement without understanding something about politics of the new social movements.

Fourth, and perhaps most important, by focusing entirely on internal developments to science, cosmological readings of the postmodern have no explanatory force when it comes to questions of power, to political economy, and to the emerging politics developing around neoliberal paradigms of globalization and global order. In order to theorize the curriculum today we argue that it is precisely accounts of the latter that are most required.

Note

1. This chapter draws on an earlier paper written jointly with James Marshall and Patrick Fitzsimmons.

Chapter 6

Curriculum and Postmodernity: Social Traits and Contours[1]

Introduction

Constituting the curriculum-society link is a very complex task in today's complicated world—characterized as it is by a severe crisis at all levels of society.[2] We say "a very complex task" because we currently lack new utopian horizons from which socio-political projects could emerge and enable a new hegemonic rearticulation of societies.[3] The changes that have occurred so rapidly around the globe since 1989, combined with the erosion of the very essences and foundations of Western thought, have put the educational field and, within it, the curriculum, in a highly complex situation.

This situation can be analyzed from a number of angles. Some of the most important are (a) the difficulty for academics to constitute themselves as subjects in the process of curricular overdetermination[4] (de Alba 1995a); (b) the complex "surface of inscription" (Laclau 1990, 63) or context that is characterized by "split subjects"[5] and by what we will call "social traits and contours" rather than by social-political projects of the type that have guided the processes of constituting the curriculum-society link in the past; (c) recognition that theoretical tools that until recently had allowed us to understand educational problems are no longer adequate for this purpose; and (d) greatly increased cultural contact and its impact on social and educational spheres.

This chapter will articulate and explore some of these characteristically postmodern issues, starting from the challenge of rethinking the curriculum in ways that will help us to recapture a purposeful, critical, and analytical stance. This means rethinking the curriculum in relation to society within the context of a rapidly ever-changing world that seems to have no obvious rudder to guide it. Here we are rethinking the curriculum in a situation of generalized structural *crisis* in which we find social traits and contours rather than political and social projects. These social traits and contours emerge as incipient moments[6] of articulation[7] among the multiple and constant movements and floating elements[8] of signification that characterize all crises. Social traits and contours appear in multiformed and multidirectional ways, affecting not only those who are decentered, but the very decentering of the center itself.

de Alba (1991) argues that the curriculum is a political-educational proposal constituted by a synthesis, or articulation, of cultural elements stemming from struggles, impositions, and negotiations among various social subjects (for example, church, state, political parties, trade unions, community organizations, etc.) that sustain broad social-political projects and assume that society will be educated in accordance with such projects.

However, as we have noted, one of the most serious problems confronting us at present in the area of the curriculum is the lack of social-political projects that would allow us to (re)constitute the curriculum-society link and to constitute subjects of the processes of curricular overdetermination. These subjects are supposed to sustain *educational* projects in relation to the *social-political* projects. The current lack of new utopian horizons and projects operates against this, however, posing the key question for curriculum under postmodern conditions: How do we constitute the curriculum-society link in societies that are in crisis and that lack any wide and ambitious social-political projects? In the recent past we had a sense of what it meant to maintain and refine the curriculum-society link. The various social subjects, the projects they represented, and the struggles among them were reasonably clear and understood and were recognized as legitimate bases for social organization and development. Under those conditions we could actively engage ourselves as subjects of curricular overdetermination, entering actively and consciously into processes that related social-political and educational projects. All this has changed, however. Indeed, many of the former social subjects are barely recognizable in the terms we had known them previously, and in some cases their very legitimation is in question.

One possible conceptual and contextual response to this question is as follows. If it is true that in moments of severe crisis, such as we are currently facing, the dislocation[9] of the established order produces an accelerated flow of elements as a result of the erosion of the symbolic order[10]— that is, erosion of condensations of meaning or discourses[11]—it is *also* true that through the processes of crisis we can observe the emergence of social traits and contours out of which new hegemonic practices can be articulated.

The main ideas to be developed here are the notions of social traits and contours. Having introduced these concepts we will then identify and describe some examples of them within the current context and suggest how they may work as contours of articulation within processes of constituting the curriculum-society link. Accordingly, the chapter is organized in three parts. The first discusses the postmodern condition and explores the notion of social traits and contours in the current surface of inscription, characterized as it is by crisis on all social levels. The second identifies and highlights what we see as some of the most important social traits and contours: poverty, "swiftness,"[12] globalization, democracy, difference, and development. By way of a provisional closure, the third section addresses the potential of social traits and contours to act as contours of articulation in the task of (re)constituting the curriculum-society link.

The Postmodern Condition as Surface of Inscription:[13] Social Traits and Contours

This section considers the concept of postmodern condition as the main meaning in the current surfaces of inscription, together with the notions of signs and social contours and related concepts. The reading has been made in the first instance from a double space of enunciation: the specific space of the Universidad Nacional Autonoma de México (UNAM)[14] and the academic space of the University of Essex.[15] This positionality overdetermines to a large extent the point of view assumed in this chapter (see note 4 above).

It is important to mention that the strength of the notion of positionality in the field of curriculum consists in its usefulness as a conceptual and political tool. Positionality is a nodal point[16] within contexts of crisis where we face social traits and contours rather than social projects. It is also important to confront the issue of positionality, and specifically our own positionality, in order to realize communication with others in our highly complex world, where cultural contact is increasing each day:

> Positionality must be understood as the psychic, cultural, social, geopolitical, economic, etc. space, from which the world is enunciated, and constructed. Discourse positionality is impacted by the strength of the social fabric from which the enunciator operates. It refers to the enunciative space (de Alba 1996, 10).

In terms of positionality taken this chapter seeks an international perspective, although from time to time concrete examples are drawn specifically from Latin America and México. In terms of temporality the chapter centers on events that occurred during the 1980s and 1990s. This is a period within a historical moment of epochal transition that is symbolically inscribed with the elements of transition from the twentieth to the twenty-first century. This critical process of transition is characterized by multiple floating elements that are provisionally rearticulated as *social traits and contours* (de Alba 1993). These inscribe themselves in the current postmodern surfaces of inscription and can be recognized as nodal characteristics of the generalized fin de siécle structural crisis.

(A) The Postmodern Condition and Postmodern Existentiality

The postmodern condition is the mainstay of the surfaces of inscription of the current social crisis. According to Ferraris (1988) postmodernity is the symptom (conscious or otherwise) of the inadequacy of the philosophical debate on modernity. Morales (1988) argues that postmodernity represents a change in rationality, while Calderón (1994) maintains that it is not only a change in rationality but also a change in ways of seeing life and of life itself. Postmodernity as a mixture of current life conditions implies, according to Morales, the thinking and rethinking of questions such as Who are we? Are humans radically different? How are we to govern in an unequal globalized economy? What are the new horizons of politics once it is no longer the monopoly of the state? How can knowledge be legitimized? Is legitimation necessary? What are the possibilities for metanarratives and what are the alternatives to them? Can an answer be given to the critique of centrality and of Eurocentrism in particular?

In 1988, Morales saw postmodernity as a horizon of a culture and identified what he saw as its main characteristics: resistance to integration into a systemic and coherent conceptual framework; the existence of a network of heterogeneous worlds; the rediscovery of contingency and difference; the end of the great horizons; the end of history as teleologically ordained; the end of ethnocentric universality; a wave of indifference to political and state power; the end of rationality based on absolute truth; the emergence of new social, political and cultural currents that are distinct from those that preceded modernity; and the rescuing of modernist ideals of modernity at higher levels of exigency, reflected in Kant's saying: "[H]ave the courage to use your own understandings."

Buenfil Burgos (1995) advances an alternative parallel account of features derived from authors such as Derrida, Lacan, and Wittgenstein:

relationalism; the floating character of the sign; the shifting or slippery nature of borders; the open character of configuration; the impossibility of establishing an overarching epistemological, ontological, political, ethical, and aesthetic proposal; the critique of fixed centers; the critique of globalizing and universalizing theories and political strategies; the critique of the transcendental, unidimensional, teleological, universal, saturated, and centered subject; the impossibility of learning the real through form, thought, or reason; the impossibility of realizing the totality of being through thought; the incomplete character of every configuration; and the constitutive character of the contingency in the formation of process.

Positivist, closed scientific and absolute knowledge, as constituted in modernism, is judged from the perspectives of postmodernism and anti-essentialism, as is the university curriculum that is informed by this knowledge. As Lyotard states:

> Our working hypothesis is that the status of knowledge is altered as societies enter what is known as the postindustrial age and cultures enter what is known as the postmodern age. This transition has been under way since at least the end of the 1950s, which for Europe marks the completion of reconstruction. The pace is faster or slower depending on the country, and within countries it varies according to the sector of activity: the general situation is one of temporal disjunction which makes sketching an overview difficult. A portion of the description would necessarily be conjectural. At any rate, we know that it is unwise to put much faith in futurology (1979, 3).

The current challenge is to take account of the changed constitution of knowledge and thought under postmodern conditions of existence (the postmodern condition) and the relationship of reconstituted knowledge to the question of power and legitimation. Modernist knowledge has been fundamental in the structured and teleological sense of modernity and has provided the basis for legitimation and sustained power. Such knowledge has openly universalist tendencies and is preoccupied with its own performance.

Anti-essentialist post-fundamental and postmodern knowledge, however, decenters and disarticulates this modernist conception. In Lyotard's words, again:

> Postmodern science—by concerning itself with such things as undecidables, the limits of precise control, conflicts characterized by incomplete information, 'fractra', catastrophes, and pragmatic paradoxes—is theorizing its own evolution as discontinuous, catastrophic, non-rectifiable, and paradoxical. It is changing the meaning of the word knowledge, while expressing how such a change can take place.

It is producing not the known, but the unknown. And it suggests a model of legitimation that has nothing to do with maximized performance, but has as its basis difference understood as paralogy (Lyotard 1979, 60).

Within postmodern parameters, the notion of science must continuously confront its formative and signifying spaces with important notions such as those of knowledge and discourse. These notions dislocate, disarticulate and transform in a definitive way knowledge that is grounded solidly in modernity. Anti-essentialism and postmodernism present a variety of ontological, epistemological and theoretical possibilities that are opposed to the various modern perspectives. We can incorporate ourselves within anti-essentialism and postmodernism and "speak" and "converse" from there only if we assume the multiplicity of meanings as the basis for dialogue in cultural contact and acknowledge the political character of cultural contact.

We need to identify as a key aspect of postmodernity an important distinction between the postmodern *condition*, to which we have referred, and postmodern *existentiality*. Postmodern existentiality[17] refers to the incorporation of postmodern conditions of existence into positionality itself: that is, incorporation of ontological, epistemological, categorical, paradigmatic, conceptual, cultural, theoretical, and ethical conditions of postmodern existence.

Such incorporation impacts on our life forms and our social visions of the past, the present, and the future, and is characterized by the precarious, the positional, the structural-temporal, the relational and the finite. These factors allow us to locate coordinates of possibilities and limits in the task of accommodating to the conditions we face. These characteristic traits of postmodern existentiality may be sketched briefly as follows.

- The precarious is understood as the floating and unstable character of any configuration or system (such as a political system, education system, family system, grammar system, etc.). It inscribes on discourse the possibility of change, transformation, and resignification.
- Positionality, as previously noted, is understood as the psychic, cultural, social, geopolitical, economic spaces from which the world is expressed and constructed.
- The spatial-structural refers to undecidable[18] structures during moments of relative stability or in moments of crisis with which and within which social subjects identify and act. The temporal refers to the characteristic of the historic moment in which debates and so-

cial practices are developed. In moments of relative stability it appears that the spatial-structural pervades or "erases" the temporal and in moments of crisis the temporal invades or erases the spatial-structural. During these moments stoppages or paralysis is produced. If the conditions (social, political, cultural, internal, or external) exist, they are "announced" as sudden possibilities of change, transformation, creation, and production.

- The relational refers, in Wittgenstein's terms, to the significance of an element in a language game or discursive configuration (social, political, educational) that is defined by its use in them. That is, the signification fields are defined by the relationships the different constitutive elements maintain among themselves.

- The finite refers to epistemic, categorical, and theoretical generational finitude as a constitutive and enabling element of thought, and of utopian thought in particular. The possibilities for constructing discursively and symbolically the present reality to which we belong, and the desired reality that one can participate in (or not) personally and existentially, depend on radical contingencies and human historicity. The reality we aspire to be part of as social subjects is constitutive of such future and desired reality.

These characteristics of postmodern existentiality are so inextricably intertwined that it is not possible to understand any of them in isolation from the others.

Precariousness and positionality direct us to the relational and open character of all social formation, as well as the position that we occupy in the various social formations to which we belong. These, therefore, locate us in very modest teleological and epistemological ambitions in relation to more profound and wider liberatory aspirations, as Laclau and Mouffe (1985) would have it. The points of departure are possibilities and limits relating to the positional, temporal, and structural, which means implication, knowledge, and proximity.

The articulation between the relational and the positional enables us to comprehend our own discourse from the tangle of signification in which it is inscribed and makes possible an open attitude and effort to understand the discourses of others emanating from the tangles in which these others are inscribed. It is interesting here to note the nature of the interrelationship and directionality of the various discourses. For instance, the visions of the authors of the First World are incorporated—in different ways—by authors from the rest of the world. A retrospective bibliographic survey of the social sciences and the humanities would show clearly the extent to which and manner in which the opposite does not occur. That is, the discourses of the authors of the First World—given their relationality and positionality—are very present in ours: for example, in those Latin American authors preoccupied with education. Nevertheless, due to our positionality and relationality, our discourses are absent in those of First World authors, except in significant and interesting exceptions (for example, the presence of the work of Paulo Freire in authors such as Giroux, McLaren, and Lankshear).

Temporality and finitude create an urgency to plan our expectations, anxieties, and proposals in terms of the possibilities and limits that they inscribe. Postmodern existentiality does not guarantee an articulation of postmodernity and critical and emancipatory positions. It does, however, contribute elements for thinking about them in relation to each other:

> [My] position sustains that precisely the open, incomplete and precarious charac-
> ter, the tension between necessity and contingency, [are] conditions for the ar-
> ticulation of diverse positions and emancipatory critical discourses, as well as
> liberal ones and even conservatives—although I don't like it. . . . This open char-
> acter of a social configuration is inconsistent with any attempt to establish a
> *necessary link* with a specific political position. . . . The plurality, the difference,
> the open, incomplete, precarious and unstable character of identities, the dis-
> semination and other conceptual values . . . do not guarantee of themselves
> emancipation but imply the assumption not of *death, end* and *abandonment* but
> the ceaseless and always renewed need of thought, of making politics and of
> imagining new utopias (Buenfil Burgos 1995, 58, 64).

This postmodern existentiality allows us, and to a certain extent obliges us, to take on visions and social and personal commitments in terms of our positionality and generational finitude. That is, in the light of the influence and weight that we exert on new generations, it allows us to recognize that it is impossible and that we do not have the right to pretend to determine the directions that future generations will build and pass through. And so our visions of the future and our constructions of uto-pian horizons must be framed within this perspective. At the same time, we must understand the strong influence we leave on new generations and, because of it, the obligations we have—together with them—to im-prove the world as best we can in the present moment.

The relevance of cultural difference from a postmodern perspective warrants special mention because it plays an important role in these vi-sions. "Difference" is an important contribution of anti-essentialist and postmodern theorists. It is important to position ourselves so that we can both use their contribution and identify certain impediments to dialogue marked by the paradoxical Eurocentric centrality of their arguments.

Analysis of the cultural field from the standpoint of a postmodern existentiality that privileges difference leads to the deconstruction of important aspects in the work of these theorists and enables us to imagine utopian horizons that act—as do the postmodern and anti-essentialist perspectives—as a hinge of articulation in constituting the curriculum-society link. This applies to the task of formulating proposals for transitional university curricula. When we locate ourselves in postmodern and anti-essentialist perspectives we can position ourselves in the discussion about the impossibility of dialogue among the islands that constitute the globalized world in which we live. It also allows us to understand that this impossibility is an obstacle to constituting the link between curriculum and society.

At the center of the impossibility of such dialogue we locate, as something simultaneously old and contemporary, something simultaneously anti-essentialist and postmodern, the problem of Western cultural megalomania. For those in the West, the world revolves around the West itself a conviction that not only permitted but actively promoted Western domination over the rest of the world. This domination has been expressed through the colonialism and neocolonialism that still today influence many countries around the world which, regardless of their level of Westernization, still are not considered part of the First World's sphere. Because the emphasis on difference can have, and in fact has had, different readings depending upon the places from which it is considered—that is, positionality—the limit situations and the crisis of sense and meanings that are privileged by some postmodern theorists assume importance for us.

In this way we get close to the edge of our own conceptualization of what we want to think of the postmodernism of cultural contact and possibility. In fact, we are assisting the always growing social and mass deconstructions of the different semiotic frameworks maintained by cultures that exist and coexist around the world. What is often interpreted by *us* as strong and energetic evidence of the kind of cultural contact that has operated for centuries and that operates today, and of the vitality of this cultural contact, is sometimes interpreted by postmodern authors as schizophrenia and cultural pastiche.[19]

It is clearer all the time that the dominant culture, rationality or rationalities, metanarratives, and colonizing narratives have severe limitations that are closely linked to the problems we experience nowadays. Other ways of thinking, other cultures, other forms of commerce and creative possibilities abound among the men and women who make up the world and who want to contribute to the task of building a better world.

Within the theoretical field—as an instance of conceptual "plays" and Lyotardian paralogies[20]—the megalomania of Western culture is characterized by the fact that it is impossible to have the dialogue mentioned above; it is interpreted as a *severe theoretical myopia*. It seems as if it is incapable of adopting the reality of the rest of the world or, rather, of the different worlds that make up the present world (world-worlds).[21] It understands other realities and interprets them only through the perspective of Western epistemological, theoretical, political, and economic domination.

As such the First World can see us—the other—only as objects of study. It can accept that it needs to understand our culture in order to analyze us more effectively (for example, through contemporary ethnology and ethnography). And it can visualize us as investment and market spaces. Nevertheless, the First World is incapable of understanding that over the centuries it has not simply been a matter of them dominating us. We, the "others," have influenced them, even if they still have the power in terms of the world economy.

From our point of view, this means that the theoretical myopia is a serious impediment to understanding the complexity of the present world. In some ways it causes impediments to the work of imagining, producing, and circulating elements that help to build the utopian horizons that could at this moment sustain proposals of new political and social projects with which our curricula could find connections.

Positionality, the postmodern condition, postmodern existentiality, and theoretical myopia are nodal points that maintain, structure, and traverse the position advanced in this chapter.

(B) Social Traits and Contours

The 1980s and 1990s developed in a climate of increasing globalized structural crisis. The fall of the Berlin Wall, the reunification of Germany, and the disintegration of the socialist bloc signaled the beginning of new situations that have had repercussions in most countries. At an international level these new situations can be characterized, albeit in complex and varying ways in different countries, in terms of the generalized structural crisis impacting their respective ideologies[22] and hegemonies. Until the 1980s these ideologies and hegemonies were capable of "speaking to" and constituting the social subjects of nation-states. They now find themselves in a process of dislocation and disarticulation, with an intensification of floating signifiers and new and incipient articulation processes. In the current generalized structural crisis multiple movements can be observed in signification elements that were previously tied to or "ossified" in certain signifiers. In this situation the "status of the 'elements' are the floating signifiers that are not able to be articulated in a discursive chain" (Laclau and Mouffe 1985, 113). Signification elements that at an earlier time made the structures appear to be strong and fixed are now in an accelerated process of dislocation and disarticulation.

Between the onset of the crisis and the moment at which new hegemonic articulations appear, we face the complex situation in which the floating elements are reconfigured in new and incipient "condensations" (moments at which signifieds and signifiers get fixed) as functions of the transformation and constitution of new social subjects (such as new political parties, new social organizations, new forms of trade unions and syndicates, new cultural groupings) who are capable of imagining new elements. These new social subjects are inclined to build new utopian horizons, which in turn allow the formulation of ideologies and social-political projects that, in the medium term, are capable of rearticulation based on new hegemonic practices.

The term *traits* refers to cases in which some new and unknown elements or elements of prevailing old social configurations appear in a significant way in the social space and fulfill two functions. The first function is to contribute to dislocating the order of things at a juncture in the general crisis. The emergence of the Zapatista National Liberation Army (EZLN) in the state of Chiapas in México at the beginning of 1994 is an example of a trait in this sense, in a way that the instigation of the North American Free Trade Agreement (NAFTA) between México, Canada and the United States at the same time was not.[23] The second function involves the display of features of elements that tend either to delineate the contours of new discursive social configurations or to lose strength and significance. In other words, traits are elements that have a limited articulation capacity and their importance lies in the *irruptive "significativity"* they acquire in the context of a general structural crisis and in their potential to become elements that tend to become empty signifiers in the new discursive configurations—although it is also the case that they can disappear during the process of crisis.

To elucidate, *contours* are shaped by a group of emerging elements articulated by a society in the process of general structural crisis. The multiple elements of the contours are the *traits* that are apparent by their invasive significativity from the first moments of crisis and through its different phases. Contours have superior articulation capacity to traits and can be observed in the advanced moments of a general structural crisis. In fact, the contours are configured as spaces of significance articulated in a new and unknown way in the genealogy of a social configuration. As such they can remain in the moment of their constitution and the process of sedimentation or be excluded from it.

The following section will identify some of the traits and contours considered most relevant to the process of general structural crisis that have expressed themselves forcefully at the end of the 1980s and through the 1990s—beginning as traits and developing into (more articulated) contours. From an analytical perspective these traits and contours are poverty, swiftness, globalization, democracy, difference, and development. These traits and contours are by no means the only ones or even the most important. Rather, they are the ones that have been privileged from the analytical perspective adopted here.

These traits and contours have diverse fields of signification according to the socio-political spaces in which they are expressed and observed as well as the signification space from which they are enunciated. A serious effort has been made in this chapter to explain the conceptual and contextual makeup of social traits and contours and the elements that shape them. Given the kind of position we have advanced, it is important that we underline the open character of traits and contours, which permits and demands that they be considered in accordance with different particular contexts within the world and in accordance with different positionalities and different spaces of enunciation.

The traits and contours will be addressed at an international level from a complex enunciation space and specific positionality, although, as noted above, specific mention is made from time to time of Latin America and México.

Some Social Traits and Contours:
Poverty, Swiftness, Globalization, Democracy, Difference and Development

The following statement about social traits and contours is heuristic and tentative. The traits and contours that are examined have an open, precarious, and flexible character. In no way are thsee accounts assumed to be definitive. On the contrary, the exercise undertaken here should be understood as an invitation to carry out other exercises that present, by various means, the traits and social contours that emerge in our societies in crisis. These can become worthwhile elements to consider with respect to constituting the curriculum-society link.

(A) Poverty: From Welfare to Structural Asymmetry[24]

To overcome poverty in our countries is a challenge that can no longer be deferred. No position or vision of the future coming from Latin America, or ideas that pretend to address the future, can avoid putting the problem of poverty at the center without the risk of weakening its credibility or legitimacy (de Alba 1993). According to a statement by the United Nations Development Program, "[t]o eliminate poverty and to improve the standard of living of the urban and rural poor is the most urgent challenge for governments, international agencies and groups and individuals with access to power and resources" (PNUD-BID-FCE 1991, 13–14).

Poverty is increasingly located at the center of concern of every country. This is especially true in those so-called Third World or underdeveloped countries that include the Latin American nations.[25] In the 1990s poverty was a theme that has demanded the attention of important international and national agencies and groups.

Together with environmental problems poverty tends to be one of the "hard knots" in the process of crisis. The conception of poverty itself is in a state of flux—floating—due to the multiple aspects that are linked to it nowadays and to its mobility and penetration into the wealthy countries/ the First World/the North. This situation has obliged these countries to begin studying this problematic issue beyond the traditional parameters of international "aid." In a broad sense, poverty is the tension between a structural state of deprivation and the efforts to overcome it; the structural situation has the upper hand, which in turn produces deprivation.

Poverty can be understood as a state of structural deprivation that is itself a necessary condition for the wealth of those who maintain the structure. It traps individuals in the condition of deprivation in two ways: (i) in terms of basic needs, and (ii) in terms of the links and processes that identify social subjects and individuals as belonging to a certain social group (a family, a culture, a nation). Poverty can be understood, then, through analysis of two facets.

The first is in relation to deprivation of the satisfaction of what are considered *basic needs*—goods and services—that affect a social group: such as food, clothing, housing, health and education. The second refers to the nodal aspects of identification of individuals and social subjects, such as the structural deprivation of the pride of ownership, honor, dignity (personal, familial, social), discipline, education and religion and/or love for one's country and one's motherland are typical examples.

It is important to consider both aspects in the proposals made for the short- and long-term plans for overcoming poverty. When the major overdetermining factors of poverty are found in the deprivation of basic needs within a conjunctural situation of crisis, poverty can be ameliorated by financial and economic support. These processes can be observed in Japan and Germany during the post–World War II period. Japan and Germany were given aid and were able to overcome their postwar cultural situation of poverty.

A very different situation prevails among peoples who for centuries have suffered structural colonialism which negates their identities. In such cases financial and economic support measures are insufficient if work is not also done to address the historical processes of structural deprivation of the second facet of poverty.

Latin American countries—particularly those with large indigenous populations—are confronted with the large and solid presence of *both* aspects of poverty in the low socioeconomic rural and urban marginal sectors.[26] From this perspective, when we consider the political and social anxieties that are shared among the multiple and diverse groups and sectors in national and international contexts, as far as building a better world is concerned *poverty* is the most serious problem that confronts us today at the global level.

Given this reality, it is crucial that university curriculum processes—in particular, the curricular overdetermination processes—must incorporate the problem of poverty as a nodal and constitutive aspect. This is necessary in order to contribute to the formation of professionals and researchers who are aware of these problems and who are able to obtain the information they need to conduct analyses and formulate proposals that will contribute to overcoming poverty. Analyses and proposals that we consider locally can affect the national and international fields. Precisely because they are formulated in such a way, they can affect the international hegemonic policies and guidelines that avoid the problem of poverty; or, perceived from the center, they represent efforts to understand problems and their complex interrelationships that are advanced from positions considered to be peripheral. This pertains not only to the professionals in the Third World but also to those professionals in the First World who make decisions in world organizations that affect poor countries.[27]

Poor countries are in an asymmetric structural relationship vis-à-vis First World countries with respect to indicators of production, wealth redistribution, consumption patterns, financial and market politics, life expectancy, pollution indices, and levels of responsibility in the environmental crisis. These are but a few of the most important dimensions considered in studies and measurements of international standards. It is important that such indicators to be impacted by the analysis, policies, and local actions of the countries concerned—starting with *their* problems—so as to dislocate the international hegemonic politics that maintain and reproduce a situation of structural asymmetry.[28]

(B) Swiftness: The Speed of Changes in the Conjuncture of the Present Crisis

When de Alba first outlined some questions about the swiftness in relation to curriculum at a 1988 conference in Guadalajara it was possible to glimpse strong tendencies in line with what was to unfold in the 1990s. At that time, however, there was no way of foreseeing the magnitude and force of swiftness as a characteristic of the conjuncture of the current crisis. The multitude of national and international events that we have subsequently been witnesses to and participants in—including the collapse of the Soviet bloc, the phenomenal rise of neoliberalism, the computerization of work, domestic, and leisure spheres, particularly within OECD countries, the privatization of public sector activity and "marketization," ethnic "cleansing" and interethnic wars, changes in communications and information flow—have wrought such changes that swiftness is nowadays considered to be a characteristic and nodal element of the general structural crisis in which we live. This is, in other words, one of the characteristic and constitutive *traits* of the crisis.[29]

Swiftness is one of the reasons why nowadays it is difficult to grasp reality using existing categories and concepts. The unexpected twists and turns taken by "reality" toward places we often cannot see with clarity refutes our illusions of having grasped that reality. It demands of us renewed efforts to open ourselves up so that we are capable of analyzing these twists and turns, without looking at a mirage that prevents us from understanding our differences, particularities, potentialities, interrelationships, and limits (de Alba 1993, 30).

Swiftness is explained through the predominance—*historically unusual and unknown on account of its speed*—of temporality (dislocation) over spatiality (structurality), through the rupture of such spatiality. In this view, spatiality is understood as a spatiality-structurality that symbolically cancels and negates temporality (understood as a fluid succession of points in the synchronic space/time chain) and is converted into a relatively stable diachronic moment (see Laclau 1990).

In order to understand better the *swiftness* of the historic moment—exemplified by some significant and representative events—let us develop an approach toward the notions of temporality and spatiality in relation to swiftness. Laclau (1990) maintains that temporality is linked to the dislocations—as well as the opening of possibilities—that are common throughout social crisis; and spatiality with structurality, with the makeup of social structures, which are understood as *spatiality that negates temporality*; starting from a repetitive nucleus that allows the symbolic makeup of *pure spatiality: the structure.*

It is of interest that in moments of crisis an understanding of disloca-tion—as pure temporality—is seen as that which irrupts the given struc-ture and opens multiple possibilities of configuration by new subjects and new structures. It can be said that swiftness is articulated with the notion of dislocation and is related to the *events* that with intense speed have irrupted the social structurality at the national and international level, dislocating it. Along these lines it is important to emphasize that "only the dislocation of the structure, only a maladjustment which is not *spatially representable*, is an event" (Laclau 1990, 42, our italics).

(i) Swiftness and Dislocation

What has been said here makes us think of *swiftness* as a phenomenon of dislocation belonging to general structural crisis that affects the most diverse fields and dimensions of social reality. This means the dislocation has an increased level of generality and abstraction. Dislocation and swift-ness mean different things, but are alike in respect of irrupting a given order. The *specificity* of swiftness refers to the speed of the dislocations within the crisis in which we live and to the effects of speed in such dislocations.

The predominance of dislocation (pure temporality) in swiftness that is characteristic of the present crisis involves an enormous volume of float-ing signifiers that flow constantly, as well as potential empty signifiers. The fields of signification lose their meanings, lose their specific signifieds; this floating and emptying of signifiers refers to the predominance of temporality, of dislocation, of movement, of the flow of *events* that irrupt and dislocate the structure of a given order.

In order to understand the articulation between the notion of *swift-ness* and *dislocation*, we will present and analyze three characteristics of dislocation: temporality, possibility, and freedom, using Laclau's perspective (1990).

(ii) Dislocation Is Itself a Form of Temporality

Dislocation is linked to movement, to change, because time implies a succession of events. Therefore, dislocation does not present itself in a predominant way in moments of relative structural stability. Temporality is not representable in a temporal way because "time cannot hegemonize anything, since it is a pure effect of dislocation." In other words, "the ultimate failure of all hegemonization, then, means that the real—including physical space—is in the final instance temporal" (Laclau 1990, 42).

Given temporality as an element of rupture, the disordering of a given structure is understood as one of the three constitutive characteristics of dislocation.

(iii) Dislocation Is Itself a Form of Possibility

When dislocation irrupts the structure (as the Lacanian "Real"[30]) it opens multiple possibilities. Laclau considers dislocation to be the very form of possibility, which includes the plurality of possibilities:

> But with dislocation there is no *telos*, which governs change; possibility then becomes an authentic possibility, a possibility in the radical sense of the term. This means that there must be *other* possibilities since the idea of a single possibility denies what is involved in the very concept of possibility. As we have seen, because structural dislocation is constitutive, the dislocated structure cannot provide the principle of its transformations. The dislocated structures thus opens possibilities of multiple and indeterminate re-articulations for those freed from its coercive force and who are consequently outside. And the very possibility of this dislocation reveals the character of *mere possibility* of the articulate ensemble forming the structure before dislocation. The pure form of temporality and the pure form of possibility thus coincide (Laclau 1990, 42–43).

The previous existence of the structure that dislocation irrupts is necessary for dislocation to occur as the very form of temporality and as the very form of possibility. This is like the Lacanian Real, incapable of being named and unrepresentable, whose double function is to dislocate *and* to be constitutive of new social traits in a new undecidable[31] structural context. In relation to this Laclau says:

> To avoid any misunderstanding, one must once again emphasize that the dislocation of a structure does not mean that *everything* becomes possible or that *all* symbolic frameworks disappear, since no dislocation could take place in that

psychotic universe: a structure must be there for it to be dislocated. The situation of dislocation is that of a lack which involves a structural reference. There is a temporalization of spaces or a widening of the field of the possible, but this takes place in a *determinate* situation: that is, one in which there is always a relative structuration (Laclau 1990, 43).

(iv) Dislocation Is Itself a Form of Freedom

The problem of freedom is one of the most complex that has been posed to different peoples throughout history, especially the Western countries, which are the ones we know best. In a way "freedom is the absence of determination" (Laclau 1990, 43). It is important to understand this statement from the perspective of the constitutive tension between the temporality and spatiality elements of a significative articulation, in this case, freedom.

Structuralism saw the subject as completely determined by the social structure. Existentialism assumed that all individuals were destined to be free because of the absence of a priori nature. Between these two extreme positions is one that considers freedom to be located between undecidable structural tension and the moment of decision of the subject:

> The subject is partially self-determined. However, as this self-determination is not the expression of what the subject *already* is but the result of its lack of being instead, self-determination can only proceed through processes of *identification*. As can be gathered, the greater the structural indetermination, the freer a society will be (Laclau 1990, 44)

According to this account of freedom, a society undergoing general structural crisis and the social subjects that make it up will be freer in proportion to the degree of structural indetermination. This is because the greater the degree of structural indetermination the greater the number and diversity of options available to social subjects, and the greater the distance is between social subjects from which they can constitute themselves, precisely, as social subjects.

These social subjects in turn and in interrelated ways make up and are made up of new structural articulations, of new signification systems. In response to the characteristics of these critical situations, Laclau and Mouffe argue:

> Hopelessness in this matter is only proper to those who, to borrow a phrase from J. B. Priestley, have lived for years in a fools' paradise and then abruptly move on to invent a fools' hell for themselves. We are living, on the contrary, one of the most exhilarating moments of the twentieth century; a moment in which new

generations, without the prejudices of the past, without theories presenting themselves as "absolute truths" of history, are constructing new emancipatory discourses, more human, diversified and democratic. The eschatological and epistemological ambitions are more modest, but the liberating aspirations are wider and deeper (Laclau and Mouffe 1990, 98).

(v) Swiftness and Curriculum

Swiftness produces multiple reactions and responses and, often, confusion and disorder. Nonetheless, it is important to recognize that given the intensity with which it is produced nowadays swiftness is a constitutive condition that opens many possibilities. Because of this, it makes the present generations freer in principle than earlier generations of the present century, in the sense that weaker structurality increases the opportunities for making interventions and envisaging new possibilities. From this perspective it would be argued that the left wing "ultras" faction among the students involved in the strike at the National Autonomous University of México (UNAM) are in a stronger position now than México City's radical students were in 1968. In 1968 the national government was also the ruling force in México City. Today, however, the fact that México City is governed at the local level by an administration under leadership other than that of the ruling national party entails a dislocation that gives additional strength to students who have projects on behalf of which they are prepared to intervene. By virtue of the possibilities and freedom it affords, swiftness permits and facilitates for the new generations an enhanced capacity to envisage a better world and pursue whatever seems possible to bring it into being. Of course, if you do not have projects and utopian horizons, you are not in a position to act in the context of weaker structurality.

In this moment, on the cusp of the twenty-first century, the university curriculum tends to be a transitory curriculum, capable of contributing responses in the context of the general structural crisis. This is why within curricular processes generally, and particularly in the processes of curricular overdetermination, curriculum subjects must consider that:

[j]ust as, in the final instance, time always overcomes space, we can also say that the character of mere possibility of any kind of arrangement imposes itself, in the long term, on all structural necessity (Laclau 1990, 43).

This quotation emphasizes that the subjects of curricular overdetermination processes can take on the crisis as a privileged context of possibilities and have freedom to be able to think and act from the present toward the future, and because of this they can take into account the importance of incorporating in curricular proposals those elements that will allow them to help young university people learn how to think and act in the context of crisis.

As Zemelman (1987a; 1987b) argues, learning to imagine reality, a reality in crisis, is to imagine not a given reality but a given–being given reality. And in our case it is the reality of a given–being given crisis. From the characteristics of this given–being given reality we need to be able to think through the crisis, to think the present through in a critical manner, and to think toward an undetermined and possible future. This is such that with the strengthening of the capability to think, young university students of all ages will be capable of creating their own utopias, their own social projects, their own social discourses that will allow them, through their everyday practices, to help to transform the world.

(C) Globalization: Changes and Conditions at World and Planetary Levels

Globalization is a phenomenon that characterizes this fin dè siècle and its general structural crisis. It results in a people, country, or group of countries or regions being impacted by the effects of situations produced within specific sites in the world. This situation is generated in the most diverse conditions and parts of the world, within specific sites that can be more or less near or distant to others geographically, politically, or culturally and whose effects on the people, country or group of countries are located in the interrelationship among these geographic, political, or cultural elements.

Globalization is the extension of spatiality in the "world-worlds" in which we live today that affects a site as pure temporality or dislocation— because the character of the phenomena or situation which has the effect in a particular site is not known (whether in geopolitical, environmental, cultural, financial or social terms) to those who are affected. Globalization is therefore the invasion of a *structural spatiality that irrupts*[32] *as pure temporality (as dislocation) in a specific structural articulation.*

The phenomenon of globalization is observed from different dimensions of reality: most notably, perhaps, from the dimensions of the environment, finance, science and technology, information, the media, the means of transportation, the problems of the minorities and majorities, the migratory movements, democracy, and culture.

We will identify and describe two key effects of globalization here. The first concerns the impact that spatiality or structurality has on a region of the world, a zone, a people, or a group of countries when they are impacted by a dislocative externality in the manner of pure temporality. A good example of this involves the question of the environment. The second effect concerns the multiple and unexpected consequences produced through the intensification of cultural contact[33] toward which globalization is disposed and which it actively promotes.

(i) The Impact of Globalization as Pure Temporality: The Environmental Question

The impact of the environmental crisis is said now to be of a planetary scale:

> Nowadays it is known that oxygen from the Amazons is as important in Manaos as it is in Stockholm and that global warming affects the North Pole as well as the Sahara Desert. For instance, the DDT concentration in the Antarctic tends to increase even though there is no agriculture there and its use has been prohibited in the countries of the North for almost 20 years. These examples show us that the human population finds itself between a dilemma and a challenge (Worldwatch Institute 1990, 1).

This statement affirms that a large number of environmental phenomena have become globalized through human activity, albeit not intentional or planned. These have been constituted as pure temporality through their dislocative effects. This characteristic bestows upon the environmental crisis a level of complexity that has obliged groups, nations, and specialists to analyze it from different angles.

One of the most important and critical matters of the environmental crisis is the patterns of consumption and wealth distribution in the world. Nowadays, it is evident that the countries that live in opulence, those that are in the widest part of the "champagne glass" of the United Nations Development Progam report (PNUD 1992), are those that have a higher level of responsibility for the globalized environmental problem. The members of this segment of humanity (approximately 20 percent) use energy intensively to live opulently. They are obliged, then, to lead the search for solutions and set about enacting them.

Two particular factors of the many components of environmental issues feature prominently in many studies. These are the population explosion and poverty. They are considered to be the main causes of environmental damage. Needless to say, our position here recognizes the magnitude of the demographic problem and its devastating effects on the environment *as well as* the depredatory character of poverty. Even so, our position obliges us to advance some qualifications and comments.

If one takes into account the relationship between population and consumption patterns, the statistics we encounter are surprising. The so-called developed countries are *overpopulated* in terms of the consumption patterns of the population. This is the case of the United States and Canada, whose populations have the highest consumption patterns at a global level. In other words, even if we say that poverty is depredatory, its environmental impacts are less than those that produce wasteful overconsumption in the industrialized countries. According to Hawken (1994, 161), "the 50 million people who will be added to the U.S. population over the next forty years will have approximately the same global impact in terms of resource consumption as 2 billion people in India."

The environmental problem is complex and has many different aspects. The gap tends increasingly to widen between the rich and poor countries. This is the key issue in efforts to solve the environmental problem. This means that answers to the environmental crisis and recognition of different levels of responsibility in relation to it are found in our understanding and analysis of the complex structural interrelationships between countries at the global level.

The most recent attempt along these lines was undertaken at the United Nations Conference on the Environment and Development in Rio de Janeiro in 1992. This summit realized some achievements in the form of signing of some accords, although in the years that have followed their fulfillment has been precarious.

In short, the environmental problem and the force and importance with which it presents itself is constituted as a historical imperative. It is not only a pure temporality that irrupts and dislocates. It also makes demands in the most diverse spheres, of which we would emphasize here the moral and the ethical. The environmental issue is shaped like a new social contour capable of acting as a nodal point or empty signifier.[34] The task of forming new paradigmatic articulations that can organize the thinking and acting of different peoples and groups that make up humanity will allow the constitution of new symbols to support utopian horizons from which it is possible to produce political and social projects for the next century.

(ii) Cultural Contact as Effect of Globalization
Bonfil Batalla defines culture as the "general field which organizes social life [and] gives . . . unity, context and sense to the human tasks that make possible the production, reproduction and transformation of concrete

societies" (1986, 7). From this idea *culture* gets special attention in relation to two trends in globalized reality that are constitutive and mutually
antagonistic. On the one hand, there is the failure of homogenizing cultural projects that have been installed in the Western countries and the
penetrating, invasive, and homogenizing cultural incursion of the "American way of life" in every corner of the world. On the other hand we find
the persistence, enrichment, and transformation of the various cultural
forms: national, regional and ethnic.

Culture and cultural issues are approached in many ways. Among the
better-known positions within educational inquiry in México are: (a) those
limited and elitist perspectives that conceive culture from the canons of a
particular culture—namely, the West; (b) cultural relativism, which peaked
in the 1970s and obscured in some ways the complex possibility of analyzing intercultural power relationships; (c) the critical multiculturalism of
theorists such as Giroux, Kincheloe, McLaren, and Steinberg; (d) Bonfil
Batalla's proposals for cultural projects and their interrelationships; (e)
Garcia Canclini's theory of hybrid cultures.

Culture in the contemporary world, in its multiple and complex manifestations, has allowed the emergence and development of a specific field
of studies that lies outside the canons of anthropology, sociology, politics,
and philosophy, while at the same time using their elements and contributions. Recently the so-called cultural studies have taken on the theme of
culture, giving it its own specific space in current societies. Stuart Hall
(1996) is a foremost author in this field.

We have appropriated the contributions of some of these positions to
examine the cultural question under the light of what we have called *cultural contact*. Cultural contact has appeared at various times in human
history and it is possible to know its characteristics from its historicity.
The present historic moment, widely understood as a postmodern condition of existence, is an important context for analysis of cultural contact,
especially from a standpoint that considers postmodern existentiality. Even
though it is true that in different periods there have been intense processes of cultural contact that in fact have given rise to cultures and peoples,
the moment has no previous historical parallels in terms of the reach,
frequency, intensity, and diversity of cultural contact. In these respects
the current moment of cultural contact is unprecedented.

Cultural contact refers to the exchange of cultural goods and the interrelationship between groups, sectors, and individuals of different cultures.
Consequently, cultural contact uses different semiotic codes that produce

changes in the different subjects that participate in it as well as changes in its contexts. These are produced in social spaces with multiple trajectories in which power relationships are exercised.

(iii) Cultural Contact Is: Relational, Unequal, Conflictive and Productive

Cultural contact is *relational* because it is generated, produced, and defined in the open and precarious relationships among its different elements. It is constituted and produced among several articulated meaning systems. That is, it occurs among diverse cultures that each has its own symbolic resources and ways of symbolization. The irruption of one culture into another and the complex and conflictive encounter among cultures produce cultural dislocation that affects the relationality of those cultural and meaning systems.

From a historical point of view it can be said that cultural contact is *unequal* in the sense that it involves different semiotic codes or language games of those who participate in a process of cultural contact, and the language games of some participants are more powerful than those of other participants. Inequality acts as both an obstacle to establishing communication and as an external dislocating element of language games themselves.

The *conflictive* character of cultural contact alludes to the interplay of power that is produced when various language games come into conflict. Wittgenstein in his *Philosophical Investigations* (1953) pointed out that conflict is provoked when different language games come into contact. That is, cultural contact is conflictive because the subjects involved in it have structural difficulties in establishing communication. They must construct elements of meaning that work as bridges among the semiotic codes of their respective cultures yet at the same time attempt to keep the constitutive traits of their identity. This semiotic and semantic construction is generated into the conflict and demand on the part of the different subjects to modify and change their very identities.

The conflict, which is constitutive of cultural contact, refers to the metonymical chains in their relation to the metaphorical chains. One can say it is the expression of different signifiers that in their fight to hegemonize the symbolic and cultural space try to constitute signifiers as empty signifiers (in order to open them up for redefinition, reconstitution, and the production of new meanings) and master signifiers.

Conflict in cultural contact is imbricated in the complexity of the social structuralities to which those language games belong. As a result the asymmetric factors perform an important role in bringing about the inequality and conflict characteristic of cultural contact. This can be exemplified by the differentials in the respective armaments capacity of groups who come into contact, or in terms of differentials in their health conditions and their ideologies. This asymmetry produces a tendency toward the dominance of one group over another through cultural contact.

Cultural contact is *productive* because the relationality, the conflictive character and the unequal character permit and accelerate the dislocation of the identities of the subjects that takes place during cultural contact. Multiple interpellations are produced among the subjects, floating signifiers proliferate, and through mechanisms of identification, new traits, new condensations, and meanings are generated. New semiotic and semantic elements permit not only communication among cultures and their subjects but also permit the transformation of subjects and cultures. In the case of long and intense periods of cultural contact, this becomes the space where it is possible to generate new meaning configurations (with nodal points), which permits the emergence of new cultures.

The productive character of cultural contact refers to moments of overdetermination and moments of articulation and to metaphorical or paradigmatic functions. In these moments one or several empty signifiers become nodal points because they condense and articulate new meanings.

Cultural contact dislocates old certainties as well as those incipient ones such as the response to the interpellation of traits and contours. Cultural contact changes around language games[35] in which the "split subject" is constituted and acts. Cultural contact changes in a radical (not merely incremental) way the rules of language games and goes much further and deeper than any of the recognized forms of multiculturalism.

All cultures are the products of cultural contacts. The Latin American countries, especially those that have a strong indigenous component, are a living example of intense cultural contact. Elsewhere, on account of its geopolitical and cultural position and history, Turkey presents another living example of intense cultural contact.

In relation to the globalized world in which we live, a very important part of this cultural contact has been described by some postmodern theorists as "schizophrenia" (Baudrillard 1983) and "pastiche" (Jameson 1983). An important critique of these authors argues that even though they criticize and help to erode pillars or nodal points of Western culture, because of their positioning[36] in the world they are still unable to acknowledge the powerful influences and transformations suffered through the centuries as the result of intense cultural contact.

The cultural question is part of a powerful movement against the current of thought and analysis that sees the globalizing process as inherently homogenizing. The idea of cultural contact works against viewing globalization as a one-way process in which a homogenous culture is imposed on everyone. Culture constitutes itself as a trench of resistance against the myth of the homogenizing phenomenon. It revitalizes the significance of difference as against processes that pretend to dissolve difference (in an apparent "buffer solution"). Culture and difference mark a potential space within which to produce new signifiers, that is, a space of new social traits and contours.

(iv) Globalization: Multiple Facets

Globalization has many facets besides those already mentioned. These include the financial question; scientific and technological advances; information and the media; trade and transportation; minorities and majorities; migratory movements—the North existing in the South and the South in the North; democracy and participation; human rights; and the issue of gender.

(a) The Financial Question. Finance is a major facet that firmly and clearly evinces the existence of globalization as a characteristic of a society currently in crisis. Nowadays, the structures of financial capital and their shifts resemble spiderwebs, since they can be built in one place one day and skillfully rebuilt in another place the following day. The fact that they group in those places where conditions are most favorable for investment affirms the point that international financial capital does not have borders or countries and moves to wherever is most convenient.

Within the framework of the globalized world-worlds we inhabit, information, cybernetics, cyberspace, the media, and transportation facilitate this flexibility and rapidity of financial movement. These factors reveal the structural aspects of present-day capitalism, which is based more on speculation than on production. This affects, in various and asymmetrical ways, the consumption patterns of world nations and generates an important problem—the loss of an appropriate balance between the proportions spent on productive and speculative capital. The capital that is diverted to speculation becomes unavailable as productive capital for the primary, secondary, and tertiary sectors. Today speculative investment predominates over productive investment. This is especially true in the poor countries, where hopes of creating employment and improving the economy are pegged to the influx of foreign investors, who then demand that countries maintain conditions of security and social peace required to invest in them.

Within globalization the impact of the financial sector affects the majority of poor countries as pure temporality, as dislocation of their social structure, their politics, and their economics. Hence, for those who work in the university curriculum, the financial question is key because it constitutes one of the major points of conflict in the general structural crisis. At the same time it is one of the elements that produces a high level of dislocation within the current structures and, because of this, creates room for possibilities and the freedom to think in new and open ways about the future.

(b) Scientific and Technological Advances. The massive and fascinating scientific and technological advances, some of which were anticipated by science fiction, are factors that simply cannot be disregarded in attempts to think about the future (de Alba 1993). Scientific and technological advances impact the most diverse facets of everyday social life, including modes of development and everyday institutional, professional, and familial practices. Although it is reasonable to maintain a critical distance with regard to these advances, ignoring them is simply not an option within new curricular proposals.

The fact that previous economic and social development models have been exhausted does not mean that we must take the naive "return to nature" path and abandon the scientific and technological advances that have been made. Nowadays we are confronted with the challenge of addressing our history and its extraordinary current advances *in conjunction with* the need to radically redress the self-destructive tendencies of the present developmental mode and the political, economic and social relations it has generated.

The scientific and technological tradition is one of the main supports Western men and women use to confront the absence of utopian horizons and the risks involved in thinking about the future. Proof of this is that both critics and proponents of proposals for sustainable development invoke the support of advanced levels of scientific and technological development in the coming years as a key pillar in their respective positions.

Indeed, returning to a "natural" world, ignoring the advances of science and technology, would be also a serious obstacle to overcoming some of the problems we experience to the extent that technological and scientific innovations can play important roles in solving these problems.

(c) Information and the Media. Media and information are linked to advances in science and technology, although their importance and specificity merits attention in their own right. Information technology is one of the greatest advances in the twentieth-century world. Day by day it

generates languages and dialects that occupy the most diverse social and institutional spaces. In a matter of minutes it is possible to establish communication with any part of the world, to send information though electronic means, and to have access to networks and general and specialized databases. Data and figures that were previously reported through print are beginning to be available through the Internet and CD-ROM discs, which facilitate their efficient handling for information and research purposes. Several of the advantages offered by these advances are the fact that it is now possible for teams to be interconnected so that they can exchange, coordinate, and download research data samples that are too large for single individuals to manage and the opportunity to consult with experts from a distance. They also open potential skills of many kinds— of networking, collaboration, etc.—through which work becomes more shared.

For these reasons it would be naive to think of reorienting university curricula without considering incorporating at least the basic computing packages required in the various professions, along with (at least) the minimum tools needed to pull down information from specialized networks that will replace traditional bibliographical consultations, skills and tools for searching the Internet, and so on.

Even though information technology has shown its enormous transformative potential in many dimensions of scientific, professional, commercial, industrial, and everyday life (to mention just a few of the more visible examples), it is without doubt true that its major impacts remain to be seen. The rapid advances of "information superhighways," the development of new superconductors such as fiber optics, and the use of satellites and remote sensors generate a cybernetic process that will revolutionize, in unexpected ways, the traditional ways of managing ourselves in the world and even human, social, economic and cultural relations. This will continue to represent one of the more notable contours of the processes of globalization in which we are immersed.

(d) Trade and Transportation. Developments in the areas of information and information technology are closely associated with the transportation of people as well as the transportation of goods and services. One of the manifestations of globalization is the establishment of the great trading blocs at regional and subregional levels. This process affects the most diverse strata of the individual countries and the regions involved in ways that go far beyond commercial objectives alone.

Some of the most relevant experiences in this process are the signing of the North American Free Trade Agreement (NAFTA) between México, the United States, and Canada as well as the quite extraordinary process of European integration that has produced significant repercussions in the political and cultural, as well as the economic, spheres.

The phenomenon of commercial globalization is associated with a marked increase in transportation. The most active commercial exchanges have facilitated the opening of new air and sea transport routes and the consolidation of the older routes as well as the improvement of land transport systems (road and rail).

(e) Minorities and Majorities. The complex relationship between ethnic, cultural, social, religious, racial, and gender minorities and majorities is one aspect of present-day reality that has contributed the most to the vertiginous social events we have witnessed in the late 1980s and early 1990s. The concept of "minority" transcends the numerical dimension and is located at the center of the exercise of power. As a result, the study of minority groups has become an object that has markedly enriched perspectives and methods within the social sciences.

Although the minorities issue is specific to each country (Asians in Germany, Africans in France, "Hispanics" in the United States) it has become a phenomenon that must be analyzed from the vortex of globalization. This is especially true when globalization begins to facilitate links to fascism: for example, the resurgence of neo-Nazi groups in European countries; and the introduction of Proposition 187 in California by governor Pete Wilson, intended to restrict public service access to the undocumented population.

The minorities phenomenon has serious implications. For example, there is also the radicalization of forms of exclusion historically used against women, children, the disabled, addicts, AIDS victims, and homosexuals, among many others. This gives rise to the establishment of an ethics sui generis that tends to justify and legitimate all sorts of excesses against these groups.

(f) Migratory Movements: The North in the South and the South in the North. Closely related to the phenomenon of the majorities-minorities relationship is the phenomenon of migration flows.[37] A typical example in modern times is the European migration to the United States during the second half of the nineteenth century and during the first decades of the twentieth century. Migration processes are always linked to the search for better life conditions, although each has specific charactersitics.[38]

At present, some interesting traits of migration flows are linked to the densities of population in relation to ethnicity and to the massive inflows of immigrants from the countries of the South to the countries of the North. This situation is related to unequal development in the different regions of the world and to the cultural components of the immigrant groups. It gives rise to the observation that areas of the Third World have been inserted into the countries in the North. As a consequence of combined and uneven development, we can find also within countries of the South enclaves of the countries of the North.

(D) Democracy and Participation

It is said that at present the world is moving toward democracy as a response to and repudiation of totalitarian regimes that took root in the socialist countries. Under this rubric the situation in Latin America demands a specific and close analysis. This is not only because unfortunate dictatorships existed in Latin American countries during this century, but also because of the unique interrelationship between Latin America and the rest of the world and, in particular, with the United States of America.

To think in terms of democracy obliges us to think in terms of social justice and of the redistribution of wealth at national and global levels, not only in terms of the freedom of the different groups to express their positions or in terms of electoral processes. The concept of democracy requires an analysis that will situate it under the spotlight of the new global considerations and the incorporation of human rights as fundamental claims.

Democratic rights from this perspective mean the rights to health, education, employment, and security. They also mean the rights to peace, to a healthy environment, and to a future. The restricted sense of democracy that is applied to mean the right to vote to elect the governing class nevertheless is predominant in the global scene. How can (and should) we rethink, for example, the concept of democracy in some of the dictatorships disguised as republics in Southeast Asia? These maintain the labor of their population at very cheap levels for the big transnational corporations; yet the high levels of income of these corporations could build the infrastructure and provide social services for the population. Can the concept of democracy be rethought in a country such as the United States where the income gap between rich and poor is increasing rapidly? Can we rethink democracy when it refers to the interior of national boundaries within a globalized world where the welfare of some rests on the inexorable sacrifice of most?

A mix of world movements is rapidly reformulating the concept of democracy so that people can participate in the processes and decisions that affect their own lives. The nongovernmental movements in relation to claims by environmental, development, human rights, and peace groups, and groups against nuclear testing is proof of that. Governments have felt the need to reformulate their social participation policies because they were quickly outsmarted by the strong social negotiation skills of these groups.

The diversity of civil organizations reflects a complex process of social struggles, commitments, and ideologies that make their characterization difficult. For example, within what is now generically known as nongovernmental organizations, a diversity of groups covers an extensive array of social and environmental objectives.

The constitution of organizations of civil society has not conformed to a particular social class, or to a particular hegemonic social subject. For this reason it is difficult to identify a factor that synthesizes and unifies their structural and functional conditions. Nevertheless, the nongovernmental movement represents one of the most interesting new social phenomena to emerge from this part of the century. It represents the most diverse spaces and social origins, ranging from academic to grassroots groups, peasants, and indigenous peoples, cutting across the private sector and religious groups that maintain a multifaceted capacity to mobilize collective action for sustainable environmental management based on participation and social responsibility.

Public participation in the processes of environmental management constitutes a typical example of the new ways that democratic forms within civil society organize and intervene in the decision-making processes of the problems that affect their lives. The sorts of examples that are presented are related to social spheres that do not deal exclusively with the discussion of democracy in electoral terms. Of course, that is important, but it is not the only concern within the context of the diverse forms of democracy that are emerging in the context of the crisis we now live in.

(i) Human Rights
The emergent struggle for human rights is one of the traits inclined to shape itself as a form of articulation between the general structural crisis and multiple institutions and social spaces, and which it is important and interesting to emphasize within the field of university curriculum.

The field of human rights gains strength day by day within the context of globalization. Struggles for human rights embrace new as well as old causes. They have revived more traditional demands for social and economic welfare and for legal justice. At the same time such struggles make demands on behalf of the new social subjects emerging within the present context of crisis. These include the demands of groups around sexual preference, AIDS, and so on. For these reasons, knowledge and analysis of human rights is a very important as well as a highly suitable form of inquiry to incorporate into the university curriculum. Human rights is one of the key facets that has the potential to form new paradigmatic articulations to guide thought and social practice in the curriculum field.

(ii) The Issue of Gender
The issues surrounding gender that have emerged in recent decades contribute new elements to the social-political and cultural analysis of the roles played by different social subjects. Among a number of important indicators, the significance of gender considerations in the formulation of the Human Development Index (HDI)—which seeks to replace the Gross National Product (GNP) as the measure of a country's development—is evidence of the importance attached at present to the gender question. The gender question is an important guideline in the task of thinking and establishing the link between curriculum and society at this critical conjuncture.

(E) Emphasis on Difference in a Context of Crisis and Accelerated Changes
The emergence of the struggle for the right to difference finds its main counterpart in the idea of equality during the French Revolution and in modernist thought. Difference becomes relevant as a nodal aspect of anti-essentialist and postmodern thought at different levels, planes and dimensions of reality: cultural, gnoseological, epistemic, theoretical, ethical, economic and political. These levels, planes, and dimensions have been used mainly by anti-essentialist theorists working from perspectives of philosophical, political, and cultural analysis. The question of difference dislocates modern thinking and makes us rethink many issues on multiple dimensions. For example, we need to think about issues such as social justice from the standpoint of difference.

The emphasis on difference is constitutive of important current struggles and makes us rethink the relationship between differences and identities. Examples of these struggles can be seen in the struggles of ethnic minorities, indigenous struggles, and struggles for autonomy. The question of difference, being nodal, is constitutive of most of the new social spaces that have emerged in this stage of the crisis and transition. A good example in which the question of difference has been central is the case of South Africa, where the proliferation of differences to a given order (apartheid) have dislocated it to construct a new order in the social and political spheres (Norval 1990).

The South African experience reveals articulation between new and productive ways of thinking, and new and productive forms of political and social constitution have taken place. This new social order has been constituted through a complex process of overdetermination in which different dimensions have been articulated from the political (as a nodal point).

The emphasis on difference is one of the most important social contours to characterize the current moment of crisis, and it has taken on new forms of expression in the 1990s. Within the field of curriculum, this emphasis presents itself as an important challenge that demands of us high levels of political, cultural, and theoretical openness, creativity and commitment.

(F) Development: On Sustainable Development and Social Development

> It is justice, not charity, that the world needs.
>
> (PNUD 1994, 16)

To speak of development at this time refers to the relationship between economic and environmental processes. On this matter, González-Gaudiano (1997a) notes that since appearing on the planet the human species has provoked an intense transformation of nature in the course of its search for nourishment and security. These changes have resulted from cultural characteristics, particularly in the forms of social organization and the use of natural resources.

With the passage of time, the effects of human activity on natural processes have reached such magnitude that they have produced changes in environments, ecosystems and natural processes, some of which are almost or completely impossible to revert (for example, extinctions of species). It is paradoxical that in spite of the high level of scientific and technological development reached, a progressive decline in the quality of life can be detected that affects a growing number of the world's population.

The desire for a development radically different from present trends implies a perspective that has productive, social, cultural and environmental dimensions, and that analyzes the characteristics of each specific region in order to modify consumption patterns, create new social values, encourage citizen participation, and conserve biodiversity, all of which will contribute to improving the quality of life and making possible the maintenance of the long-term productive capacity of the ecosystem. The results should in turn be associated with the consolidation of rural communities. Above all, it is crucial that the present discussion of development be redirected to incorporate both sustainable development and social development.

(i) Sustainable Development

Although the idea of sustainable development emerged in the 1970s, it only acquired international importance after the publication in 1987 of the Bruntland Report, *Our Common Future*. The key theme of the report is that sustainable development means development that satisfies present needs without compromising the capacity of future generations to satisfy their own needs.

Nevertheless, the concept of sustainable development has been subject to all sorts of controversies associated with positions taken to address problems. The countries of the North, for example, emphasize the importance of actions directed at *conservation*. Countries of the South prioritize those issues associated with *development*. Other criticisms (Bifani 1993) point to the North-South asymmetry, notably in social-economic respects, and emphasize the sentiment that satisfaction of the North's needs must not compromise the South's present and future needs.

Sustainable development[39] is not an easy concept to measure and, hence, to compare. Nonetheless, it is one of the new social contours that, from our perspective, demands further attention, and will have to be considered henceforth in curriculum proposals and revisions that are undertaken.

Neither is sustainable development a question of temporal transactions or transfers from one generation to the next. Before beginning to act on the problem of future generations it is imperative to look after those that at present find themselves in dire straits. This is because the difficulties of sustainable development increase in relation to the existing "social lag" and the requirements of demands that are still to be satisfied. Hence, the problem will be ever more complex if existing production and consumption patterns are reproduced along with other cultural values and technological schemes that cause deterioration.

In short, moving toward sustainable development involves a new worldview, a restructured relationship between the state and society, and a major social intervention in the decisions and institutional and cultural changes for the next generation of social values. It also involves an emphasis on stabilizing and distributing populations more effectively and modifying production and consumption patterns—*above all in the developed countries and in the wealthy sections of the population in the poor countries*—a technological reorientation in order to lessen impacts and reduce risks, and redesigned policies, institutions, and norms. These aspects cannot be taken on board in a fragmented manner since interconnectedness is the key to understanding the complexity and possibilities of sustainable development.

(ii) Social Development

One of the most complex and important discussions of the 1990s is about social development. Those themes discussed in the section on sustainable development, and advances that have been made with respect to them, are linked to the nascent concept of social development. Among the voices from the many nations concerned with these issues are some that call for a social development that will incorporate sustainable development as a nodal aspect.

If social development incorporates sustainable development, what is the specificity of social development? The first thing that must be pointed out is that incorporating sustainable development within social development is a new way of configuring the nodal points of signification in what is a very old struggle. In relation to such points of signification, and taking into account the open, precarious, and unstable character of all configurations, two aspects form part of social development (which is the most inextricably and intertwined contour of those we have identified within the utopian horizons for the next century).

These two constitutive aspects of social development are overcoming poverty and preserving the environment. Having already elaborated on the second aspect let us take up now in more detail the first aspect: overcoming poverty.

From 6–12 March 1995, the World Social Development Summit was held in Copenhagen, Denmark. This has become the most relevant event with regard to development since the Rio Summit in 1992. Three central themes were discussed in Copenhagen:

(1) Eradicating poverty
(2) Creating productive employment
(3) Social integration

At the time of the summit México was immersed in deep economic and political crisis. Notwithstanding this, México participated actively in both the preparatory[40] stages and in the development of the summit. The tenor of the summit is encapsulated succinctly by Carrasco and Hernández Puente as follows:

> Eradicating poverty cannot be attained simply through implementing programs that will combat it. It demands democratic participation and changes in the economic structures so everyone is guaranteed access to resources, opportunities and public services. It also necessitates providing social protection to those who cannot fend for themselves and aid to victims of unexpected natural disasters. At the individual or collective level, natural, social or technological . . . poverty is inextricably connected to the lack of control over resources: land, skills, knowledge, capital and social relations. . . . [P]overty eradication demands universal access to economic opportunities that will favor the existence of sustainable means of life (1995, 47).

(iii) The Human Development Index (HDI)

Despite the complexities involved in both notions, conceiving development from the standpoint of either a sustainable or a social perspective requires ensuring that development processes are directed toward satisfying human needs. This relies on indicators that include economic and social factors, thereby replacing the traditional method of relying on Gross National Product (GNP) alone.

Since 1990, the United Nations Development Program (UNDP) has proposed the Human Development Index (HDI).[41] This combines indicators of national income, life expectancy, and level of education. The UNDP subsequently proposed the Index of Human Freedom and the Index of Political Freedom as indicators that would allow for evaluating the level of freedom and the exercise of human rights corresponding to generally accepted concepts and values. Work has been undertaken toward developing a theoretical and methodological understanding of these two indices that will permit quantification of the HDI. The UNDP exercise has been useful in approaching a national average that is adjusted for the internal disparities between the sexes, among ethnic groups, in income, across regions and between rural and urban inhabitants.

The 1998 UNDP report pays close attention to consumption. Such exercises can only contribute constructively to redefining the corresponding scale in ways that address the high level of consumption of energy and natural resources as well as the production of emissions and toxic and dangerous wastes derived from the levels of opulence and consumption patterns in some countries. These aspects significantly obstruct the possibility of achieving enhanced levels of quality of life.

The HDI and other efforts to transform existing instruments and develop new ones for measuring development is one of the most important social traits within constitutive and development processes to be considered by those in the curriculum field facing the task of addressing the curriculum-society link. It tends to transcend ideas, proposals, and lineaments of a higher level of abstraction and generality.

In Closing: Social Traits and Contours as Curriculum Articulation Contours

This chapter has engaged in a conceptual and contextual exercise that attempts to contribute some elements to the debates in the complex field of curriculum during this period of transition toward the twenty-first century. The chapter began by posing the question: Can we construct the link between curriculum and society within societies that are in crisis and that lack broad and ambitious socio-political projects?

The central question that has occupied this chapter has dealt with establishing the curriculum-society link in those societies that live in a process of general structural crisis. If we accept that curriculum—as a political-educational proposal—is linked in diverse and complex ways to the political and social projects that exist in a wide social context, and if, at the same time, we accept that there is an absence of utopian horizons and broad and ambitious social projects to which these political-educational proposals can be connected, then the problem we face from the curriculum perspective is conceptual as well as contextual and pragmatic.

It is helpful to remember that in moments of general structural crisis, such as the one many societies are currently experiencing, what is readily apparent about utopian horizons and broad and ambitious social projects is the weakness of those very elements that previously acted as supports for their social, economic, and political development. Hence, the hegemonic projects of the twentieth century are in crisis, have been seriously weakened, or else have even disappeared. Those that survive lack credibility, which means we face a serious lack of new projects.

The absence of credible utopian visions and broad and ambitious social projects puts us in a very complex situation in the curriculum field. In response to this, we have posed the possibility of social traits and contours as social contours of articulation in constituting the curriculum-society link; to the extent that these social traits and contours are considered expressions of new social movements and present characteristics of our society that are socially and politically constituted through the logic of articulation, they are suitable for hegemonic practices. Thus, on the conceptual plane social traits and contours are tools that help us understand new attempts to form and solidify new hegemonic practices. They are tools of connection that allow us to think about and establish the link between curriculum and society in moments of crisis.

These two points comprise the main contribution of this chapter and of the account of social traits and contours advanced within it. The chapter is a preliminary and necessarily incomplete exercise that attempts to show what are, from our perspective, *some* of the most important traits and social contours of the 1990s in the process of transformation leading up to the twenty-first century. A key aspect in any social proposal—including proposals for the curriculum-society link—is one that recognizes our view of the possibility of new utopian horizons from which new social and political projects can emanate and re-hegemonize social spaces presently in crisis. Our position may be synthesized in the idea of thinking and acting in the plural, and pushing to one side the singular. In the present context of the absence of utopian horizons and projects we do not believe we can find a single utopia or project that would serve for the world as a whole.

As we have said throughout this chapter, the present general structural crisis affords us multiple opportunities to direct our actions within a wide framework of social aspirations and new social horizons which are not very clear at present. The emergence of social traits and contours point to many possible configurations of utopian horizons and make us recognize the wide spaces of freedom in which we operate. As Laclau says:

> Our time is more conscious than any other of the precariousness is and contingency of those values and forms of social organization, which the naive optimism of earlier ages considered, guaranteed by some immanent need of history. But it is the experience of this constitutive contingency itself which leads, paradoxically, to a higher consciousness of freedom and human dignity—that is to say, to the recognition that we ourselves are the exclusive creators of our world, and the ones who have a radical and non-transferable responsibility towards it (1990, 173).

Notes

1. This chapter has been developed within the theoretical framework of the Essex School of thought based on the work of Ernesto Laclau. Where appropriate, we have used endnotes to amplify points for readers who are unfamiliar with Laclau's work.

2. A crisis manifested at all levels of society is considered a generalized structural crisis in the sense that Laclau and Mouffe conceptualized Gramsci's notion of organic crisis. As they point out:

    A conjuncture where there is a generalized weakening of the relational system defining the identities of a given social or political space, and where, as a result there is a proliferation of floating elements, is what we will call, following Gramsci, a conjuncture of organic crisis (Laclau and Mouffe 1985, 136).

3. We share Laclau's (1988) view that neoliberalism is also in crisis. In that sense, one cannot consider it to be a hegemonic social-political project.

4. The process of curricular overdetermination refers to the social processes among several subjects in their struggle to give their own direction to a curricular proposal. In that process, the lack of an ultimate literality of their very identities works both as a condition of possibility and impossibility of constituting such a proposal as a symbolic order, as a precarious fixation of its identity. The curricular proposal has many senses and an excess of meaning. In "sedimented societies" such as those that we lived in during earlier times, this process of curriculum overdetermination was easier. In a crisis situation, however, it is much more difficult to take part in this process and struggle for projects as subjects of the process of curricular overdetermination.

    Regarding the concept of overdetermination, it is important to identify three key points in Laclau's position:

    (a) The symbolic—that is, the overdetermined—character of social relations implies that they lack an ultimate literality (which would reduce them to necessary moments of an immanent law).
    (b) The claim that "everything existing in the social is overdetermined" is the assertion that the social constitutes itself as a symbolic order.
    (c) According to Laclau and Mouffe (1985, 97–98), the concept of overdetermination is constituted in the field of the symbolic, and has no meaning whatsoever outside of it.

    By way of further elaboration:

    There are not *two* planes, one of essences and the other of appearances, since there is no possibility of fixing an *ultimate* literal sense for which the symbolic would be a second and derived plane of signification. Society and social agents lack any essence, and their regularities merely consist of the relative and precarious forms of fixation which accompany the establish ment of a certain order (Laclau and Mouffe 1985, 98).

In overdetermination, "far from there being an essentialist *totalization*, or a no less essentialist *separation* among objects, the presence of some objects in the others prevents any of their identities from being fixed. Objects appear articu- lated not like pieces in a clockwork mechanism, but because the presence of some in the others hinders the suturing of the identity of any of them" (Laclau and Mouffe 1985, 104).

5. The split subject "is merely the distance between the undecidable structure and the decision" (Laclau 1990, 39). In other words, "[s]ubject equals the pure form of the structure's dislocation, of its ineradicable distance from itself" (Laclau 1990, 60). There is an inextricable interrelation between the split subject and the "con- stitutive lack" of the subject. In Žižek's words:

    The subject is a paradoxical entity which is, so to speak its own negative, i.e. which persists only insofar as its full realization is blocked—the fully realized subject would be no longer subject but substance. In this precise sense, subject is beyond or before subjectivation: subjectivation designs the movement through which the subject integrates what is given him/her into the universe of meaning—this integration always ultimately fails, there is a certain left-over which cannot be integrated into the symbolic universe, an object which resists subjectivation, and the subject is precisely correlative to this object. In other words, the subject is correlative to its own limit, to the element, which cannot be subjectified, it is the name of the void which cannot be filled out with subjectivation: the subject is the point of failure of subjectivation (1990, 254).

6. Compare: "The differential positions, insofar as they appear articulated within a discourse, we will call *moments*" (Laclau and Mouffe 1985, 105).

7. Articulation refers to "any practice establishing a relation among elements such that their identity is modified as a result" of such a practice (Laclau and Mouffe 1985, 105).

8. Element refers to "any difference that is not discursively articulated" (Laclau and Mouffe 1985, 105).

9. Laclau elaborates on the notion of dislocation in two ways that are crucial to our argument. He says:

    (a) "It is important to note that by dislocation and unevenness we do not mean 'contradiction' in the classical Hegelian-Marxist sense of them. Contradiction is a necessary moment of the structure and is therefore internal to it. Contra- diction has a theoretical *space* of representation. As we saw, dislocation is not a necessary moment in the self-transformation of the structure but is its failure to achieve constitution and is mere temporality in this sense. For that reason it opens different *possibilities*" (Laclau 1990, 47); and

(b) "We must . . . emphasize that the dislocation of a structure does not mean that *everything* becomes possible or that *all* symbolic frameworks disappear, since no dislocation could take place in that psychotic universe: a structure must be there for it to be dislocated. The situation of dislocation is that of a lack which involves a structural reference. There is a temporalization of spaces or a widening of the field of the possible, but this takes place in a *determinate* situation: that is, one in which there is always a relative structuration" (Laclau 1990, 43).

10. It is important to say that when we are talking about the symbolic order it means reality—that is, discourse, the discursive or the discursive practices—and in that sense, it is convenient to point out the following basic points in order to obviate the more common misunderstandings in this position. In this respect, the following ideas advanced by Laclau and Mouffe are apposite:

(a) The fact that every object is constituted as an object of discourse has *nothing to do* with whether there is a world external to thought, or with the realism/idealism opposition. An earthquake or the falling of a brick is an event that certainly exists, in the sense that it occurs here and now, independently of my will. But whether their specificity as object is constructed in terms of 'natural phenomena' or 'expressions of the wrath of God', depends upon the structuring of a discursive field. What is denied is not that such objects exist externally to thought, but the rather different assertion that they could constitute themselves as objects outside any discursive condition of emergence.

(b) At the root of the previous prejudice lies an assumption of the *mental* character of discourse. Against this, we will affirm the *material* character of every discursive structure. To argue the opposite is to accept the very classical dichotomy between an objective field constituted outside of any discursive intervention, and a discourse consisting of the pure expression of thought. This is, precisely, the dichotomy which several currents of contemporary thought have tried to break. . . .

(c) Finally, we must consider the meaning and productivity of the centrality we have assigned to the category of discourse. Through this centrality, we obtain a considerable enlargement of the field of objectivity, and the conditions are created which permit us to think numerous relations placed before us by the analysis" (Laclau and Mouffe 1985, 108–109)

11. Discourse is

a meaningful totality which transcends the distinction between the linguistic and the extra-linguistic. . . . [T]he impossibility of a closed totality unties the connection between signifier and signified. In that sense there is a proliferation of "floating signifiers" in society, and political competition can be seen as attempts by rival political forces to partially fix those signifiers to particular signifying configurations (Laclau 1993b, 435).

Or, in other words: "The structured totality resulting from the articulatory practice, we will call *discourse*" (Laclau and Mouffe 1985, 105).

12. Swiftness means speed *and* difficulty or impossibility of thinking, articulating. Swiftness erases spatiality—that is, swiftness implies dislocation.

13. "The main feature of a surface of inscription is its incomplete nature: if the inscription process was complete, there would be an essential symmetry between the surface and the inscription left on it, thus eliminating any distance between the act of expression and what is expressed by it. But if the process is never complete, the symmetry is broken and our view is displaced from what is inscribed to the process of inscription itself" (Laclau 1990, 63).

14. Alicia de Alba is a researcher at UNAM's Center for the Study of the University (CESU-Centro de Estudios sobre la Universidad).

15. During the period in which this chapter was written Alicia de Alba was a visiting research fellow at the Centre for Theoretical Studies in the Humanities and Social Sciences and the Discursive Analysis Seminar at University of Essex, England.

16. "Any discourse is constituted as an attempt to dominate the field of discursivity, to arrest the flow of differences, to construct a centre. We will call the privileged discursive point of this partial fixation, *nodal points*" (Laclau 1990, 112).

17. From a very particular reading, it could be said that one way of adopting the postmodern existential condition is to refer to the incorporation of the positional itself—in ontological, epistemological, categorial and paradigmatic spaces—in a discursive articulation made up of Wittgenstein's language games, Laclau's discourse, the Lacanian triangle of the real, the symbolic and the imaginary. This configuration transforms the speaker's position.

18. What the "principle of structural undecidability does mean is that if two different groups have taken different decisions, the relationship between them will be one of antagonism and power, since no ultimate rational grounds exist for their opting either way" (Laclau 1990, 31).

19. See Baudrillard (1983) and Jameson (1983).

20. For the concept of paralogy, see Lyotard (1979).

21. World-worlds refers to the differences in the world. That is, differences in the conditions of existence and differences in the way that the world is read from the diversity of positionalities. It refers to the ways that the world is named: First World, third world, developing world, world on the way to development, etc. (de Alba 1995b).

22. In Laclau's terms:

> The ideological would not consist of the misrecognition of a positive essence, but exactly the opposite: it would consist of the non-recognition of the precarious character of any positivity, of the impossibility of any ultimate suture. The ideological would consist of those discursive forms through which a society tries to institute itself as such on the basis of closure, of the fixation of meaning, of the non-recognition of the infinite play of differ-

ences. The ideological would be the will to "totality" of any totalizing discourse. And insofar as the social is impossible without some fixation of meaning, without the discourse of closure, the ideological must be seen as constitutive of the social. The social only exists as the vain attempt to institute that impossible object: society. Utopia is the essence of any communication and social practice" (Laclau 1983).

23. The EZLN is the Zapatista Army of National Liberation. This could be seen as a social trait at its point of arrival on 1 January 1994 because it *was* some new and unknown element *and* it both contributed to dislocating the symbolic order and displayed features of elements that tend to delineate the *contours* of a new discursive social configuration. On the other hand, we do not think of NAFTA as comprising a social trait on 1 January 1994 because it was not some new and unknown element and did not dislocate the symbolic order or tend toward delineating contours of a new discursive social configuration.

24. We are indebted to Aurelio de Alba for his personal contributions on the nodal aspects of the conceptualization of poverty proposed here. The following two aspects are of particular importance:

(a) the second group of factors of poverty he calls subjective aspects which in a sense belong to a structure, a culture, and we call aspects that relate to the makeup of social and individual subjects who belong to a group, a social sector, ethnic group, people or country;

(b) the aspect relating to the taking up of and treatment of poverty in different countries, taking as a nodal element, for example, the process of colonialization that many countries in the world have gone through in different ways in the last five centuries.

25. México deserves special mention because, despite its "entrance" into the Organization for Economic Cooperation and Development (OECD) in 1994, it remains a poor country.

26. In the context of the 1990s special mention must be made of those studies in relation to poverty written at the international level by the United Nations Development Program (UNDP)—at times referred to also as the PNUD, its Spanish language acronym.

27. The terms poor and rich countries, First World, developed countries, developing countries correspond to the geopolitical and conceptual spaces of enunciation which, in turn, are determined by the different positionalities of those who construct discourse.

28. In relation to these ideas I am taking González-Gaudiano's (1998) phrase "think locally, act globally," which goes against the international environmental and sustainable development maxim "think globally, act locally."

29. Because of the character of swiftness, we can say in analytical terms that this is to be considered more as a trait than a contour according to our notions of trait and

contour. It is necessary to add, however, that it is impossible to trace the limit between trait and contour in the manner of a frontier separating two territories.

30.   We are using "Real" in the Lacanian sense. For an introduction to his thought bearing on this idea, see Lacan (1973, 54).

31.   See note 18.

32.   Our use of the term "irrupts" throughout the text involves three characteristics: (a) an irruption is something unexpected; (b) it appears suddenly with force and energy; (c) it tends to have an effect on the symbolic order or reality.

33.   The notion of cultural contact will be developed below.

34.   According to Laclau (1988, 15), "A signifier is emptied as it separates from an specific meaning and symbolizes a long chain of equivalent meanings. It is this dislocation and enlargement of the signifying function that constitutes a symbol."

35.   "Language game" is used here from Wittgenstein's perspective. See Wittgenstein (1953).

36.   "Positioning" is understood as the expression of a discursive practice that contains cultural, epistemic, theoretical, and other aspects.

37.   It can be said that the migratory phenomenon is inseparable from the development of intelligence in the human species when in search of food sources. This in spite of the fact that animal species possess migratory capacities (such as the tropical tuna, monarch butterfly, many species of birds, and mammals such as the bison). The American continent, for example, was populated by migratory flows coming from Asia through the Bering Strait during the last ice age and through the Pacific Ocean by taking advantage of marine currents, according to the most accepted theories.

38.   From this perspective, many differences can be ascertained in what we call migration processes and processes of conquest and domination that also form part of history. The former includes flows of "civil" populations and the latter includes those strategic deployments of the military and political class. Their objectives are also different; nevertheless we cannot deny that under certain circumstances one is the result of the other.

39.   The concept of sustainable development readdresses the principles of ecodevelopment and strengthens them with elements of economics which, while validating the need for productive strategies that do not harm the environment, emphasize the need to raise the standard of living of those from low social-economic backgrounds. They also make the industrial countries accountable for underdevelopment and the environmental crisis. The main requirements are:

(a) The modification of consumption patterns, especially in the industrialized countries in order to maintain and increase the resource base and revert the damage done by present and future generations through the following steps: (i) disseminating a better understanding of the diversity of ecosystems and putting measures in operation that are locally adaptable in order to solve environmental problems; (ii) improving the monitoring of environmental impacts produced by economic activities; (iii) respecting social-cultural guidelines, especially those of indigenous peoples and incorporating a gender perspective in project development.

(b) Undertaking work following these strategic guidelines:
- Eradication of poverty and distribution of resources in a more equitable manner.
- Use of natural resources in a sustainable way and cleanup of the environment within a given territory.
- Making social, economic, and environmental realities more compatible with each other.
- Promotion of organized and effective social participation.
- Promotion of state reform and production of a genuine social-economic strategy.
- Reduction of population growth and an increase in standards of health and education.
- Establishment of more equal and open internal as well as external trading systems. This includes raising production for local consumption.

Considering the latter, the new sustainable development project can be summarized in the following work areas:

(a) Decreased dependence on fossil fuel sources, especially oil and increased use of renewable, less polluting and more efficient sources of energy.
(b) Development of more labor-intensive technologies that are better adjusted to the resource base and cleaner.
(c) Improvement and support, in a dedicated fashion, of recycling programs and reuse of wastes and residues.
(d) Management of natural resources with the aid of knowledge and technologies that are based on ecological and equity principles.
(e) Increased efforts directed toward priority regions.
(f) Institution of administrative and political forms that are more decentralized and that are better supported by local communities. These should take into account all their social-cultural characteristics and gender-based perspectives.
(g) An end to the expansion of cities and excessive consumerism.

In order to ensure that development processes are oriented toward the satisfaction of human needs we must rely on indicators that include social and economic factors, even though they are very complex, rather than the traditional practice of relying solely on the Gross National Product (GNP). In this respect, the efforts of the UNDP during the 1990s is essential in the formulation of the Human Development Index (HDI) to which we will refer later. Other perspectives emphasize different aspects when they list the general principles that should guide a sustainable society:

(a) Respect and care for the living community.
(b) Improvement of quality of human life.
(c) Preservation of the vitality and diversity of the earth.
(d) Reduction of the exhaustion of nonrenewable resources.

(e) Maintenance of the earth's carrying capacity.
(f) Changes in personal attitudes and practices.
(g) Training of communities to care for their environment.
(h) Provision of a national framework of reference for the integration of development and conservation.

40.   In relation to the Latin American position, two meetings took place to prepare for the Mexican Social Development Summit Conference held in Oaxaca in 1993, and the XXV round of negotiations of the Economic Commission for Latin America (ECLA) in Cartagena de Indias, Colombia, in April 1994, where the document "Basis for a Latin American and Caribbean Consensus on the Social Development Summit" was approved (Carrasco and Hernández Puente 1995).

41.   In 1992 the UNDP offered three principles toward a formulation of the HDI:

(a) Sustainable human development must give priority to human development. Environmental protection is vital but it is a means to promote human development. This includes securing the long-term viability of world ecosystems, including their biodiversity. *All* life depends on them.
(b) Developing countries cannot choose between economic growth and environmental protection. Growth is not an option; it is an imperative. The question is not how much economic growth is necessary but what *type* of development.
(c) Each country must set its own environmental priorities. These will differ between industrialized and developing countries.

Chapter 7

Literacy Policy and Postmodern Conditions[1]

Introduction

This chapter will identify and analyze some current prevalent constructions of literacy in education policy proposals in North America, Britain and Australasia. It begins by distinguishing five broad constructions of literacy, referred to here as "the 'lingering' basics," "the 'new' basics," "elite literacies," "foreign language literacy" and "information literacy." The discussion will then identify six important characteristics shared to a greater or lesser extent by each construction of literacy. These literacy constructions and their associated characteristics will then be considered as instances of postmodern conditions using ideas based on work by Jean-François Lyotard. The chapter concludes with an assessment of current literacy policy agendas and suggestions about where literacy educators might work in the spaces between formulations of literacy policy and their implementation in classroom practice, with a view to promoting more progressive and generous conceptions and practices of literacy.

The present education policy moment reflects the elevation in status of literacy from a marker of marginal spaces that is used mainly in relation to marginal people ("illiterates"), to a lofty mainstream educational ideal. Not surprisingly, literacy currently spans a wide spectrum of meanings. Some meanings remain close to literacy's earlier connotative and denotative associations, as in lingering constructions of basic, functional, and remedial literacy. Others stretch to encompass sophisticated levels of analysis, abstraction, symbol manipulation, and theoretical knowledge and application—particularly in science, math and technology (as in constructions of higher order literacy). This wide range of meanings and connotations is evident in the account of literacy constructions that follows.

Our approach has been to review an array of key education policy texts and commentaries, with an emphasis on U.S. English, and Australian exemplars. Over successive readings we have looked for recurring patterns relevant to meanings of literacy, using a sociocultural sense of "meanings." This includes conceptual accounts of literacy, values encoded in these accounts, and kinds of practices and relationships they prefigure for literacy in social, cultural, and institutional settings. The patterns emerging from these readings provide two useful ways of organizing constructions of literacy. First, the reform texts reveal a range of *types* of constructions of literacy: that is, several "literacies" that vary from each other significantly in kind or degree. Second, for all the differences between these constructions, they share more or less in common a number of *characteristics* that are important and contentious from a normative perspective. These two axes offer a structure for identifying and critiquing dominant meanings of literacy in current reform proposals. They also provide leverage with which to critique agendas proposed for literacy in educational reform texts and with which to act on this critique with a view to enacting alternative projects for literacy.

Five Contemporary Policy Constructions of Literacy

Five different constructions of literacy have emerged in key policy texts. Four of these are well established. We call them the lingering basics, the new basics, elite literacies, and foreign language literacy, respectively. In addition, an emerging construction of information literacy is becoming apparent in literature intended to inform literacy education policy. This construction is often more inchoate than it is fully and clearly articulated in formal policy statements. The five constructions are described in turn.

1. The Lingering Basics: Recovering Marginals for Baseline Incorporation

Literacy conceived as the mastery of fundamentals of encoding and decoding print texts (including elementary math operations) has an ambiguous position in education policy today. On one hand, it is believed that survival-level reading and writing competencies are no longer enough to participate effectively in the economic and social mainstream. *A Nation at Risk* laments that "in some metropolitan areas basic literacy has become the goal rather than the starting point" (NCEE 1983, 14). On the other hand, it is acknowledged emphatically that integration into public life demands, minimally, the ability to negotiate texts encountered in the course of everyday routines. A 1993 U.S. report cites statistics claiming that 21 to 23 percent—or between 40 and 44 million U.S. adults—would perform at the lowest level of prose, document, and quantitative proficiencies on the test used, ranging from those who could perform few or no items at all on the test to those who could not perform above the lowest level (Kirsch et al. 1993, xiv). *Goals 2000* pledges more adult literacy programs to help improve "the ties between home and school, and enhance parents' work and home lives" (U.S. Congress 1993, Goal 6B, iv).

Policies address basic and functional literacy competencies at both school and adult education levels, although the constructions differ between these levels. At the school level policy documents mainly frame basic literacy in terms of mastering the building blocks of code breaking: knowing the alphabetic script visually and phonetically and grasping the mechanism of putting elements of the script together to encode or decode words, to separate words, or to add them together to read and write sentences. Proposed approaches to remedial literacy work focus heavily on accuracy and self-correction during exercises that are read aloud, and correct spelling in written work. Typically, official policy statements recommend that remedial learners be subjected to batteries of word recognition and dictation activities and tests, as well as letter identification and print concept exercises. Teachers are to be required to maintain accurate and comprehensive records for diagnosis, validation, accountability, and reporting purposes.

For example, key strategic components of the recently developed National Plan for Literacy in Australian schools include: assessment of all students by teachers as early as possible in their schooling; early intervention strategies for learners assessed as having difficulty with literacy learning; development of literacy benchmarks for Years 3, 5, 7 and 9, against which the literacy achievement of all students will be measured; and progress toward reporting student achievement against the benchmarks (DEETYA 1998, 10). This policy replicates procedures and trends already well established in Britain and in many North American states.

For adults, basic literacy is defined more in terms of baseline functional competencies or life skills all adults should have, emphasizing ability "to perform specific literacy-related tasks in the context of work, family and other 'real-life' situations" (U.S. Congress Office of Technology Assessment 1993, 32). The literacy test that was used in the U.S. survey reported by Kirsch and colleagues (1993) defines basic literacy in terms of bottom line prose, document and quantitative proficiency. *Prose proficiency* tasks at Level 1 include identifying a country in a short article and locating one piece of information in a sports article. Level 2 tasks include locating two pieces of information from a sports article and interpreting instructions from an appliance warranty. *Document proficiency* tasks at Level 1 include signing one's name and locating the expiration date on a driver's license; at Level 2, locating an intersection on a street map and identifying and entering information on an application for a Social Security card. *Quantitative proficiency* task examples at Level 1 include totaling a bank deposit entry, and at Level 2, calculating total costs of a purchase on an order form and determining the difference in price between tickets for two shows.

Basic literacy competence for school learners, then, relates to mastery of generalizable techniques and concepts that are presumed to be *building blocks for subsequent education*—decontextualized tools that are a means for accessing subsequent content and higher-order skills. By contrast, policy statements define adult basic/functional literacy competence in terms of completing immediate tasks that are *their own ends*, and that are directly and functionally related to daily survival needs.

2. The New Basics: Applied Language, Problem Solving and Critical Thinking

A central motif in many education policy proposals is that the "old" (that is, "lingering") basics are no longer sufficient for effective participation in modern societies. It is widely accepted by education policy writers that qualitative shifts in social practices associated with transition from an agro-industrial economy to a postindustrial information/services economy; from Fordism to post-Fordism; from more personal face-to-face communities to impersonal metropolitan and even virtual communities; from a paternal (welfare) state to a more devolved state requiring greater self-sufficiency, and so on call for more sophisticated (smart), abstract, symbolic-logical capacities than in the past. Some policy authors see this in terms of a generalized shift toward a more metalevel modus operandi, captured in emphases on higher-order skills as the norm. In this context, it is argued, the old basics are not enough, and the level of what we accept as basic skills needs to be raised.

This sentiment is captured in claims such as the following, from the National Commission on Excellence in Education (NCEE), which claims that many school leavers

> do not possess the higher-order intellectual skills we should expect of them. Nearly
> 40% cannot draw inferences from written material; only one-fifth can write a

persuasive essay; and only one-third can solve a mathematics problem requiring several steps (NCEE 1983, 9).

The NCEE is concerned that schools may be overemphasizing such rudiments as reading and computation at the expense of other essential skills such as comprehension, analysis, solving problems, and drawing conclusions.

Critical thinking is often used as a grab bag for such higher-order skills as comprehension, problem solving, and analysis and is conjoined with reading, writing, speaking, listening—or, in short, communications—to encapsulate the "new basic literacy." Maxson and Hair, for example, frame their conception of critical literacy in just this way: "Critical literacy, a relatively new term, combines the concepts of critical thinking and communications" (Maxson and Hair 1990, 1; see also Brandon 1998).

In a similar vein, *Australia's Language: The Australian Language and Literacy Policy* (DEET 1991a; DEET 1991b) identifies as its primary objective that all Australians "develop and maintain effective literacy in English to enable them to participate in Australian society" (DEET 1991a, 4). Effective literacy is defined as "intrinsically purposeful, flexible and dynamic and involves the integration of speaking, listening, and critical thinking with reading and writing." It "continues to develop throughout an individual's lifetime," with "the support of education and training programs" (5, 9).

Such constructions remain abstract until they are put into explicit contexts. Concrete embodiments are provided most regularly and graphically in terms of life on the floor of "new times" workplaces: their demands for teamwork (requiring communication skills), self-direction (calling for problem solving and troubleshooting capacities), and responsibility throughout the entire enterprise for producing the efficiency and competitive edge (abilities to innovate, maintain quality, continually improve) enhances the success of the enterprise and, to that extent, improves workers' prospects of job security. In a well-known statement, Motorola's corporate vice president for education and training observed that the rules of manufacturing and competition changed during the 1980s and Motorola had to rethink their approach to workplace literacy and training. Line workers now have to "understand their work and equipment," "begin any troubleshooting processes themselves," "analyze problems and then communicate them." Hence,

from the kind of skill instruction we envisioned at the outset, we moved out in both directions: down, toward grade school basics as fundamental as the three

Rs; up, toward new concepts of work, quality, community, learning, and leadership (Wiggenhorn 1991, 71–72).

Such claims are now commonplace in "new capitalist" accounts of education and training for front-line work (Gee, Hull, and Lankshear 1996).

3. Elite Literacies: Higher-Order Scientific, Technological, and Symbolic Literacies

Reform proposals based on "education for excellence" affirm that post-elementary education must emphasize *academic* learning and pursue greatly increased academic subject standards (Toch 1991, 1). The key underlying notion here is that high impact innovation comes from applications of theoretical knowledge. Claims such as the following, advanced in U.S. reform proposals, are echoed in many other Western countries. At a time when

> knowledge, learning, information, and skilled intelligence are the new raw materials of international commerce . . . our once unchallenged preeminence in commerce, industry, science, and technological innovation is being overtaken by competitors throughout the world (NCEE 1983, 7, 5).

According to a National Academy of Sciences task force, "those who enter the workforce after earning a high school diploma need virtually the same competencies as those going on to college" (National Academy of Sciences Task Force 1984, xi). This is reflected in *Goals 2000* proposals; the objective of Goal 6 (v) states that the proportion of college graduates who demonstrate an advanced ability to think critically, communicate effectively, and solve problems will increase substantially.

Elite literacies consist of high-level mastery of subject or discipline literacies, understood in terms of their respective languages and literatures (Hirst 1974). The *language* of an academic subject/discipline is basically the logic and process of inquiry within that field. The *literature* of a subject/discipline consists of the accumulated attainments of people working in the field, who have brought its language to bear on its existing literature in order to extend knowledge, understanding, theory, and applications within everyday life.

Command of the language and literature of subject disciplines enables critique, innovation, variation, diversification, and refinement when applied to work. This ranges from producing entirely new approaches to managing organizations or new kinds of computer hardware and software (from mainframe to PC from DOS to Windows, the addition of sound and video) to producing new reporting processes for literacy attainment and new ways of conceiving literacy; from variations within architectural and engineering design to variations on mass-produced commodities that provide a semblance of individuality or novelty.

This is very much the literacy of Robert Reich's symbolic analysis and Peter Drucker's knowledge work, which they see as the real value-adding work in modern economies (Reich 1992; Drucker 1993). Scientists, historians, architects, software designers, composers, management theorists, and electronic engineers all manipulate, modify, refine, combine, and in other ways use symbols contained in or derived from the language and literature of their disciplines to produce new knowledge, innovative designs, new applications of theory, and so on. This is seen as adding maximum value to raw materials and labor in the process of producing goods and services. Knowledge work, then, contains a critical as well as a creative or innovative dimension. As will be suggested later, the *critical* dimension of knowledge work is valued almost entirely in terms of value-adding economic potential, thereby confining critique to *internal* criticism.

4. Foreign Language Literacy: Proficiency for Global Dealings?

Following decades of decline in the percentage of students who were learning a foreign language in schools, colleges, and universities, recent education policies have given renewed attention to extending second-language proficiency (DEET 1991a, 15; Toch 1991, 8). Strategies include increasing foreign language enrollments, maintaining community languages, and maximizing ESL proficiency among groups from non–English-speaking backgrounds.

Justifications advanced in policy documents and supporting texts often foreground "humanist" considerations in support of foreign language proficiency and bilingualism. Sooner or later, however, economic motives generally emerge as the real reasons behind efforts to promote foreign language proficiency.

For instance, *Australia's Language* gives as its first reason the fact that it enriches our community intellectually, educationally, and culturally, and second, that it contributes to economic, diplomatic, strategic, scientific, and technological development (DEET 1991b, 14–15). However, Australia's location in the Asia-Pacific region and its patterns of overseas trade are the only relevant factors explicitly mentioned with respect to developing a strategy that "[strikes] a balance between the diversity of languages which could be taught and the limits of resources that are available" (ibid., 15). Influential statements are often considerably more direct and less ambiguous: for example, U.S. Senator Paul Simon's reference to tongue-tied Americans trying to do business across the globe in a world where 10,000 leading Japanese businesspersons speak English to less than 1,000 Americans, and where "you can buy in any language, but sell only in the customer's" (Kearns and Doyle 1991, 87).

Two main factors have generated the resurgence of second language literacy education as a new (and pressing) means to capitalist ends. First, trading partners have changed greatly for Anglophone economies, and many of our new partners have not been exposed to decades (or centuries) of colonial or neocolonial English language hegemony. Second, trade competition has become intense. Many countries now produce commodities previously produced by relatively few countries. Within this context of intensified competition, the capacity to market, sell, inform, and provide support after sales in the customer's language becomes a crucial element of competitive edge.

5. Information Literacy: Literacy for the Knowledge Economy

Current education policy statements abound with talk of harnessing new information and communication technologies to literacy practices and integrating new technologies into literacy education. Less clear, however, is the extent to which these policies provide coherent new constructions of literacy in addition to those identified above. In most instances, policy statements simply recognize the growing significance of digital-electronic information processing and communications and advocate adding a new technology dimension to already familiar literacy constructions. In a typical example, *Australia's Language* observes that "information processing is becoming more sophisticated, for both social participation and economic performance," and that "literacy development is . . . influenced by prevailing technologies," with the result that many people now learn literacy skills through computers and word processors (DEET 1991b, 36–37).

Until recently, perhaps the most obvious contender for a new construction of literacy based on new technologies was the notion of computer literacy. As Bigum and Green (1992, 5) observe, however, computer literacy typically serves as shorthand for the idea of possessing an appropriate or acceptable amount of computer-related knowledge or know-how, rather than providing a cogent construction of *literacy* in the manner of those already addressed here. It is, in other words, more a notion of technology proficiency than a conception of literacy.

In 1996, President Clinton's announcement of America's Technology Literacy Challenge brought talk of technological literacy to official policy prominence. Here again, however, the central concept is severely limited as a construction of literacy. Technological literacy is defined loosely in terms of "communication, math, science, and critical thinking skills essential to prepare [students] for the Information Age" (Winters 1996). Communication skills include the ability to learn through use of computers and the information superhighway and to handle modern computers efficiently. Framed in this way, technological literacy appears to be little more than "the new basics" harnessed to information and communications technologies.

The closest we can get, perhaps, to a recognizable post-typographic construction of literacy is the attempt to formulate a coherent notion of "information literacy." A recent report commissioned as a guide to education policy in Australia argues that the knowledge economy demands a competency that "links information management skills, systems thinking and learning skills and information technology competency at various levels of sophistication" (Tinkler et al. 1996, 73–74). The report defines information literacy as:

> a literacy that combines information collection and analysis and management skills and systems thinking and meta-cognition skills with the ability to use information technology to express and enhance those skills. In a society of information "glut" the ability to detect "signal" from "noise" will become increasingly valued (74).

Furthermore,

> [S]tudents will require the development of information literacy to be effective citizens and workers in a knowledge economy, while teachers/learning facilitators will require this literacy to be able to develop it in their students and to carry out their professional responsibilities as knowledge workers (ibid.; see also Lankshear et al. 1997, volume 1, 103–106).

This is more than a mere adding on of information technologies to extant constructions of literacy, such as new basics and elite literacies. It is an attempt to frame a distinctive conception of text-information handling practices integral to post-typographic conditions; to come to terms with "the rapid movement towards ubiquitous electronic networking through convergent technologies, combining text, voice, image and kinaesthetics (simulations and virtual reality technologies) with interactivity that enables multiple authoring of communication" (Tinkler et al. 1996, 73).

Some Emerging Trends and Issues

Although more could be said about each of these constructions of literacy apparent in current educational reform proposals, the descriptions provided are enough for our purposes here. It is clear that Guthrie's point (1993) that current education policies in general tend to subordinate wider educational purposes to functional—and, notably, *economic*—purposes holds true particularly for literacy. It is interesting, for example, to compare rationales for adult literacy provision that were advanced in the 1970s, when a strong adult and community education ethos was in place, with mainstream statements today. In the 1970s the supporting rhetoric for provision was very much centered on values of personal enrichment—reading for pleasure, participation, self-development and the like—as well as for more functional or instrumental ends. These values have now been swamped by a functionality motif increasingly cast in terms of workplace productivity and efficiency demands.

Because this tendency is at the level of *encoded values* and *policy frames*, it remains open in principle to the pursuit of wider purposes within actual pedagogical practices. At the same time, we should recognize that how we come to value a practice has a strong influence on how we come eventually to practice it. From this perspective, it may be sobering to reflect on the extent to which our everyday talk and operations as educators and educationists are in fact constrained by structured demands and processes in which economic and other functional purposes are central, if not almost exhaustive: and the extent to which we may *already* be walking and talking the functionalist-intrumentalist walk and talk in our everyday routines, albeit as the line of least resistance within our institutions. We need to *name* this situation explicitly if we are to contest values encoded in reform proposals rather than allow them free rein over our practice.

Interestingly, various tensions—if not potential contradictions—exist among some of the literacy constructions identified here: notably, between the lingering basics and the new basics. As literacy *crisis* talk gets recycled yet again, the emerging policy predilections for test-based benchmarking and batteries of standardized diagnostic, remedial, and reporting procedures cast strongly in a lingering basics mold threaten a new regime of teaching to the test. For those students judged to be most at risk, there is a real possibility that time spent in diagnosis-remediation cycles may undermine their opportunities to acquire the new basics.

It has been argued elsewhere (Lankshear 1997) that we may be facing a potential emergence of a new *word* order that corresponds to differential access to social and personal goods associated with mastery of the varying literacies identified above. If the likelihood of such an outcome *is* enhanced by current framings of literacy within reform proposals, it has serious implications for agendas of access, equity, and inclusive education. To advance the argument, we will now consider a range of characteristics associated with the constructions of literacy in question.

Characteristics of Literacy Constructions in Education Policy

1. A New Word Order?

Within postindustrial economies work is becoming increasingly dominated by polarized forms of service work: namely, "symbolic analytic services" on one hand, and "routine production" and "in-person" services on the other (Reich 1992, 177). Furthermore, modern organizations aim to infuse a sense of responsibility for the success of the enterprise throughout the entire organization, and to push decision-making, problem-solving, and productive innovation as far down toward front-line workers as possible.

Symbolic-analytic work involving elite literacies provides services in the form of data, words, and oral and visual representations. These include diverse problem-identifying, problem-solving, and strategic brokering activities that spans the work of research scientists, all manner of engineers (from civil to sound), management consultants, investment bankers, systems analysts, authors, editors, art directors, video and film producers, musicians, and so on. The discourse of new capitalism (Gee, Hull and Lankshear 1996) presents symbolic-analytic work as *the* substantial value-adding work within the postindustrial information economy and, hence, the best-paid work. By contrast, routine and in-person service work are typically presented as low value-adding work. Moreover, the new capitalist literature stresses that there are huge (global) labor pools of service workers. Hence, this work is poorly paid. According to typical accounts, beyond demands for basic numeracy and the ability to read, routine work often calls primarily for reliability, loyalty, and the capacity to take direction and, in the case of in-person service workers, "a pleasant demeanor" (Reich 1992, 177).

This polarization captures the order of difference between elite literacies and lingering (old) basics literacy. The hierarchy is complicated somewhat by the changed rules of manufacturing and competition mentioned by Wiggenhorn. Many workers not involved in symbolic-analytic work are now required to solve many of their own problems, operate self-directing teams, and understand concepts and procedures of quality, continuous improvement, constant innovation, and so on. Such work is seen as requiring mastery of the new basics. As with the earlier category of routine work, this mid-range work often is not well paid, despite being said to demand a higher-order basics than before.

In this way, then, we may currently be witnessing the emergence of a *word* order—ranging from elite literacies to new basics to lingering basics, via information literacy—that is broadly aligned with structural characteristics of a postindustrial *work* order. These are simultaneously orders (hierarchies) of conditions, rewards and possibilities. The pressing question is Where does current literacy policy stand in relation to this situation?

2. The Emphasis on Standard English

In key reform statements literacy means, first and foremost, Standard English. In Australia, current literacy policy statements affirm that "proficiency in English literacy is of major importance for every Australian's personal, social and cultural development" (DEETYA 1998, 7). "English only" policies are resurgent in Britain and the United States—with California's recently legislated Proposition 22, "English for the Children," reflecting the general direction of the policy tide. Increasingly, the intended force of reform proposals is that Standard English become the sole medium of instruction and learning in all subjects other than foreign language education in mainstream classes. The rationale is that Standard English proficiency has a vital bearing on the labor market prospects and general welfare of individuals; this is made absolutely explicit in much supportive rhetoric of educational reform (for example, Kearns and Doyle 1991, 86–87). The meaning of literacy as "Standard English literacy" has two main origins. Migrants from non–English-speaking backgrounds have a strong presence within our labor markets, especially in *routine* manufacturing and in-person service work sectors. Employers and policymakers accept that efficient production and service delivery in these sectors depend upon workers having English language competence. They interpret this to mean ensuring that students whose first language is not English, and who will make up a high proportion of tomorrow's work force, master English at school. In addition, Standard (American) English has thus far emerged as *the* international language of the information age.

3. The Clamor to Technologize Literacy

Regardless of particular constructions, literacy increasingly entails computer-mediated text production, distribution, and exchange. This is a facet of our enforced learned dependence on computer applications in work and other daily routines. Education policies make prominent references to "technological literacy," technologized curricula, and technologized administration. Aronowitz and Giroux (1993) go so far as to claim that "the whole task set by contemporary education policy is to keep up with rapidly shifting developments in technology" (48).

Promoting technological literacies in tune with labor market *production* needs is part of the story here. In addition, however, we also have to reckon with *consumption* "needs"—as Ivan Illich (1971, 1973) has long reminded us. New electronic technologies directly and indirectly comprise key *products* of new capitalist economies. As "direct products," they include all manner of hardware and software, for which worldwide markets need to be generated and sustained. As "indirect products," new technologies include information and communications services, such as Internet access provision, on-line ordering and purchasing facilities, manuals and guides, networking and repair services, Web page design, and so on. Education policy agendas play a key role here in helping to create and maintain enlarged markets for products of the information economy—extending beyond curricular exhortations to advocate the extensive use of new technologies for administrative tasks in restructured schools.

President Clinton's Technology Literacy Challenge policy package of February 1996 has set the standard and pace subsequently for initiatives across the West and beyond. It was a direct response to such claims as that of the National Science Board (see Toch 1991, 16) that "alarming numbers of young Americans are ill-equipped to work in, contribute to, profit from, and enjoy our increasingly technological society." The Challenge asserts the goal of making all U.S. children technologically literate by "the dawn of the 21st century." Its strategy is to ensure that all teachers receive the necessary training and support "to help students learn via computers and the information superhighway"; to develop "effective and engaging software and on-line learning resources" as integral elements of school curricula; to provide all teachers and students with access to modern computers; and to connect every U.S. classroom to the Internet (Winters 1996, n.p.).

4. Literacy as Individualized, Standardized, and Commodified

Education policies construct literacy as an intensely *individual* perfor-mance. Literacy is framed in terms of measurable capacities of individual learners. Achievements are to be compiled in personal portfolios, to serve in part as an accountability mechanism and, for adults, as a fundamental criterion of employability. At a time when individuals in well-supplied la-bor market sectors must be prepared to move around to find employ-ment, "portable certified literacy competence" acquires strong functional value.

Such proposals encode values of "possessive individualism" (Popkewitz 1991, 150), which is a key operating principle of current reform initia-tives. According to Popkewitz, possessive individualism is grounded in a liberal conception of persons and society, wherein "society is composed of free, equal individuals who are related to each other as proprietors of their own capabilities. Their successes and acquisitions are the products of their own initiatives, and it is the role of institutions to foster and support their personal development"—not least because national revital-ization (economic, cultural, and civic)—will "result from the good works of individuals" (150).

Literacy policies also propose *standardizing* literacy performance against benchmarks, profiles, and other accountability procedures predi-cated on notions of economic efficiency and competitiveness, cultural cohesion, and national allegiance. A clear tendency toward standardiza-tion exists in requirements that teachers observe and map student progress using designated "tools," texts and tests. Here again, it does not follow that such proposals will necessarily result in highly standardized practices and outcomes. At the same time, we need to acknowledge that teaching to the test is already common practice. Under conditions of intensified accountability, burgeoning class sizes, fiscal restraint, and diverse student and linguistic populations, recourse to narrow definitions of outcomes backed by packaged methods and resources may well prove increasingly attractive to many teachers. In Queensland (Australia), for example, where a Year 2 Diagnostic Net was introduced in 1995 (DEQ 1995a), early indications suggested that many Year 1 and Year 2 teachers quickly be-gan teaching to the requirements of the Diagnostic Net, despite a consid-erably wider brief defined by that state's English syllabus (DEQ 1995b).

Many current reform proposals also encourage strongly *commodified* views of literacy by promoting assessment, evaluation, and validation packages; remedial teaching and textbook packages; and teacher profes-sional development packages. These hold out the promise of recipes and resources for securing required performance outcomes. In many cases, this is intensified by narrow and mechanistic models of literacy competencies and by the encouragement of public and private providers to generate income by selling professional development and literacy packages to clients in schools and workplaces (for an extreme statement, see NBEET 1996). In addition, identifying literacy largely, if not primarily, as an *exchange* value to be cashed in as a credential or as a form of scarce expertise valued by employers, is to perceive and value literacy as a commodity.

5. Literacy as Instrumentally Valuable: Economized Language

An increasingly crass instrumentalism is never far from the surface in contemporary literacy policy statements. For example, emphasis and value is attached to elite literacies most explicitly in terms of the fact that high-impact innovation comes from the application of theoretical knowledge. The new industries of the last century, such as electricity, steel, the telephone, and the automobile, were invented by "talented tinkerers" (Bell 1974) rather than through applications of scientific theory. The big-impact inventions of this century, however, such as "the computer, jet aircraft, laser surgery, the birth control pill, the social survey . . . and their many derivations and applications" have emerged from "theory-driven scientific laboratories" (Levett and Lankshear 1990, 4). Symbolic analysts manipulate, modify, refine, combine, and in other ways use symbols contained in or derived from the language and literature of their disciplines to produce new knowledge, innovative designs, new applications of theory, and so on. These can be drawn on to "add maximum value" to raw materials and labor in the process of producing goods and services.

6. "Incorporated" Critique

Although many education policy proposals emphasize "critical" forms of literate practice—couched in terms of a critical thinking component of effective literacy, or as text-mediated acts of problem solving—it is important to recognize the nature and limits of the critical literacies proposed. They are typically practices that permit subjecting *means* to critique, but take *ends* as given. References to critical literacy, critical analysis, critical thinking, problem solving, and the like, have, "in the current climate . . . a mixture of references to functional or useful knowledge that relates to demands of the economy and labor formation, as well as more general claims about social inquiry and innovation" (Popkewitz 1991, 128). The closer literacy proposals are to the world beyond school, the more functional and instrumental critique becomes, with an emphasis on finding new and better ways to meet institutional targets (of quality, productivity, innovation, improvement), but these targets themselves are beyond question. This is critical analysis and critical judgment directed toward innovation and improvement *within* the parameters of a field or enterprise rather than criticism in larger terms that might hold the field and its applications and effects, or an enterprise and its goals, up to scrutiny. The logic here parallels that seen by Delgado-Gaitan (1990, 2) as operating in notions of empowerment construed as "the act of showing people how to work within a system from the perspective of people in power."

The Postmodern Condition of Literacy Policy

Much about the ways in which literacy is constructed within contemporary education policy can be seen as characteristically postmodern. Although much more can be thought and said about this than space permits here, we will argue that contemporary policy constructions of literacy can usefully be understood by reference to Lyotard's account of performativity as the response of decision makers to the epistemological and institutional crises of legitimation.

Lyotard's account of postmodernity builds on the claim that "traditional" modernist metanarratives have collapsed, generating a crisis of legitimation in the foundations of knowledge and of our institutions. The (modern) role of metanarratives had been to provide foundations for knowledge, morality, and aesthetics and the various institutions based on them— notably, education. Lyotard argues that belief in metanarratives as legitimating devices has collapsed, and we find ourselves in a moment marked by "incredulity toward metanarratives"—which is how Lyotard *defines* the postmodern (Lyotard 1984, xxiv). In other words, postmodernity is characterized by a seemingly incurable suspicion that all grand, sweeping narratives perform their legitimating role by masking the will to power and negating the interests of others.

The rule of consensus, which governed the Enlightenment narratives and constructed truth as a product of agreement between rational minds, has, from this standpoint, finally been rent asunder. The narrative function has been dispersed into many language elements, each with its own pragmatic valences. We are left only with "language particles," a heterogeneity of language games. There is no neutral ground upon which to adjudicate between competing claims, no synthesizing master discourse that can reproduce the speculative unity of knowledge. The linguistic turn of twentieth-century philosophy and the social sciences does not permit the assumption of a metalinguistic neutrality or foundational epistemological privilege.

Lyotard invokes the plurality of language games to advance an attack on the conceptions of universal reason, the unity of language, and the unified subject. There is no one reason, he argues, only *reasons*; no one form of reason takes precedence over others. Lyotard emphasizes the multiplicity and proliferation of forms of reason, defined by the rules of particular discourses or language games.

Using Wittgenstein's concept of language games as his procedural method, Lyotard seeks to show how the legitimation function of metanarratives has been broken down and dispersed into incommensurable modes of discourse. Each of these has its own irreducible set of rules. These rules, however, do not have any rock-bottom justification— they are contingent historical discursive productions. Neither do they carry with them their own legitimation. From this basis, Lyotard develops a general view of language as an "agonistics" (Lyotard 1984, 10), where to speak is, as it were, to fight. He elevates this conception into a model for understanding society in general, claiming that

> the society of the future falls less within the province of a Newtonian anthropology (such as structuralism or systems theory) than a pragmatics of language particles. There are many different language games—a heterogeneity of elements. They only give rise to institutions in patches—local determinism (xxiv).

Herein lies the crisis of legitimation. The approach taken by decision-making power elites to address this crisis is writ large in the very policies of literacy at issue here (as well as across the spectrum of public institutions and at all levels of their operation). Lyotard provides two complementary accounts which, together, provide a basis for interpreting and critiquing literacy policies—and education policy generally—under conditions of postindustrial capitalism.

First, Lyotard argues that decision makers try to manage this heterogeneity of language games, these "clouds of sociality," by imposing commensurability upon them under the rule of efficient performance: that is, by overriding the irreducible differences between language games, negating difference, treating all discourses/forms of life as though they were commensurable, and conjuring a de facto "legitimation" by providing a criterion and procedures for the exercise of power in the public domain.

> The decision makers . . . attempt to manage these clouds of sociality according to input/output matrices, following a logic which implies that their elements are

commensurable and that the whole is determinable. They allocate our lives for the growth of power. In matters of social justice and scientific truth alike, the legitimation of that power is based on its optimizing of the system's performance—efficiency. The application of this criterion to all of our games necessarily involves a certain level of terror, whether hard or soft: be operational (that is, commensurable) or disappear (xxiv).

That is how education comes to be treated under the same rules and criteria of productivity as business: Education is to be made over ontologically into the same "stuff"—subject to the same laws—as business by imposing the same logic upon it as applies to business. What holds for the language game of education as a whole applies more specifically to literacy, as constructed by the policies of these same decision makers.

This account, from *The Postmodern Condition*, takes us so far. Lyotard's explicit insistence, in his "Svelte Appendix to the Postmodern Condition," that the problem of legitimation in knowledge and education cannot be separated from an analysis of capitalism takes us farther still. He argues that capitalism "is one of the names of modernity." In a vein highly reminiscent of *The Postmodern Condition*, he adds that

capitalism has been able to subordinate to itself the infinite desire for knowledge that animates the sciences, and to submit its achievements to its own criterion of technicity: the rule of performance that requires the endless optimization of the cost/benefit (input/output) ratio (Lyotard 1993, 25).

He speaks of the "penetration of capitalism into language," and "the transformation of language into a productive commodity" which reduces phrases to encoded messages with an exchange value—information that can be stored, retrieved, packaged, calculated, and transmitted. Lyotard acknowledges his debt to Marx, framing his analysis within the ambit of commodification (albeit a *representational* commodity system): in effect, the Marxist analysis of commodity fetishism as it applies to knowledge and education.

At this level of his argument, the issue for Lyotard is to understand and provide a critique of capitalist forms of insinuating will into reason and the way this is manifest primarily in language. He addresses this concern in *The Postmodern Condition* in relation to the performativity principle (Lyotard 1984, 47–49).

Performativity is the principle of optimizing the overall performance of social institutions according to the criterion of efficiency or, as Lyotard puts it, "the endless optimilization of the cost/benefit (input/output) ratio" (Lyotard 1993, 25). In the operational terms we are most familiar with, perhaps, this involves framing goals in terms of "ever narrowing demands of reporting," where "accountability is measured by outputs" (Marshall 1998). At the level of policy rhetoric and rationale, the argument is that the shrinking welfare dollar (fiscal restraint) calls for small government (the public sector equivalent of lean and mean enterprises) that manages welfare institutions like education in ways that ensure that maximum outputs are obtained from welfare-dollar inputs.

The locus of operation is no longer based on questions of educational aims and ideals in the old sense that drew on language games involving values, aspirations, conceptions of and beliefs about humanity, potential, personal worth and autonomy, emancipation and dignity, and the like. Rather, attention has moved from aims, values, and ideals to a new focus on "means and techniques for obtaining [optimally] efficient outcomes" (Marshall 1998, 8). That is to say, the education language game has been forced into commensurability with the varieties of technicist language games, and is required to play—to perform—according to the technological criterion of efficiency. The problem of legitimation, which is ever a problem of rationalizing *power*, is addressed by making efficiency the basis of legitimation and then extending this logic across *all* the language games of the public-social institutional domain.

At the level of daily practice, performativity in education at all levels calls for our schools and universities to make "the optimal contribution . . . to the best performativity of the social system" (Lyotard 1984, 48). This involves creating the sorts of *skills* among learners that are indispensable to maximum efficiency of the social system which, for societies like our own, is a system of increasing diversity and players in the marketplace of global capitalism. Accordingly, two kinds of skills predominate:

(1) Skills "specifically designed to tackle world [economic] competition," which will vary "according to which 'specialities' the nation-states or educational institutions can sell on the world market"
(2) Skills which fulfill the society's "own needs." These have to do with maintaining the society's "internal cohesion." Under postmodern conditions, says Lyotard, these cohesion skills displace the old educational concern for *ideals*. Education is now about supplying "the system with players capable of acceptably filling their roles at the pragmatic posts required by its institutions" (48).

As Marshall (1998) notes

educational institutions . . . will be used to change people away from the former liberal humanist *Ideals* (of knowledge as good in itself, of emancipation, of social progress) to people who through an organized stock of professional knowledge will pursue performativity through increasingly technological devices and scientific managerial theories (12).

Against this background, reading our policy constructions of literacy and their shared characteristics as "postmodern conditions" is practically unavoidable. Although Lyotard's focus was on higher education and the condition of knowledge as research production, the frame he presents speaks powerfully to literacy policy at all educational levels. In particular, the account provided of a new *word* order inherent in policy priorities and its functional coherence with the emerging new *work* order (Gee, Hull and Lankshear 1996) resonates disturbingly with the notion of performance at pragmatic posts.

It is, however, important not to advance simplistic arguments of structural correspondence and make the unwarranted assumption that what policy dictates is what will be implemented in practice (see Lankshear 1998). At the same time, we have to be able to account for such policy trends as the fact that the recent resurgence of interest in foreign language education has emphasized very different languages from the narrowly Eurocentric focus that typified earlier postwar decades. As with adult literacy, the justifications are unashamedly different: The ideals of a liberally educated person who would travel, converse, and experience different "cultures" is giving way increasingly brashly to capitalist desires to sell in world markets.

We might similarly read the "English first/English only" emphasis under the description of society's need for internal cohesion identified by Lyotard above. To some extent, the standardization emphasis can be read the same way—although standard units for measurement are, of course, crucial for determining outputs. Similarly, the insistence on treating literacy as a private or individual possession has good cohesion value. It militates against "collective" conceptions and practices of literacy (see Kell 1996) that can develop and sustain group solidarity and oppositional or resistant discourses.

What is arguably of most significance is the way policy constructions of literacy education practices would socialize teachers, learners, administrators, parents, researchers, and others involved in literacy education into the ways of performativity under the command: "be operational (that is, commensurable) or disappear" (Lyotard 1984, xxiv). Policy formulations would permeate the entire school literacy enterprise with technocratic rationality and a reductionist logic that values practice as technique. This is as apparent in current moves toward "benchmarking" as it was in the 1980s in the fetish for highly mechanical operationalizations of "competence."

As one would expect under capitalism, technicism and commodification come together in this scenario. Literacy is profoundly commodified within the current reform agenda in relation to assessment, evaluation packages, validation packages, remedial teaching packages, packaged standards, profiles, curriculum guidelines, textbook packages, and teacher professional development packages promising recipes and resources for securing the required performance outcomes. Sometimes this commodification reaches almost bizarre levels, as in a model promulgated in Australia (NBEET 1996), in which it is proposed that industry sectors build literacy competencies into their respective competency standards. The idea behind local competency standards and associated competency-based training is to make Australian industry as competitive as possible by creating a "smart" work force of high-quality and efficient performers by means of up-to-date training programs that prepare workers cost effectively for the kinds of tasks they will be doing on the job. Competency standards comprise so many *units of competence*: for example, "participates in daily team meetings and discussions." These are broken down into *elements of competence*. For instance, "participates in daily team meetings and discussions" contains, as one of its *elements of competence*, "reads team meeting documents." Each element of competence has associated *performance criteria*, and a specified *range of variables*, that plot various dimensions along which performance will have to be demonstrated (such as in a range of contexts, or with reference to a range of materials or tasks, in which the performance of, say, "initiating discussions" might occur). Finally, an *evidence guide* for assessing competent performance has been produced for each unit of competence.

What Is to Be Said?

It is important to remember that our concern here is with constructions and associated characteristics of literacy at the level of policy proposals, *not* with concrete implementations of proposals as actual programs. As is often observed, reform proposals are rarely implemented in practice as they are framed on paper (Thomas 1994; Beare and Boyd 1993). The constructions of literacy we locate in policy formulations may differ significantly from those that subsequently emerge in concrete responses to these proposals. Indeed, in the present context it is to be hoped that this is so. This chapter builds on the belief that it is very important to address and understand the extent to which, and ways in which, policies can influence the range of meanings and practices subsequently realized in material sites within and beyond classrooms.

To interrogate policies for constructions and characteristics of literacy is to ask what we are being rallied and directed to *become* (and not become) as teachers and learners of text production, transmission, and reception/retrieval, and what we are being enlisted to *make literacy into* (and not) as lived conceptions and practices. It is important to do this kind of work as a form of cultural critique. Reform proposals are like scripts, frames, or "cultural models" (Gee, Hull and Lankshear 1996). They encode values intended to change people and social practices—values that will change people and practices to a greater or lesser extent depending on how fully they get implemented in practice. From this perspective we must look at educational reform proposals in terms of a much broader context than formal educational sites alone. Those who propose educational reforms intend them to mesh with scripts for doing life as a whole. The key questions here are What kinds of "visions" for life, people, and practices more generally, are encoded in these scripts? What do we think about them? and How do we intend to respond to them?

The vision of literacy underlying education policy predicated on performativity has some serious flaws. We outline briefly three of these here.

1. Viable Alternative Literacies Are Silenced

It has long been recognized that school discourses silence many established cultural forms of literate practice (see Scollon and Scollon 1981; Michaels 1981; Heath 1983; Jones 1986; Delgado-Gaitan 1990; Gee 1996). Current policy formulations are by no means the only silencing devices operating in schools. By the same token, implementing them seems likely only to extend and intensify an already established tendency. Moreover, in many cases implementation may actually work *against* the criterion of efficiency. The recent work of Catherine Kell (1996) and Michele Knobel (1997) illustrates how the ways that current policy proposals frame literacy as an individual possession may undermine collaborative and cooperative literacy practices and the functional efficiencies made possible by such practices.

Kell (1996) describes the work of an African National Congress (ANC) activist, Winnie Tsotso—a local ANC branch organizer and long-standing member of the squatters' civic association, who serves on the local health, preschool, and Catholic welfare and development committees. Tsotso also runs a soup kitchen for pensioners—purchasing, preparing, and serving the food—and is a qualified first aid worker, among many other things. By means of social procedures she has developed with others she easily manages the print requirements of her various roles, despite having strictly limited "print competence." In these respects and domains, although not in others, she is literate in the sense of handling the language requirements of multiple Discourses (Gee 1996). Yet her superiors pressured her into entering formal literacy training. Kell contrasts Tsotso's struggling efforts to deal with literacy learning in a beginners' class, and her greatly diminished sense of personal efficacy, with her fluent competence in diverse text-mediated social practices.

Knobel (1997, 1999) contrasts the in-school and out-of-school literacy performances of a Year 6 student named Jacques. Relative to the sorts of demonstrated print competencies enshrined in measurement procedures like "benchmarks," "levels profiles," and the like, Jacques performs badly. His teacher describes him as "having great difficulty with literacy." His spelling is poor, he shuns writing in class wherever possible, and he has developed elaborate strategies for avoiding classwork. He regularly displays genuine signs of not understanding the metalevel explanations and metacognitive literacy strategies the teacher has explained with great care. The same student has elaborate out-of-school language and literacy practices. These include doing door-to-door "witnessing" as part of his religious affiliation and engaging in demanding reading, speaking, and exegesis activities in theocratic school. He has also produced a sophisticated and elaborate flyer that he posted in local letterboxes that established a very successful lawn-mowing route. As with the case described by Kell, Jacques' out-of-school performances involve close collaboration with family members. His performances, like those of Tsotso, are embedded in mature versions of social practices through which he has acquired a sound understanding of purposes, props, and scaffolds.

So far as efficiency is concerned, effective literacies are, by definition, ways of handling textual requirements within social practices: in situ. Interestingly, the very kinds of efficiency most at stake in performativity demands—such as economic competitiveness and optimal productivity outputs—are often sought precisely via arrangements involving distributed expertise, collaboration, teamwork, and the like (Gee, Hull, and Lankshear 1996, ch. 3). Yet what is a proven modus operandi within many "insider" versions of social practice is *systematically negated* in policy constructions of literacy and formally required accountability, diagnostic, and reporting procedures. By these means, many students will be effectively cut out of future selection for entry to social practices they would otherwise perform effectively in. In such instances, which could be repeated endlessly, legitimation via performativity is secured at high price.

2. Effective Literacy Is Subverted

The cases just mentioned illustrate, among other things, the tension between a narrowly operational-mechanistic-technicist approach to literacy and a socioculturally informed approach. To a large extent, the tension between policy perceptions of "efficiency" at school discourse level and efficiency-driven social practices in workplaces and other sites where collaboration and "distribution" are emphasized is precisely the tension between operational and sociocultural approaches. New capitalist ideology has bought heavily into insights from sociocultural theory and tried to appropriate them for economic ends.

Two decades of sociocultural research and theoretical work pertaining to literacy strongly indicates that effective literacy is best seen as having three interlocking dimensions—the operational, the cultural, and the critical—that bring together language, meaning and context (Green 1988, 160–63; Green 1997a; Green 1997b). An integrated view of literacy in practice and in pedagogy addresses all three dimensions simultaneously; none necessarily has any priority over the others.

The *operational* dimension refers to the "means" of literacy, in the sense that it is in and through the medium of language that the literacy event happens. It involves competency with regard to the language system. To refer to the operational dimension of literacy is to point to the manner in which individuals use language in literacy tasks to operate effectively in specific contexts. The emphasis is on the written language system and how adequately it is handled. From this perspective, it is a question of individuals being able to read and write in a range of contexts in an appropriate and adequate manner. This dimension focuses on the language aspect of literacy (see Green 1988; Green 1997a; Green 1997b; Lankshear et al. 1997, vol. 1).

The *cultural* dimension involves what may be called the meaning aspect of literacy. It involves competency with regard to the meaning system and recognizes that literacy acts and events are not only *context* specific but also entail a specific *content*. It is never simply a case of being literate in and of itself but of being literate with regard to something, to some aspect of knowledge or experience. The cultural dimension of literacy refers to the ability to understand the meanings of texts in context—and not only the meaning of the text, but the meaning the text must make in order to be appropriate and how contexts make for appropriate or inappropriate ways of reading and writing. For example, the context of making a written application for a job will typically require a formal prose style and addressing the relationship between the job requirements and one's personal capacities and achievements. Writing a chatty note to the boss at head office inviting her for a beer would indicate a failure to understand the cultural context and what makes for an appropriate text. If we take the case of a worker producing a spreadsheet within a workplace setting or routine, it is clear that this is not a simple matter of "going into some software program" and "filling in the data." Spreadsheets must be *compiled*—which means knowing their purpose and constructing their axes and categories accordingly. To know the purpose of a particular spreadsheet requires an understanding of relevant elements of the culture of the immediate work context; to know why one is doing what one is doing now, how to do it, and why what one is doing is appropriate (Green 1988).

The *critical* dimension of literacy has to do with the socially constructed nature of all human practices and meaning systems. In order to be able to participate effectively and productively in any social practice, humans must be socialized into it. But social practices and their meaning systems are always selective and sectional; they represent particular interpretations and classifications. Unless individuals are also given access to the grounds for selection and the principles of interpretation they are merely socialized into the meaning system and unable to take an active part in its transformation. The critical dimension of literacy is the basis for ensuring that participants can do more than merely participate in a practice and make meanings within it, that they can in various ways transform and *actively* produce it (Green 1988).

As we have seen, policy constructions of literacy severely constrain its critical dimension. Furthermore, their emphasis on narrow and decontextualized forms of measurement and reporting constrains the cultural dimension as well—as endlessly replicable examples (like Winnie Tsotso and Jacques) reported in literacy research attest. The points at which current policy formulations are most clear and explicit are, precisely, points dealing with diagnosis, remediation, quality assurance, and accountability on the operational dimension. This is not enough, whether seen from a more traditional "ideals" perspective or, indeed, from more imaginative and far-sighted perspectives on performance and efficiency.

3. Policy Constructions of Literacy Are "Unreal"

The heavy emphasis on standardized measurement, test packaging, and decontextualized literacy activities and assessment evident in policy formulations pertains at all levels of literacy education. This often generates highly distorted effects. For example, recent international adult literacy surveys conducted across several OECD countries draw on assessment instruments that bear little relationship to the lived literacy reality of many people. The test items (for examples, see Kirsch et al. 1993) are allegedly stand-ins for what adults are supposed to (have to) do in their everyday lives. It is readily apparent from Australian data, however, that *many* people do not do their lives the way these items do their testing.

Besides the formal assessment component, the Australian survey contained a "qualitative" component that surveyed what respondents actually do on a daily basis in terms of literacy tasks and how they rate their capacity to do these things (ABS 1997a; ABS 1997b). Some interesting findings emerged. A very significant 28 percent of those who self-rated their reading skills as excellent were subsequently assessed at the two lowest levels of performance. Conversely, only 79 percent of those who rated their mathematical skills as poor scored at the lowest level. In other words, there were significant differences between the subjective and objective assessments. The ABS report comments as follows on the reading aspect:

> It may seem incongruous that some people who were objectively assessed as having relatively poor literacy skills rated their skills as excellent or good. One possible explanation for this is that people with lower skill levels (as measured by the objective assessment) who had little need to use advanced skills in daily life may consider that their skills are good enough to meet the demands placed on them, and, accordingly, rate their skills *for the needs of daily life* as good, or even excellent (ABS 1997a, 9).

This is sufficient to raise reasonable doubt about the relationship between survey items and what people actually do in their daily lives, and the ways they set about negotiating information, meaning, and other communication demands. Moreover, relatively small proportions of those assessed at the lowest level in the Australian study used (14 percent) or wrote (10 percent) reports, articles, magazines, journals, invoices, bills, spreadsheets, etc., on anything like a daily basis. This is not to say that they *should not* be able to do these things well or that they will not need to do them routinely in the future. It *does*, however, imply that large numbers of people experience themselves as functioning competently under present real life conditions with what they can already do—and that this is being adjudged poor and, by extension, inadequate. Equally significantly, the Australian figures provide empirical support for the *unreality* of policy constructions of literacy: something that teachers and educationists who have not already sold their souls to performativity are well aware of.

The qualitative survey was nonetheless overridden in the official reporting of Australian levels of literacy attainment as a basis for international comparison. Subsequent policy initiatives were likewise based squarely on the quantitative survey. To the extent that such cases illustrate larger tendencies under performativity regimes, they call us as educators to engage in critique and oppositional activities.

What Is to Be Done?

In the context of developing an agenda for sociocultural studies of literacy, James Gee (1998) develops a useful distinction between "enactive work" and "recognition work." This is work done by human beings—largely unconsciously—in their everyday discursive practices. Gee argues that social worlds are created and sustained by human beings as they organize and coordinate materials in ways that others (come to) recognize, to see as *meaningful*. These materials are, of course, the stuff of Discourses: "people, things, artifacts, symbols, tools, technologies, actions, interactions, times, places, ways of speaking, listening, writing, reading, feeling, thinking, valuing," etc. (Gee 1998, 15). Our discursive practice involves "attempting to get other people to recognize people and things as having certain meanings and values within certain configurations or relationships" (14). Enactive work refers to these attempts (which, of course, are often unconscious—they come with recruitment to Discourses—but can, equally, be conscious—as in witting acts of transformative practice). Recognition work refers to the efforts by others to accept or reject such attempts—"to see or fail [refuse] to see things our way" (15).

These attempts and recognitions are precisely what produce, sustain, challenge, and transform particular discursive effects. Enactive and recognition work is, then, political and ethical. And the stakes of such work are "always 'up for grabs'." Actors, events, activities, practices, and Discourses do not exist in the world *except through* active work, work that is very often unstable and contested" (Gee 1998, 17).

Attempts to construct literacy in particular ways through policy formulations that may have particular discursive effects are instances of enactive work. Educators have both enactive and recognition strategies available in responding at the level of policy implementation. They can engage in critical recognition work, refusing whatever aspects of policy implementation they find unacceptable and looking for ways to subvert it in practice. They can also, and ideally would, engage in critically informed and deliberate enactive work. Struggling to build support for a socioculturally informed three-dimensional view of literacy is an important option here. In the short run this involves working in ways that accommodate performativity demands at a level sufficient for avoiding punishment, while refusing the identities pushed by the policies. In the longer run it means organizing and working politically through unions, professional associations, school-level programming and planning committees, and so on in support of more educationally expansive policy constructions of literacy.

Such work calls for developing a critical perspective on current policy and working to build alternative visions. This chapter has attempted to outline at least the beginnings of a critical perspective and to point toward an alternative vision. The next chapter will look at some aspects of what this might involve nearer the chalkboard.

Note

1. The first part of this chapter draws on articles published in *Educational Theory* 48, no. 3, and *The International Journal of Inclusive Education* 1, no. 4.

Chapter 8

Technological Literacies: Postmodern Tendencies

Introduction

With the exponential growth of the "digital-electronic apparatus" (Ulmer 1989) during the past two decades, technological literacy has emerged as an increasingly visible item on learning agendas worldwide. It is, of course, an ambiguous item. Initially, "technological literacy" implied achieving an acceptable level of know-how with new electronic technologies (see Bigum and Green 1992). To be technologically literate simply meant knowing one's way around a range of new electronic gadgets and applications (from being able to program a video to being au fait with various computing applications). In this sense, technological literacy often served as a synonym for "computer literacy."

More recently, however, the idea has taken hold among literacy educators that in addition to being literate in terms of conventional print media and texts, learners must now acquire *some new kind of literacy* associated with the burgeoning use of computer-mediated communications technologies in everyday life. It is as if in the past we had literacy, pure and simple, and now we have technological literacy—or, as many would have it—a whole range of new technological literacies.

Of course, any notion that literacy has become *technological* with the emergence of the digital-electronic apparatus involves a kind of conceptual and historical blindness. Understood as some form or other of *written* language, literacy is always-already "technologized," in the sense that it comes into being only in and through available technologies of information and communication.

Literacy is best understood, historically, in terms of particular formations of language and technology. It only comes into being through available technologies of information and communication: such as marks on natural surfaces, the alphabet and other symbol systems, stylus and pencil, the printing press, and the digital-electronic apparatus. Whatever the particular technologies involved in specific cases, technology is always necessarily inherent in literacy (Lankshear et al. 1997, 1: 20; see also Bigum and Green 1992).

The spate of contemporary talk about *technological literacies* seems to reflect the tendency for those technologies integral to conventional (print) literacy to become invisible because they have always been there and, consequently, have become naturalized. The emergence of a new literacy medium suddenly makes its associated literacy, or literacies, appear to be technological. When we recognize this historical blindness for what it is, we understand conceptions of "technological literacy" to be variations on the theme of practices in which texts are digitized electronically.

As with "conventional" literacy, technological literacy can assume all manner of forms. To use Brian Street's metaphor, technological literacy may be seen as a shorthand for the myriad (actual and potential) social practices and conceptions of producing, transmitting, receiving, and engaging digitally encoded texts (see Street 1984, 1). Research and theoretical work undertaken since the 1970s in sociocultural studies of literacy has alerted us to the sheer variety of ways in which human beings construct literacy as social practice and to issues and implications arising from this for formal literacy education and classroom learning.

Important issues with respect to conventional and technological literacies alike include the degree of "fit" between classroom constructions of literacy and forms of literacy engaged in contexts of social practice beyond the school—particularly those that provide greater access to social goods (Gee 1996)—and the relationship between the varying literacies and funds of literacy knowledge learners bring with them to school and those they encounter in school (see Moll 1992). It is also important to consider curriculum and policy directions in education in relation to trends in student achievements and to trends in literacy practices within real-world settings.

At this time we know very much less about constructions of technological literacy than about conventional literacy and, hence, about the sorts of issues mentioned here as they pertain to technological literacy. Indeed, the fact that the digital-electronic apparatus is so new at the mass level means that technological literacies remain to a great extent embryonic or inchoate, rather than realized. The development of new technologies has implications for changing forms and practices of literacy, thereby compelling attention to the notion of new and emerging literacies and associated new forms of human subjectivity (see Green and Bigum 1993; Lankshear et al. 1997, vol. 1). About such matters we know remarkably little at present.

This chapter briefly describes six examples of practice from formal and informal educational settings in which the production of digital text artifacts was integral to planned learning activities. We identify and discuss the salient features of these practices. It is important to note that the examples addressed represent something of a forced choice, in that the informal cases have been chosen precisely because they contrast significantly with the school cases—and to that extent serve a useful heuristic purpose. Although the formal (classroom) examples are typical of much current practice within schools, they do not exhaust the range of what might be found there. Nor can the informal examples be taken as representative of constructions and practices of technological literacy within informal educational contexts. Even so, the examples have been selected as a way of providing a base for beginning to theorize possibilities and limits within settings where contextual factors are significantly different.

Some Technological Literacies in School Settings: Three Vignettes

During 1996–1997 a national research project undertaken in Australia investigated links between literacy and technology in classroom-based teaching and learning, with particular emphasis on the use of new information and communication technologies (Lankshear et al. 1997). Twenty classrooms ranging from lower elementary to upper secondary levels spread evenly across urban and rural settings participated.

Sites were selected because they provided informative and illuminating examples of what was actually going on in everyday classroom learning mediated by new technologies across a broad range of conditions and circumstances. Variables included different professional knowledge bases on the part of teachers, varying policy arrangements and access to physical and human resources, and diverse geographical locations and subject areas.

The classrooms varied widely in terms of the technological tools being employed and the relative extent to which and ways in which they were applied in learning activities generally and in literacy education more specifically. Some classrooms used Internet access (e-mail, the World Wide Web) and an array of (other) multimedia applications—for example, moviemaking software, CD-ROMs, presentation software, digital cameras, sound and animation software—on a daily basis. In one case, a site had indirect access to a CD-ROM copier, by which HyperCard presentations were published as CD-ROMs. Others ran the hardware gamut from the venerable Apple IIe to the latest Pentium-powered PC, using diverse word-processing, drawing, painting, graphics, and desktop publishing software.

In what was possibly the most pedagogically sophisticated site, a Year 6 class in a low socio-economic status area worked twice weekly on an integrated, cross-curriculum, theme-based unit of work on inventions. During two consecutive 90-minute sessions, small groups of students worked their way twice through a sequence of three 20-minute rotations: one each for reading, writing and discussing, and work at a computer. The linchpin of the project involved making a short movie involving an invention, using MS 3D Moviemaker. The unit of work was organized around the state English syllabus, which required students to become familiar with a range of genres. Students' work traversed several genres during any single session as they researched and compiled biographies of inventors, scripted their movie narratives, wrote evaluations of inventions from different points of view (corresponding to social groups differently affected by the invention), designed posters to advertise their movies and invitations to their premieres, justified decisions taken about scenes, characters, etc., and compiled an information report on an invention, which also provided the basis for an oral presentation to the class at the end of the unit. Social, cultural, economic, political, and ethical aspects of inventions were addressed, along with technological aspects. Activities were scaffolded by way of strategic tasks, questions, hints, and the like which the teacher integrated into worksheets and whole-class discussion—all designed to make *explicit* the concepts, categories, and techniques being learned. Student portfolios included work ranging from computer-generated and "polished" texts to handwritten worksheets, scribbled notes that played formative roles in discussions, props for the oral presentation (assessed by the class with reasons provided for their assessments), etc.

Elsewhere, the sessions observed in the site studies tended to be rather narrower in range, less integrated, more fragmented and stand-alone. For example, a snapshot from a second site captured students trying to access information on the World Wide Web and, when it was not available, sending an e-mail request to the relevant Web site personnel. This was a self-contained activity with no clear connection to other learning tasks. A snapshot from a third site captures *SuccessMaker* and *SentenceMaster* software being used to improve mastery of basic literacy skills. Examples from other sites describe teachers and students working together to format e-mail interviews for presentation on the Web, to present reports (for example, on local endangered species) as a series of Web pages; and to create individual student Web pages. In most cases, Web work—indeed, computer-produced work in general—was roughed out first using pen and paper before being produced in electronic form. Other examples capture students using computers for producing five-minute plays and for jointly constructed retellings of individual pages of children's stories, producing newspapers reporting stories about the school, making Christmas cards, and producing brochures about aspects of the local town. HyperCard presentations were popular forms. These ranged from sequences of individual stories (including voice-overs and illustrations to supplement straight text) to a presentation designed to augment the principal's end-of-year speech, to information reports on Olympic athletes, a history of the school, environmental project reports, and the like. At the primary school level, many students produced stories using a range of computer applications. These activities ranged from producing interactive stories based on modern myths and legends to more straightforward productions using storyboard panel formats and software that simulated storybook space. The following vignettes provide more detailed pictures of typical cases (for full accounts see Lankshear et al. 1997, vol. 2).

1. Taunton Elementary: Computer-Mediated Literacy Education in a Combined Year 5–7 Rural Classroom

Taunton is a very small remote rural town, several hundred kilometers from an Australian state capital city. Its primary/elementary school serves around fifty students organized into three multi-year/level classes: Preschool/Years 1 and 2; years 3 and 4; Years 5, 6, and 7. The Year 5–7 class we observed had eighteen students and was housed in a spacious classroom. Desks faced a blackboard extending along one wall. The other walls were crammed with commercial posters, student artwork, and teacher-prepared information and procedural charts designed to assist learning. Off one side of the room was an enclosed verandah containing print resources for learning and three computers at workstations. A second verandah ran off the opposite wall. It contained more books, comfortable "lounging" space, and led to a small room housing a fourth computer that had a modem link. This resource had been provided by the state government for use by Year 6 and 7 students, all of whom are mandated by state policy to learn a Language Other Than English (LOTE).

The Year 5–7 class was equipped with two Apple IIe computers connected to Image Writer II printers, a Macintosh LC 630 computer shared with the Year 3–4 class, and a Macintosh LC 475 with modem, dedicated phone line, microphone, and a Conferlink telephone. The LC 475 ran an external CD-ROM drive and had an HP Deskwriter 600 printer attached. The class used a range of software including HyperCard, Claris Works, and various drill and skill games. In addition to these school-owned computing resources, Taunton also had occasional access to more specialized equipment by way of an education adviser for learning technologies (see below). This included a digital camera, scanner, a Macintosh LD 630, a CD-ROM copier, and cable links for connecting computers to VCRs.

The Internet Service Provider (ISP) used at Taunton was expensive and unreliable—a function of telecommunications infrastructure in remote areas. Phone equipment and lines were outmoded by "leading edge" standards. When computer hardware failed and needed repair it had to be sent hundreds of kilometers for servicing. Technical advice for glitches that could be fixed on site involved phone calls to the regional school support center, also hundreds of kilometers away. The fragility and vulnerability of equipment inclined the teacher, Teresa, against unsupervised student use and doors were kept locked when necessary. A recent hard drive crash had put the class's best computer out of action for an entire school term.

Teresa had worked ten years at Taunton Primary. She had majored in computer studies in her pre-service teacher training and had been the school's computing coordinator throughout her tenure. Although her programming-based training in BASIC and LOGO had fired her interest in computers, she had subsequently found little applicability for it in her teaching. Under state provisions, the school had access to an education adviser who specialized in learning technologies (read: computing in learning). The adviser, Georgia, was responsible for promoting effective use of learning technologies in the many schools that dotted the several thousand square kilometers of remote countryside comprising her domain. Not surprisingly, her visits to Taunton were infrequent, and "urgent" assistance requirements often met with unavoidable delays—at times up to several weeks.

Georgia's work involved providing technical advice about school technology resources, running lessons for teachers and students in hardware and software applications, conducting in-service professional development sessions for teachers at the regional support center base, and arranging and coordinating exchanges of equipment and advice among schools in her area—as well as working with the teacher to envisage and plan computer-mediated learning activities and participating in such activities as appropriate and possible. Her preferred pedagogical mode was to work with teachers to develop activities around applications she was trialing. At the time of the research, Georgia was exploring the potential uses for learning of a digital camera and scanner in conjunction with use of the Internet and HyperCard. Georgia would work with the teacher to conceptualize learning activities and projects, train the teachers and students in relevant applications, and coordinate with schools in her area to visit on a schedule that would keep the various activities moving forward, since schools could only access certain equipment when she visited.

Two examples were indicative of practice at Taunton. The first involved use of the school's computer-mediated communications facilities to implement the state's mandated foreign language learning policy with Years 6 and 7. The state department of education had provided remote schools such as Taunton with the networked computer and Conferlink phone. Twice a week Taunton's Years 6 and 7 students joined students from four other remote schools in an electronic uplink to a French teacher located at a regional center. The students at the four schools were to gather round a computer and download graphics pertaining to the lesson. These were fed in at distance by the French teacher while he spoke to the students by Conferlink phone. Phone connections regularly dropped out because of the aged infrastructure. The computer often froze because it came with insufficient memory for handling the various functions required of it (and there was no budget for upgrading). The visual and audio receptions were often so far out of sync with each other that the French teacher's instructions were rendered either irrelevant or inadequate. Important parts of lessons got lost as students in one or more sites at a time could not hear the teacher or other students. These difficulties were exacerbated by the low levels of backup support available.

The second example involved literacy education activities mediated by computer technologies. As in many small schools in the state that operated multi-age or composite classes, Taunton used a pedagogical approach based largely on self-directed learning built around activities designed by the teacher for individuals and small groups. Group work relied heavily on peer assistance and tutoring, with the teacher acting mainly as facilitator and guide. Groups were organized on the basis of needs and abilities to get optimal matches among students that would work pedagogically. "Units of work" were developed around a common theme. Activities appropriate to different age/year/ability levels were incorporated into the units of work to ensure coverage of state-mandated learning objectives (content, skills, processes) as laid down in the syllabus.

Language and literacy education based on the English syllabus emphasized genre-based learning. Units of work featured biography and information report genres. For both units of work Teresa assembled wall charts
addressing key features of the genres and strategies for information gathering, assembly and elaboration, text production, etc. She also collected
sets of relevant print resources from the school library and elsewhere.

In the unit of work on biography, students collectively produced a
HyperCard presentation on Olympic athletes. They did research using
mainly print resources to gather and arrange information for producing
biographies to the recommended format. Much of the work was roughed
out on pen and paper, and after successive drafts was produced on the
computer—including photographs taken with the digital camera. Once in
electronic form the biographies were assembled as a HyperCard presentation. This was then reproduced as a CD-ROM by Georgia at the regional resource center.

The information report project involved a unit of work on space. In
place of HyperCard technology, the computing focus shifted to using the
Internet. Teresa located suitable Web sites to share with the students.
Besides Internet sites the class used books from the library that had been
assembled as a resource set by the teacher, CD-ROMs containing information on space and instructional wall charts. Once again, students worked
through conventional pen-and-paper drafts before committing their
(pen)ultimate copies to the computer.

The process of using the Internet in this project was plagued with
technical hitches. We visited the school to observe an Internet session
that had been designed by Teresa to allow students to access on-line
information about planets. The previous day after school Teresa had run
a search for relevant sites, bookmarking them so that the students could
conduct a "planned search" on the day we visited. Since the room holding
the networked computer was so small, Teresa called out the Year 7 students first, explaining to the others that they would get their turns in due
course and asking them to proceed with their math activities meanwhile.
However, the Internet connection could not be made. Teresa made repeated attempts, without success, to log on, while the Year 7s returned to
their math.

2. Calhoun Elementary School: Using Multimedia
to Support Year 2 Multicultural Students

Calhoun is a K–6 school located in a culturally diverse district of an
Australian metropolis. Students at the school represent more than thirty

nationalities, with Vietnamese, Chinese, Khmer, and Serbs being the largest groups. Just 10 percent of students are from native English-speaking backgrounds. The school's enrollment had dropped 20 percent during the five years prior to the research period. Unemployment in the area runs at 40 percent, and the "transient population" is calculated officially at 30 to 35 percent. High-density housing prevailed.

The Year 2 class of 22 students was housed in a room that seemed small and dark—windows on each side notwithstanding. Desks and chairs were arranged around the perimeter, maximizing open floor space. Although the teacher, Doug, had his desk in one corner, he spent most of the time during lessons seated on the floor, calling students to him when appropriate or responding to them when they came to him on their own initiative to discuss work or get help. Samples of student work hung from string that crisscrossed the room. Chalkboard and walls were covered with different kinds of displays: student drafts and "brainstorms," suggestions and instructional processes related to literacy and learning (for example, a model for building a good story based on analogy with a three-story building), day and weather charts, and class rules as negotiated at the start of the year.

The school's resourcing in general, and learning technology resourcing specifically, reflected its officially designated status as a "Special Fitness" school falling within the state's Disadvantaged Schools Program (DSP). Staff could be selected by reference to locally specified criteria, such as ESL expertise. Funding under the DSP enabled the school to establish a "balanced literacy program" and to access a series of workshops for staff on multimedia, Hyperstudio, Claris Works, digital cameras, and other hardware and software applications. Under its balanced literacy program the school had mobilized a literacy learning team comprising ESL teachers, support teachers, an "Ethnic Aide," and a school counselor to provide specialized literacy education backup for regular classroom teachers. The Year 2 classroom had two stand-alone (not networked) computers with multimedia capacity. Software available included Claris Works (for writing, drawing and graphics), MS Word, Kidpix Studio (for multimedia), Corel Draw 5, Excel, MS PowerPoint for slide shows and other presentations, a range of drill-and-skill and problem-solving software, some gamesware, and specialized literacy instruction software (for example, *Wiggleworks*) for individual student use and for use with input from the language and literacy support specialists.

The teacher (Doug) was in his tenth year of teaching and was studying part time for a master's degree in literacy and technology. He had lived through the transition from no computer technologies in classrooms to his current situation where computers are such a taken-for-granted facet of classroom routines that they are practically invisible. During his tenure language and literacy education had moved from being based almost entirely on whole language programming to having a strong genre-based component, with explicit emphasis on understanding and using a range of text types.

The literacy education activities observed in the research focused on the narrative genre of stories. Students moved between working in pairs with paper, pencil, crayons, paint, scissors, glue, lettering books, etc., and working in the same pairs at the (two) computers as they became available. At the time of our observations, students were involved in a new collaborative writing activity. Each pair was jointly to produce a re-telling of one page of *The Magic Flute*. When they had all completed their work it would be assembled into a collective slide show presentation. They first sketched out their text and illustrations on large pieces of white chart paper. Those pairs working at the computers were producing slide show versions of other stories they had previously worked on—using text, graphics, and sound recordings of their texts.

One pair of boys worked on their presentation of *The Three Little Pigs*, making multiple takes at recording their text. The first time they discovered they had selected the "no sound" option on each slide, and at their second take the sound was too soft. A pair of girls worked on a story about dinosaurs. They had prepared a narrative using an eight panel storyboard, roughing out their text and illustrations on paper. Using this draft they prepared slides for their final presentation using drawing and painting tools in Kidpix. They drew a purple dinosaur with a red mouth, then deleted and retrieved it several times in the process of finally changing its color to yellow. They completed the slide by keying in "*Marie's Dinosaur* by Marie and Lin." During the draft production phase, Doug worked with students, discussing their illustrations and texts and helping them clarify their intentions.

3. Text Processing in the English Program at Technology High

Technology High opened in 1991 as the first purpose-built technology high school in the state. It was located in the heart of a burgeoning middle class suburb undergoing large-scale housing development. Almost 40 percent of the local population did not have English-speaking backgrounds. Students from forty-eight different linguistic communities attended the school. Cantonese and Mandarin formed the largest foreign language groups. Originally built for 850 students, the school had an enrollment of more than 1,200 at the time it was studied, and additional portable classrooms had eaten considerably into recreational space. Partnerships with hardware and software companies had assisted with resourcing throughout the school's life.

The school aimed to provide "a comprehensive curriculum which embraces technology in theme and delivery" (Goal 2, School Strategic Plan 1994–98). Teachers revisited this goal by considering the distinction between being a "technology high school" and a "computers high school"— defining a *technology* high school as one that develops skills to work in teams and solve problems creatively using a range of technologies across the curriculum. Issues at stake in the difference between the two kinds of school, and challenges involved in pursuing the technology high school philosophy, were readily apparent in observed practices.

Technology High was originally built around three PC-equipped labs and a media editing suite. Discrete music, animation and robotics, and CAD facilities had evolved and had been equipped with scanning facilities, other recent innovative applications, and upgrades. In addition, regular classrooms were progressively being computerized, with small withdrawal rooms between classrooms being provided with six to eight machines and Internet access.

Teachers without access to such facilities, including the English teacher (Alison) in the case to be described here, had two options. One was to negotiate for access to a lab for which computer technology subjects had priority status. The other was to book a class set of laptops from the library. Getting physical access to equipment for a lesson was rarely a problem. As Alison explained, "something is always available, or someone is always willing to negotiate access." A school survey indicated that 85 percent of students had home computer access, and 35 percent had home Internet access.

Alison's English home classroom, where she taught classes in Years 7 through 11, was arranged in seven blocks each of four desks. It appeared cramped and overcrowded, partly due to its having been built as a science lab containing a space-gobbling chemistry bench. Alison was in her third year of teaching English. She saw herself very much as belonging to the computer generation, used computers heavily for lesson preparation and administrative tasks, and said that having grown up with computers displacing handwriting and spelling meant she could not read her own writing. She felt comfortable using computers and information technologies, enjoyed experimenting, and was always willing to try out new applications and to incorporate into her teaching "anything new, as long as students are still learning and it's not a game or a time filler."

The two snapshots which follow, involving Year 7 and 8 students, respectively, illustrate some of the challenges teachers confront as they try to live up to the school's philosophy.

The Year 7 class had returned to working on their newspaper project after a gap of several weeks during which they had shifted to the debating component of the English program. The class worked in groups of four or five. Their assignment was to compile a four-page newspaper built around stories to do with the school; the project was designed to take two to three weeks. Alison had printed out the work already done by the groups several weeks previously to remind them where they were up to. She told them to go into Windows and then into Ami Pro (which would let them produce text in columns) and then to retrieve their existing work from the collective floppy disk on which they had saved it. Because some of the groups were quite large (up to five students), Alison recommended that one or two students in each group attend to the "typing" while the others wrote new articles. A group of girls showed us where in the menu they looked for graphics to illustrate their articles. They explained how they wrote their drafts by hand into their English books before entering them into the computer. As we watched this group, two girls worked on writing articles while two entered the stories from hand-written copy, editing as they went and running the spell check over the text before printing out. At the end of the lesson Alison took the disk from group to group to have them save their work. She instructed the class to exit through Windows and turn the machines off properly.

In the second snapshot, Year 8 students were working in groups of four and five in the English home room. Each group had a laptop running an external disk drive. They were producing five-minute plays to perform before the class. One or two students per group would key material in while the others dictated dialogue, designed costumes, sketched characters on sheets of paper, constructed simple props and costume items, etc. Roles would switch when members felt like a change. Although tasks were always divided up the groups maintained themselves as units, discussing plot or character development as they went about their respective tasks. When a member had something to add to the text, s/he would momentarily take over the keyboard to make the addition, which sometimes signalled a transition in roles. As the end of the hour approached, students were instructed to "start saving" and to "pack up the machines." One student from each group returned a machine to the library while the others put chairs away and tidied up.

Features and Factors

These are quite unexceptional vignettes that will immediately be recognizable to anyone familiar with classroom appropriations of new technologies in literacy education (as well as wider subject studies). They were repeated with minor variations time and again throughout the other sites in the larger study in which they were involved (Lankshear et al. 1997, vol. 2), and they resemble countless descriptions in the research literature on educational computing (see, for example, *Journal of Educational Computing Research*, all issues). In many ways, the challenge for researchers who are interested in getting beyond the "industry" of such mundane pretend activity is to find examples that are substantially qualitatively different from ones such as these.

When we step back from such cases, several features of the ways in which technological literacy is constructed in the classrooms stand out. We will identify five key features here before turning to factors which may help us understand how such constructions come about.

First, the way technological literacy is constructed in the cases observed might fairly be described as "old wine in new bottles." It is more or less *routine* school literacy with new technologies added here and there. Much of what we saw might not unfairly be described as 1970s to 1980s process writing (draft, conference, redraft, conference, publish the final copy) and children's and young adults' literature being harnessed to computers. That is, we find long-standing classroom language and literacy education routines being undertaken as slide show and Web page presentations rather than as literal "cuttings" and "downloadings" from print resources, followed by literal "pastings" into workbooks, as was formerly the case. The final format, however, is all that changes, since the physical dimension of pen-and-paper space typically provides the medium all the way to the publishing stage.

The "old wine" syndrome was affirmed by teachers' accounts of how they understood practices at the interface of literacy, new technologies and learning. When, for example, Teresa was asked what she anticipated in the way of new literacies emerging in the future around new technologies, she replied: "People will be using old skills but applying them in new ways." She saw the skills used in research for the students' HyperCard presentations as being "the same, and set up the same ways" as those used in pen-and-paper contexts. All that is different is the mode of presentation. In her view, the major variable undergoing change is the sheer *amount* of information now available. Students will need to be(come) more picky as they negotiate this mass of information, but they will

essentially just be doing the same thing as previously: reading and deciding what is relevant; reading critically; indeed, *reading*. In a variation on
the same theme, Alison spoke approvingly of what she saw as the capacity of computing technologies to "make students more aware of the *presentation* aspects of their work." She wanted them to "take pride in their
work"—evinced in cleanness, sharpness, and tidiness of presentation—
and gestured to work displayed on the walls with visible pleasure and
satisfaction.

The second feature is how quintessentially school-like the practices are
in structure and content. Using new technologies as tools for telling and
retelling stories and for presenting biographies of national sports personalities are *absolutely* the kinds of things anyone familiar with elementary
school classrooms would expect to see going on. The same holds for
production of newspapers and five-minute plays in high school English
classrooms (see Hodas 1996 for an explanatory account of this within a
larger historical context).

A third feature is closely related to the second. It is that from the standpoint of efficacious learning, the ways technological literacy is constructed
in these classrooms often seems odd and/or mysterious. The example of
children in an elementary school with a 90 percent non–English-speaking
background (NESB) population producing retellings of fairy tales as slide
shows is an illustrative case in point. In fact, the issue has less to do with
what counts as appropriate activity in multicultural classrooms than with
the general requirements for learning to be efficacious, where what a person does *now* as a learner "must be connected in meaningful and moti-
vating ways with 'mature' (insider) versions of related social practices"
(Gee, Hull, and Lankshear 1996, 4). What we see in much classroom
practice that attempts to integrate new technologies into literacy education is a subset of a larger phenomenon: namely, that "schools don't
merely separate learning from participation in 'mature' Discourses. . . .
They render the connection entirely mysterious" (15).

Finally, relative to expansive ideals of effective literacy, the classroom
constructions of technological literacy observed were overwhelmingly one
dimensional. From the standpoint of effective sociocultural practice, as
foreshadowed in the previous chapter, literacy should be seen as having
three interlocking dimensions—the operational, the cultural, and the critical—which bring together language, meaning, and context (Green 1988,
160–63). An integrated view of literacy in practice and in pedagogy addresses all three dimensions simultaneously; none has any necessary priority over the others. The operational dimension involves competence

with the tools, procedures, and technical aspects of a practice. (In the case of literacy, it involves competence with the language system.) The cultural dimension involves competence with the meaning system of a practice: knowing what it *means* to be "in" this practice/discourse and how to make and construe meanings appropriately within the practice. The critical dimension involves awareness that any social practice is selective: It includes particular representations and classifications (values, purposes, rules, standards, perspectives, etc.) and excludes others. Critically competent participants in a practice understand the grounds (such as they are) for selection and thereby can be involved in *actively* producing and transforming the practice rather than being "submerged" in it.

By and large, the vignettes reflect constructions of technological literacy that are confined to *operational* aspects. Genres such as narratives/stories, information reports, projects, and the like serve as vehicles for introducing students to specific software applications—which are typically detached from understanding the *meanings* of practices mediated by digital text production and from notions of what is included within and/or written out of the practice (such as could readily be done, for example, by reflecting on assumptions and values that come with slide show templates or, indeed, with the very production of presentation software itself).[1]

How might these features of typical constructions of technological literacy and attempts to integrate new technologies into classroom work be understood? Why are they like they are? It is important *not* to approach description and critique of classroom constructions of technological literacy and technology-mediated pedagogy simply as a critique of individual teacher adequacy and performance but rather to see them as highly regular forms of discursive production intimately linked to aspects of the "deep grammar" of schooling as well as to aspects of policy development and implementation, resourcing trends, professional preparation and development, and so on. The deep grammar of school refers to structural characteristics of schooling as a phenomenon that occur in schools generally, notwithstanding superficial differences in detail that exist between individual schools.

In terms of its deep grammar school constructs learning as teacher-directed and "curricular" (see Illich 1971). Schooling operates on the presumption of the teacher as ultimate authority on matters of knowledge and learning. Hence, whatever is addressed and done in the classroom must fall within the teacher's competence parameters, since s/he is to *direct* learning. The notion of learning as "curricular" means that classroom learning proceeds in accordance with a formally imposed/officially sanctioned sequenced curriculum that is founded on texts as information sources. School learning is accessed primarily through reading and writing texts. In relation to this, Seymour Papert (1993, 9) observes the long-standing and pervasive tendency in the education literature "to assume that reading is the principal access route to knowledge for students." The world, in other words, is accessed via texts (books; school is book space). This imposes a pressing and profoundly instrumental value and significance on the capacity to read. It also promotes and encourages a view of (school) literacy as operational in the first instance (which, unfortunately, is often the last instance as well): that is, reading as a matter of competence with techniques of decoding and encoding.

From this standpoint, literacy is framed as the essential tool for accessing curricular knowledge and demonstrating competence in acquiring curricular knowledge (having learned). As a classic representative statement of this construction, the recently developed National Literacy and Numeracy Plan for Australian Schools identifies its first purpose as being the development of strong foundational literacy and numeracy skills for students in the early years as the basis for progress in all future schooling (DEETYA 1998, 9).

These aspects of the "deep grammar" of schooling impact on classroom adoption of new technologies and on classroom constructions of technological literacy in important ways as they intersect with contingencies operating in and on classrooms. Current policies to technologize learning intersect, for example, with a teaching work force that is largely un(der)prepared for the challenge of *directing* computer-mediated learning in the role of teacher as authority. The on-the-ground reality is captured succinctly in Chris Bigum's assessment:

> . . . [A] significant proportion of the teaching workforce still makes little use of computers. In a climate of shortage, schools value almost any computer skills in teachers. In practice, this means that low-level operational or technical skills and knowledge predominate (1997, 250).

Under pressure of policy implementation and notwithstanding the predominance of low "skill levels" and constraints on the quality and extent of professional development, teachers are expected (and expect themselves) to act as if they have expertise, are authorities, and can direct learning that integrates the use of new technologies. Practices are widely generated and consolidated under pressure-cooked conditions with whatever knowledge and facility teachers have available.[2]

The prevailing conception of literacy as a tool for learning in turn helps promote constructions of new technologies as tools for reading (accessing learning) and writing (demonstrating learning/producing outcomes). To this extent, technological literacy is constructed as information accessing and presentation of work by electronic means. So, for example, technological literacy within many elementary classrooms becomes a matter of learning and practicing decoding and encoding skills by such means as telling and retelling stories, since "narrative" is a key medium for teaching reading and writing.

The pervasive reductionist framing of literacy and computer alike as "tools for learning" is deeply entrenched. As Bigum further observes, arguments used to justify classroom use of computers have been given a "strong social framing," in which the classroom context (including teacher professional knowledge and expertise) "shapes and mediates the role of the technology"—and is, therefore, much more important than the computer in shaping what emerges as learning and how learning is practiced. In these arguments the computer is framed as merely "a neutral tool/technology"; a "means to educational ends" whose "purpose is defined in use" (251). The motif of the technology as a "mere" tool, which leaves the locus of control and power for shaping pedagogy with the teacher, has often been used to enlist and reassure teacher novice users and/or those who fear that large-scale adoption of new technologies might threaten teacher jobs and deskill and downgrade teacher work (251).

Not surprisingly, teachers look for ways of fitting new technologies into classroom "business as usual." Since educational ends are given by curriculum, and technologies are mere tools, the task of integrating new technologies into learning is often realized by adapting them to familiar routines. One corollary of this is that making learners "technologically literate" is largely reduced to teaching them how to "drive" the new technologies. As our vignettes demonstrate, the emphasis is very much on technical or operational aspects: how to add sound, insert a graphic, open and save files, create a HyperCard stack, and so on.[3]

The process can become confusingly circular. Adding sound, for example, becomes a way of (re)writing a story—as a means to leaning how to read and write in the conventional sense. (Re)writing a story—as a means to learning how to read and write as the precondition for curricular learning—becomes the pretext for learning how to add sounds, open and save files, and so on as operational/technical skills constitutive of "technological literacy."

This logic can be seen as a specific instance of a much larger phenomenon: the systematic separation of (school) learning from participation in "mature" (insider) versions of Discourses that are part of our life trajectories. School learning is learning for school; school as it always has been. The burgeoning adoption of new technologies simply gives us our latest "fix" on this phenomenon. It is the "truth" that underpins many current claims that school learning is at odds with authentic ways of learning to be in the world and with social practice beyond the school gates. The reason why many school appropriations of new technologies appear odd in relation to real-world practices—with which children are often familiar and comfortable—has to do with this very logic. It is precisely this deep grammar of schooling that cuts schools off from the new (technological) literacies and associated subjectivities that Green and Bigum (1993) say educators are compelled to attend to. To put it another way, new literacies and social practices associated with new technologies "are being invented on the streets" (Richard Smith, personal communication). These are the new literacies and practices that will gradually become embedded in everyday social practice: the literacies against which the validity of school education will be assessed. But the deep grammar of school is in tension here with its quest for legitimation in a high-tech world—which is potentially highly problematic for schools.[4]

In recent work, Lankshear and Bigum (1998) have addressed some of the issues involved here by referring to a fruitful distinction made by John Perry Barlow (in Tunbridge 1995), between "immigrant" and "native" (or "newcomer" and "insider") mindsets bearing on the "space" of new technologies.[5] Barlow distinguishes between those who have, as it were, "been born and grown up" in the space of "the Internet, virtual concepts and the IT world generally," whom he calls "natives," and those who have, as it were, migrated to this space. The former (natives/insiders) understand this space; the latter (immigrants/newcomers) do not. Barlow's distinction is between mindsets that relate to how this space is constructed and controlled in terms of values, morals, knowledge, competence, and the like. Since immigrants lack the experience, history, and resources available to them that the natives have, they cannot—to that extent—understand the new space the way natives do. On fundamental points and principles of cyber/information/virtual space, says Barlow, immigrants "just don't get it." Barlow illustrates differences between the mindsets by referring to their respective understandings of cyberspace economics and the issues of pornography on the Net.

Barlow argues that the native-immigrant distinction falls very much along age lines:

[G]enerally speaking, if you're over 25, you're an immigrant. If you're under 25 you're closer to being a native, in terms of understanding what it [i.e., the Internet, virtual concepts and the IT world generally] is and having a real basic sense of it. (Barlow in Tunbridge 1995, 8).

Notwithstanding the potential dangers inherent in Barlow's terminology (see note 5), we may use "immigrants" and "natives"/newcomers and insiders as markers for two competing mindsets: one that affirms the world as the same as before, only more technologized; the other that affirms the world as radically different precisely because of the operation of new technologies (Lankshear and Bigum 1998, 11).

The deep grammar of school—embedded in its administrative systems, policy development, curriculum and syllabus development, systemic planning, etc., as well as in its daily enactment within classroom routines and relations—institutionalizes the privileging of the immigrant mindset over the native mindset. Those constructions of technological literacy addressed here are classic instantiations of immigrant understandings of literacy grounded in the familiar physical world (book space) that have been imported into cyber/virtual/information space, where they operate to control and construct that space within curricular learning. This generates familiar tensions for schools: tensions that may, however, be seen as choice points—where choice about mindsets is in principle open and up for grabs.[6]

For example, schools already face sizable cohorts of "insiders" largely indifferent to and bemused by the quaint practices of schooling. This is a cohort that is in tune with and largely at ease with the dizzy pace of change, with the development of new technologies, and with social and economic shifts that cause pain to many immigrants (Lankshear and Bigum 1998, 14). A further tension/choice point relates to the grounds for deciding when and how to use new technologies in learning. Joseph Weizenbaum (1984) has written eloquently of the dangers of allowing computers to do things solely on the basis that they *can be done* using a computer. He distinguishes between computing "cans" and computing "oughts." From his perspective, applying a computer to a task should be approached very much as a *moral* issue, one not to be determined solely on efficiency grounds. To "newcomers," workability is almost entirely a matter of efficiency. To natives, however, it is much more: Workability for them includes a sense of elegance and beauty (Gelernter 1998), appropriateness, and other criteria which we, as immigrants, still perceive but dimly. Across the two broad mindsets, we have two very different perceptions of workability.

For learning, then, the "application test" is arguably not so much whether the computer does the job but rather the extent to which the practice is inclusive of the sensibilities of the natives. This is no easy matter and is always confounded by the dominant views that teachers, schools, parents, and systems "know what is best." For perhaps the first time in human history, however, new technologies have amplified the capacities and skills of the young to such an extent that many conventional assumptions about curriculum seem to have become inappropriate (Lankshear and Bigum 1998, 13).

This, it seems, is not the way many school education authorities understand matters and certainly not in the local contexts of our vignettes. Affirmation and further consolidation of the deep grammar of schooling and a resounding restatement of the immigrant mindset are, for example, readily apparent in the statement of Learning Technology Competencies for beginning teachers laid down by Education Queensland in its *Schooling 2001 School Kit* (Education Queensland 1997, 45–49).

This policy document identifies competencies pertaining to classroom uses of new technologies that prospective teachers must demonstrate upon completion of their training programs. Evidence is to be provided at interview as a portfolio that is "signed off" by recognized "authorities" (practicum supervisors, IT lecturers, etc.). Learning technology competency goals are identified for the dimensions of IT skills, curriculum applications, school planning skills, and student-centered learning.

The deep grammar of school and the "immigrant" character of the policy are self-evident within the competency statements. For example, the IT skills competency goal states that teachers should be able to produce documents for their own use (for example, timetables, workbooks, certificates, worksheets, etc.) in their school and classroom setting. Performance indicators are provided for using hardware, software and telecommunications. Typical examples are as follows: *Hardware* ("can recognize basic components of systems and input devices, determine the configuration, start up and shut down system or software"); *Software* ("can use files and folders, menus and desktops, virus protection, document and editing functions, open and save files"); *Telecommunications* ("can use basic functions of WORLD WIDE WEB browsers, send and receive an e-mail message").

The competency goal for curriculum applications (including classroom planning and management) is that teachers be able to incorporate use of computers as teaching and learning tools in achieving and extending curriculum goals—ensuring equitable access, participation and outcomes. Indicators of competence are provided for selecting worthwhile activities, organizing worthwhile activities, and classroom management. Typical examples are as follows: *Selecting worthwhile activities* ("is familiar with Education Queensland's *Computers in Learning Policy* and *Guidelines for Use of Computers in Education*," "has explored a range of software and on-line applications," "has used prepared evaluations of projects or software"); *Organizing worthwhile activities* ("has organized student access to the Internet or CD-ROM resources for projects," "has designed computer-based learning tasks which have explicit links to curriculum goals," "has delivered and assessed student learning activities using at least one curriculum software and one generic software package"); *Classroom management* ("can organize student use of computers, design a timetable of student use providing flexible/varied duration access, and adjust student access to computers depending on the kind of learning activity—whole class, individual, small group") (Education Queensland 1997, 45–49).

Similar orders of competency statement obtain for school planning skills and student-centered learning. The future is seemingly well embedded in the same deep grammar and control paradigm as has operated in the past.

Some "Non-Formal" Technological Literacies: Three Vignettes from a Community Site

Between 1992 and 1997 a series of nonformal educational projects that included an emphasis on using new technologies developed out of an evolving community-based network in Brisbane (Australia). Funded on the basis of competitive grant applications to a range of community arts and local and federal government schemes, projects grew out of an earlier community-based youth theater initiative, CONTACT Youth Theater Inc., begun in 1989. CONTACT was concerned with exploring cross-cultural, youth, and indigenous peoples themes through performance art. By the mid-1990s the network had established a project called "Making Space" with the key aim of developing a multipurpose youth cultural and entertainment center. This goal was met in 1995, with the establishment of GRUNT.

By 1996, CONTACT was recognized nationally for its youth arts and cultural development work, which was based on a double agenda:

- a strong social justice agenda focused on issues of access, participation, equity, and empowerment, with particular emphasis on disadvantaged young;
- a strong cross-cultural agenda, founded on work with ATSI (Aboriginal and Torres Strait Island) communities, but which subsequently evolved to include non–English-speaking background (NESB) groups at large and, finally, to become a generic cross-cultural ethos and perspective running through all projects.

In 1995, CONTACT began using on-line technologies and multimedia within its repertoire of tools, at the same time developing networks and support bases within the private (as well as pubic) sector using e-mail and the Web. CONTACT's work increasingly reflected the growing significance of information technologies as networking tools *and* as art form. CONTACT experimented with modes for using computer technologies in "grounded" community work, adding on-line contact to its earlier communicative modes of touring, consulting, performing, organizing exchanges, and hosting conferences. The drop-in center that became GRUNT was designed to accommodate the familiar "meatspace" (physical space) modes as well as the new mode of cyberspace.

GRUNT became both a physical meeting, learning, training, and production space and a distinctive cultural agenda. It was established in accordance with its germinating (1992) idea to establish a safe space for young people in the Valley area of Brisbane's inner city. The Valley is a well-known part of town that has in the past been synonymous with marginal life and activities. It has for decades been a magnet for displaced, homeless, drifting folk, many of whom have addictions or histories of substance abuse. In addition, the Valley was formerly a well-known site of vice: prostitution, graft, and various forms of racketeering. In the late 1980s, the Criminal Justice Commission's inquiry into corruption at high levels resulted in some of the Valley's best-known personalities being convicted and imprisoned. On the other hand, the Valley is also home for Brisbane's Chinatown, a bustling and thriving center of restaurants and businesses serving the long-established Chinese community. More recently, other Asian ethnic groups have also established a cultural presence there, and different Asian communities find in the Valley a zone of ethnic familiarity and comfort.

During the 1990s the heart of the Valley underwent a dramatic facelift. Its mall has been upgraded, new shopping centers have been established, and existing businesses revitalized. The mall is now home to many outdoor cafés, sidewalk bars, tourist-related businesses, and trendy nightclubs. This caters in part to a new clientele of tourists as well as to more affluent social groups who want somewhere to go that is a little exotic and "on the edge." At the same time, the Valley retains its traditional gritty base. Street kids, aged alcoholics, young unemployed men hanging out in video game parlors, bag ladies, lingering Mafia-like groups, and so on maintain a visible presence, albeit a less conspicuous one than previously.

One consequence of these recent changes has been the "rewriting" and "sanitizing" of the Valley for sale as a tourist destination and yuppie playground. As a result, the long-standing marginal youth users of the Valley—many of whom who are among the traditional "owners" of this space and its activities—have been written out of new official representations of the Valley and pushed still further to the margins. As a project to offer a safe and welcoming space for young people in the Valley area, GRUNT had a strong and important sense of purpose. It also maintained the clearly defined philosophies of and agendas for cultural productions of meanings and identities, and for providing training, framed by CONTACT. In part, GRUNT aimed to equip youth with skills and strategies relevant to earning a living. At the same time, the project was strongly committed to offering activities that would promote a sense of self-identity and interconnectedness with other identities and contexts in a world where many young people seemed increasingly to have no place.

GRUNT occupied 400 square meters of warehouse space on the first floor of a building in the center of the Valley. It was divided into three subspaces. One was used mainly for regular art exhibitions and performances. Another was a general purpose meeting, hanging out, and administrative space, furnished with deep comfortable chairs and decorated with paintings and collages, plus the occasional prop from previous performances. The third was GRUNT's main digital production area. Making the space as "un-school-like" as possible was an explicit operating principle. Multimedia equipment available to GRUNT users included color flatbed scanners, up-to-date sound, text, and image authoring software, Internet browser software and hypertext mark-up language (HTML) editors, data panels and projectors, digital cameras, conventional cameras, video cameras, and the like. The emphasis was on support for enterprise and self-sufficiency. Unlike more conventional drop-in centers and similar facilities, GRUNT, with its on-line telecenter and multimedia laboratory, worked to provide inner-city youth with "training in vocational skills, in the mastery of the new information technology and in planning, management and life skills" (Stevenson 1995, 4).

Cultural production was often built on visits to marginal communities—especially traditional indigenous communities in central Australia—and subsequent performance and artistic productions were based on what participants learned about others and themselves.

A Murri (Aboriginal) girl gets involved in a cross-cultural project at CONTACT, culminating in a performance tour of Cape York communities. While there she finds a grandmother she did not know she had and returns to Brisbane with a skin name.

A Murri boy, who could easily pass as "white," joins a workshop and participates in several projects. He buys a "how-to-play-didge" (didgeridoo) cassette and teaches himself to play, blowing through plastic pipe into water to strengthen his cheeks and lungs. The didgeridoo becomes a pathway to his Aboriginality, to the Central Desert, and to a profession (musician).

An Anglo boy joins a street theater workshop and does projects variously as actor, writer, and programmer of a CD-ROM project—coming and going over several years. He currently studies neuropharmacology (Doneman 1997, 137–38).

At its zenith during 1997 GRUNT had developed a policy of public access to the Internet and associated skills and training. The Web could be accessed by members of the public for $2 per hour (a quarter of the cost in Internet cafés and the like at the time). The telecenter was available for community groups to run experimental and training sessions involving communications and information technologies and was used regularly by more than thirty young people from socioeconomically disadvantaged backgrounds. GRUNT Youthspace also emphasized enterprise development, aiming to kit young people with skills and confidence to enter the workplace as professionals. A resident company in the network brokered skills and projects among keen and able youth users of the space. Products and services undertaken on a commercial basis included interactive CD-ROM design and production, Web authoring (HTML, Java, Javascript, CGI, database applications, Shockwave, audio, VRML), graphic design, desktop publishing, and training.

Among the projects undertaken between 1995 and 1998, three in particular typify constructions of technological literacy in GRUNTspace.

1. Black Voices
Other theater companies in Australia besides CONTACT were working with Aboriginal young people during the 1990s. These included the

Corrugated Iron company in Darwin and Yirra Yaakin in Perth. Under the auspices of GRUNT, the Black Voices Web site was developed to broadcast information about these groups and their performance-based projects.

The Web page for CONTACT provided information about three projects: The Third Place, Wirkinowt, and Famaleez. Famaleez (a phonetic rendition of "families") was a theatrical production "based on the extremely sensitive issue of alcohol and substance abuse in indigenous communities." The project focused on "the traditional aboriginal construction of 'family' and the way it used to give people structure and meaning" and built on the theme that invasion of Australia by Europeans had resulted in "a whole range of social dislocations and problems through the destruction of the extended family structures of many groups." The Famileez page contained a graphic of a moment in the performance, information about where it played/toured, and a link to CONTACT for those wanting more information. The Workinowt page followed the same structure—graphic of a scene, overview of plot, playing season, and link for further information. In Workinowt white boy meets black girl "but family problems intervene." Besides the friction across race, "there is a further division: gender." "The fathers of each family are the source of most friction, while the mothers tend to be more conciliatory and eventually prevail" (all references from the now-defunct "Perfect Strangers" home page on the World Wide Web).

2. Virtual Valley
Between 1995 and 1997, GRUNT conducted two projects, each with an on-line (or "virtual") component, based on the Valley: Virtual Valley I and II. They addressed the theme of young people who have strong affinities with the Valley and whose identities are bound up with the Valley, being pushed out of the process of its redefinition and re-"development" (as described above).

Virtual Valley I ran in 1995. It aimed to produce "an alternative user's guide" to the Valley that would provide different readings and writings of the Valley from those in official municipal promotions and tourist brochures, particularly the sepia-inked "historical walk" guides that listed a range of "must-see" sites and landmarks connected with the colonization of the Valley area by Europeans in the 1800s.

As an oppositional cultural response, Virtual Valley I presented work by nine young people who used the Valley on a daily basis for work and recreational purposes. These youth "held strong opinions about the Valley's role" in the life of Brisbane, then being promoted by the Queensland state government as Australia's most livable city. Participants' work was presented in two formats: a Web site and a booklet to help guide visitors "through a number of interesting sites using maps and postcard images" (which could be pulled out and used as real postcards) based on these young people's identities, values, worldviews, experiences, and ways of locating themselves personally and collectively in time and space within the Valley. The focus was on encouraging young people "to map the Valley area in ways that [were] culturally relevant to themselves and their peers." Places of interest presented in the Virtual Valley Web site included the location of a large clock (used by youth who do not have or wear watches), and favorite places for dancing, eating, getting coffee, finding bargains, and meeting friends. These were incorporated into Web pages built around an on-line street map that contrasted graphically with tourist maps, such as an official "heritage trail" that mapped points of interest from the standpoint of colonialist history. The hard-copy booklet provided a picture postcard collage of images—including some from the Web site—that ranged from snapshots of a gutter and a tidy line of garbage bins to a crowded Saturday market scene in the Mall.

Virtual Valley II included students from an Aboriginal (Murri) and Torres Strait Islander independent community school, which aimed at providing a culturally appropriate pedagogical balance between Aboriginal funds of knowledge and culture and those of mainstream white Australians. Students spent half a day each week at GRUNT exploring aspects of identity using conventional artistic means of painting, drawing, and collage as well as learning operational aspects of Web page construction—including basic HTML and Web page design principles, using digital cameras, manipulating digital images and anchoring them to Web pages, and using flatbed scanners.

Students gathered material for their Web pages on walks through the Valley using digital and disposable cameras, sketchbooks and notepads. They created large annotated collages of aspects of the Valley that were significant to them, using photocopies of digital and camera images they had taken of themselves, their friends, family members, and the Valley area, plus drawings and found objects (for example, food labels, ticket stubs, bingo cards, etc.). These were edited down to key images and chunks of text and reorganized as flow charts to guide design and construction of Web pages.

The pages yielded a series of readings and writings about the cultural phenomena of the Valley, combining photographic images of the students with captured features of the Valley that serve as icons or tropes for its multicultural life. One showed a Murri student sitting in the lap of a large Chinese doll statue in Chinatown while others captured the students against pagodas and symbolic gates. Such images (re)present the enacted identity of these Aboriginal young people "rubbing up against" key elements of Asian ethnic identities. Further images capture elements more directly involved in their own cultural identities, such as photographs of Aboriginal mosaic designs set in the sidewalks, and others bring kinship together with vital aspects of popular youth culture and taste, such as the photograph of a Murri student drinking a McDonald's milkshake purchased by an Aunty he met on his "field trip." Additional images of popular culture abound: students lined up at a McDonald's counter and photographs taken while playing video games at Time Zone and Universal Fun City.

3. Digitarts

Digitarts (<http://digitarts.va.com.au>) is an on-line multimedia project space constructed by young women for young women that explores alternative perspectives on style, food, everyday life and commodities and expresses different conceptions and constructions of female identity through poems, narratives, journal pages, "how-to-do" texts, and digital images. The project is "dedicated to providing young women who are emerging artists and/or cultural workers with access to the knowledge and equipment necessary for the development of their arts and cultural practices in the area of new technologies" (see Welcome page). It aims to challenge "the 'boys toys' stigma often associated with electronic equipment" and to "provide young women with access to information technology in a non-threatening 'girls own' space, to encourage involvement in technology based artforms." Digitarts provides a venue for emerging multimedia artists to showcase their work, and seeks to attract young women to the field by providing six to eight-week "Web development" courses for beginners. Other training provisions have included a twelve-week advanced Web-development course, a twelve-week digital animation course, and the collaborative production of four issues of GRRROWL (an electronic zine, or e-zine: <http://digitarts.va.com.au/grrrowl/>), using "only two machines [computers] augmented by a scanner [and] a printer."

The Digitarts project is currently managed by a part-time coordinator with a background in visual arts, theater, community and youth arts, and Web-based cultural work. Originally conceived and developed in the spaces of GRUNT, Digitarts is now supported by several government and self-funded youth-based or arts-oriented organizations. Individual projects are mainly funded through successful applications for money from government agencies.

The Web site documents "sub-projects" enacted since 1995. These include Girls in Space (<http://digitarts.va.com.au/gis/>). This project was prompted by the low visibility of young women in public spaces and the lack of research in Australia about women's recreational and public space needs. It gathered information from young women who made use of public spaces and those who didn't and made this information available to public policy makers. The information was also used to generate models of service/activity delivery designed to increase young women's participation in a range of public sites (for example, recreation and public parks, sporting venues) and to promote collaboration between local government and community organizations. Spin-offs include an on-line gallery of poster art inspired in part by some Girls in Space participants' reflections on women and public spaces (see: <http://digitarts.va.com.au /masses/gallery.html>) and an on-line "pajama party" (found at <http:// digitarts.va.com.au/grrrowl3.5/front.html>) that explores real and virtual spaces in participants' lives.

The e-zine GRRROWL (<http://digitarts.va.com.au/grrrowl/>) is an ongoing, collaborative publishing endeavor. One of its early issues focused on grrrls and machines. Each contributor constructed a page that is either a personal introduction—much like a conversation—or contains poems or anecdotes about women and technology. Hotlinks to similar Web sites on the Internet also define each writer's self, and her self as connected with other selves. Other issues of GRRROWL provide alternative readings of fashion trends and body image, with contributors/coeditors showcasing their most favorite item of fashion wear (for example, a reconstructed bicycle helmet made to look like something a Viking would have worn, a collection of handbags garnered from local second hand shops), or "surveying" what people are wearing on their feet in the Valley this spring (everything from gold thread-embroidered Doc Martens to nothing), or presenting a "fashion diary" along the lines of "one day in the life of . . ." Still other issues focus on action, showcase virtual reality (VRML) programming constructions, and the like.

GRRROWL #4 (<http://digitarts.va.com.au/grrrowl4/>) investigates its title theme, "Simply Lifeless," by "documenting on-line, the everyday lives of young women in Darwin and Brisbane." Its thesis is: "Our culture informs our everyday activity. Our everyday activity informs our culture." The issue celebrates the "everyperson" (cf. Duncombe 1997), with eight young women, ranging in age from 12 years to 25 years, who broadcast by Web pages snapshots of their lives—including digital videos of key elements (composing music on a much-loved guitar, a daughter feeding a pet chicken, etc.), or hypertext journals that span a day or a week of her life and that also include personal digital images (family album snaps, etc.), hand-drawn graphics, digital artwork, and so on (see, especially, twelve-year-old Gabriell's page: <http://digitarts.va.com.au/grrrowl4/ gabriell/typicalday.html>). By documenting the "banal" and "everyday," this issue of GRRROWL aims at "increasing the range of criteria by which our cultures are measured and defined" (<http://digitarts.va.com.au/ grrrowl4/>).

The Digitarts projects embody what we have identified as three-dimensional literacy. Each Digitart project engages its participants in developing a range of "operational" technology and literacy skills needed to produce effective Web pages (for example, becoming fluent in Web page design skills, HTML and VRML, scanning images, hyperlinking files, digital photography and image manipulation, embedding digital video clips in Web pages). On the "cultural" dimension, items in the Digitarts portfolio are steeped in cultural analyses of everyday life as well as in processes that properly blur the relationship between effective Web page construction in cyberspace and meaningful social practices in "meat space." This includes broadcast publishing of on-line magazine–type commentaries, the use of the Internet to establish and nurture interactive networks of relations between like-minded people, and the exploration and presentation of cultural membership and self-identity through writing, images, and hyperlinks. The critical dimension of Digitarts' work resides in its keen-edged critique of "mainstream" Australian society. For instance, the editorial in the third issue of GRRROWL explains how to override/subvert the default settings on readers' Internet browser software and encourages young women to override/subvert other socially constructed "default settings" that may be operating in their lives. It challenges social scripts that allocate various speaking and acting roles for young women that cast them as passive social objects or as victims (for example, "This is not about framing women as victims—mass media vehicles already do a pretty good job of that" Girls in Space), and that write certain types of girls (or grrrls) out of the picture altogether (cf. Duncombe 1997, 65–70). Digitarts offers a very real alternative to the commodification of youth culture—that is, youth as a market category—by making space for young women to become *producers*, and not merely consumers, of culture in the way it privileges the personal over the commercial (cf. Doneman 1997, 139; Duncombe 1997, 68, 70).

Features and Factors

It is not our purpose here to force contrasts or dichotomies, frame "good practice" versus "bad practice" dualisms, or to extol nonformality per se and denigrate school. Rather, it is to begin thinking about ranges of possibilities, relationships between contextual features and the forms social practices take, and about possible options for doing "technologically mediated life" under foreseeable conditions. Obviously, projects and outfits such as GRUNT are not subject to the same operating assumptions and conditions as schools—although they *do* have to meet project goals and conditions, establish accountability and viability of practice to funders, create and sustain clienteles, ensure the safety and welfare of employees and learners, and so on. They by no means have a free hand, and sheer economic survival is usually tenuous.

> This kind of work doesn't get done often because it eats you. To imagine and then operationalize "alternatives" is by its nature an activity which will not usually generate much of an income or even much in the way of peer support (Doneman 1997, 138).

Whatever "spaces" for alternatives such projects open are opened at the price of risk: Choices are made and consequences lived with (in some cases, living on the breadline and remortgaging homes to continue financing the dream).

Our point here is to get a clearer sense of possible choices/options and their attendant risks and constraints. If schools are profoundly *modernist* institutions (Lankshear, Peters, and Knobel 1996) that have to negotiate various postmodern conditions, to what extent might outfits like GRUNT represent emerging *postmodern-like* "institutions" that have to make their way amidst still largely modernist modes of thinking and operating? To what extent do our school examples and GRUNT embody different options for negotiating education under changing conditions of technology and sensibility? What, if anything, can we learn by addressing them in proximity?

The nonformal, experimental, loose-coupled, community-based, "project-ive," "enactive" (Gee 1998), "subject-ive" nature of GRUNT is reflected in the ways the young people, project-brokers, and support persons constructed practices of technological literacy. Although this theme bears closer investigation than is possible here, we will suggest by way of a preliminary account that GRUNT's constructions of technological literacy are characterized by five important features.

First, there is a vital sense in which these literacies use new technologies within processes of reading and writing the world; in practices designed to access and represent everyday social structures and processes, and their experienced consequences, "in the raw." For example, the very act of having grade 5 and 6 Aboriginal students go out to photograph, draw, and otherwise "record" the Valley involved considerable existential risk and tension. "A lot of Aboriginal people are very careful about sending their kids to the Valley . . . Code for 'police harassment', basically." Yet, what was ultimately encoded as digital textual products encapsulated rich readings of "world," and of "identity" in relation to "world." For example:

> They [the schools] would send one Aboriginal assistant and one white teacher with the kids and we struggled, and we struggled, and we struggled and the kids would like disappear, they would go for this sort of shoot up the Valley, take photographs and they would come back one less and they wouldn't see the kid for the next three days at school because he would have found an "uncle" or "aunty" [extended family member] on his journey. (Interview transcript—GRUNT personnel)

> Every one of those Murri school kids did take a photograph of the Police Beat [the policing base in the Valley] or their cars. . . . (Interview transcript—GRUNT personnel)

> "When I walk past in the morning the ice-cream lady is just sitting there.
> In the middle of the day she yawns.
> In the afternoon she eats the ice-cream she's supposed to sell.
> In the evenings she goes home with no profit."
> (Text by eleven-year-old George, from his Web page)

Second, this reading and writing of the world was constructed as an *open* and *interactive* literacy, where participants sought and gained access to others' subjectivities and spaces of representation. In particular, adult participants were open to experiencing new windows on shared space. One noticed a clock figuring prominently in young people's virtual mapping of the Valley. He checked out the railway station mall and found what he had never seen before: "this enormous clock right in the fucking middle of it" (interview transcript). This virtual codification of the environment provided a basis for re-experiencing and problematizing that space.

> For example, I walk around with a watch on my wrist most days and consequently I'm not aware of public clock faces around the place. Now, if you're a kid and you don't wear a watch you become quite aware as you move through the city of where the public clock faces are, and clock faces around the city become part of

your navigation of the city in a way that is not part of mine. [Finding the clock there] actually changes my perception of the space I'm moving through. . . . [It's] actually quite profound because it gives you a window on the environment you inhabit that otherwise you would not have had, and that window has opened for you by young people because of the restraints that they live with . . . and if you're concerned with kids that are coming from socially, economically disadvantaged backgrounds then that's a wave crisis, you know, for comfortable middle-class intellectuals to understand bits of the world that normally we screen from ourselves (interview transcript,—GRUNT personnel)

The literacies were interactive in a more material sense as well. The pedagogy involved considerable collaboration in the process of actually producing the digital artifacts. For instance, university students enrolled in cultural studies, leisure studies, drama, computing studies, and so on, played unpaid pedagogical assistance roles in GRUNT's production of "curriculum and pedagogy on the fly." Some taught HTML and other aspects of Web page production when learners were ready to put their representations on the Web. Others helped construct role-plays in which Murri students negotiated meaning and relationship in the Valley. Others (such as members of the local Murri community) collaborated by accompanying the young people on their journeys into the Valley.

Each of these forms of collaboration was present in Justin's virtual tour of the Valley. His text, which appeared in large and brightly colored fonts on his Web page, read as follows:

People allsorts
Ice-cream parlour allkinds
Timezone fun
Dragons
Temples colourful
China Town lots of people
susan pretended to be opal
winney [Oprah Winfrey] and we was the audience

one group was police the others
was murries and shop owners after all
that we did some drawings

then we had lunch I had two banans
and three sandwhiches

I also had a drink of coke cola
there was plenty for us to have
seconds. My friend Louis ate lots of
cakes and so he had an belly

ache. After that we went for a walk
in the valley we saw dead ducks
with their heads still attached.[7]

This text was augmented by two photographic images captured and encoded digitally. The first image captured the cultural diversity of the Valley's people. The second inscribed fun experiences at Time Zone, showing a video game in action. At lines 7–11, the text referred to a role-play which dealt with the students' frustration and anger on their excursions at being watched by shopkeepers "as though we were going to steal something every time we walked into a shop" (interview transcript).

The third key feature of technological literacy practices constructed by participants at GRUNT is their nature and role as elements of "enactive projects"; their "project-ive" nature (Gee 1998). They formed integral parts of planned projects that aimed to promote values, ways of being, an ethos, etc., and to "recruit" others to them by *enacting* them within public spaces (real and virtual). Hence, the Perfect Strangers Web site was the textual vehicle and marker for networking and advocacy of a certain kind of youth arts practice, as well as being an information display of work. "It sought to mix and match work from three distant locations in Australia, to highlight good cross-cultural and indigenous work for the purpose of encouraging the groups to look at each other's work, to encourage more of the same, and to coax support from funding bodies—at a time when there was very little ATSI and cross-cultural work in the youth arts/performance field" or, for that matter, on the Web (Michael Doneman, personal communication). The same, of course, is true for the ongoing Digitarts initiative, whose co-founder had earlier been involved in producing the Perfect Strangers site that featured Black Voices.

The fourth feature of GRUNT-style constructions of technological literacy is their strong and explicit "subject-ive" character and purpose. They explore, experiment with, express, and represent diverse subjectivities; problematize and celebrate cultural diversity; explore issues of identity and the relationships between who one is and the discursive spaces, practices, and social relations one inhabits, creates, and endures; and enact counternarratives—"little stories" that resist being incorporated and being made commensurable with some more powerful "language game" or representation. For example:

I guess what we're trying to say, in a kind of roundabout way is that we're a colourful bunch, not
easily pigeonholed . . . we are varied in age, in lifestyle, in attitude, in personality and can think of

only three things that unite us
1 a need to know and understand what "the digital" can do for us
2 a desire to have our views and creativity represented
3 a love of food—any variety
oh yeah, sorry four things . . .
4 we're all chicks (<http://digitarts.va.com.au/frames.html>).

The construction of technology-mediated literacy practices for exploring, addressing, communicating, and negotiating subjectivity and identity has been an abiding feature of work at GRUNT and allied groups, with early origins in a CONTACT project called The Third Place. This project set out to create a "third place," where "people from [different] cultural groups can meet, without surrendering their own cultural values but also without compromising these values, mixing them down, integrating them with others. It is not a bland, neutral space, but a dynamic one conditioned by principles of equity, tolerance and participation" (From The Third Place formerly on the Perfect Strangers Web site. See note 7).

Finally, constructions of technological literacy within GRUNT projects are "multi-mediated." Electronic technologies are fused with other technologies—including the body as performance tool—to encode and decode meaning. In part, this multi-mediating quality has to do with work at GRUNT continually being about negotiating the interface of physical ("meat") space and cyber ("virtual") space. All GRUNT projects were informed by a strong awareness that successfully negotiating the present and the future would involve being at home in meatspace as well as cyberspace, of moving across the borders, between the spaces, possessing the requisite understandings and skills. Moreover, as we discussed with respect to the work of Digitarts, literacy was constructed as multidimensional: operational, cultural, *and* critical. This was a function of the enactive and subject-ive nature of the practices in which the textual work was embedded.

GRUNT had its own "grammar," in terms of which we can understand much about how technological literacy was constructed in its projects. Learning was avowedly "noncurricular" in the *school* sense. Curriculum and pedagogy were developed "on the fly" with whatever resources were available in relation to broad project goals. Adults did not *direct* learning but, rather, aimed to "broker" learning opportunities.

In the development of *curriculum on the fly*, perhaps a first step for youthwork leaders is to "fence the paddock", to define ground rules, define what a project is *not*, then step back. (Doneman 1997, 140)

The absence of timetabling and programming offered flexibility and informality that encourage skill sharing and collaboration across a wide resource range. The ready availability of technologically adept persons meant there was no problem of having to master new technologies in the process of using them in learning activities. Moreover, because GRUNT had personnel available (including a good proportion of "insiders") who were familiar with uses of new technologies in "mature" versions of social practice, projects were designed from the outset in ways that would accommodate applications of an entire range of technologies—including new information and communications technologies—in organic ways. Hence, there was never any question of having to "look for ways" to "fit new technologies in."

Consequently, participants came to learning situations where what was on offer were predominantly "authentic" technologically mediated practices, where they could be apprenticed to "mature" versions of practice and experience "guided participation" (Rogoff 1990, 1995), yet where they could "push" maximally in directions of personal interest in the presence of readily available skill assistance. In some important ways, GRUNT functioned in the manner of Ivan Illich's "convivial institutions" (Illich 1971), although Illich might well reject the hi-tech component. It was a noncompulsory, non-teacher-directed, non-curricular resource, with minimal social distance across the age range of those involved. Since attendance was voluntary and people were "teaching" what they knew from a basis of existential commitment to it, networks of collaboration and expert-rich communities of practice could evolve, transform, and change direction as participants chose.

> The GRUNT model proposes the conscious overlapping of "class rooms" towards a dynamic and creative *sloppage* of ideas, impulses, attitudes and values. An underlying social-democratic politics determines a basic moral-ethical system and curriculum is composed on the fly around a set of access strategies and protocols. Delivery systems are informal and culturally appropriate (Doneman 1997, 145).

Activity at GRUNT was steeped in a paradigm of value that Barlow identifies with information/cyberspace, and which natives grasp. Barlow distinguishes between paradigms of value operating in "physical" space and cyberspace, respectively. In physical space, says Barlow, controlled economics increases value by regulating scarcity. To take the case of diamonds, the value of diamonds is not a function of their degree of rarity or actual *scarceness* but, rather, of the fact that a single corporation *owns* most of them and hence can regulate or control scarcity. In this paradigm, scarcity has value. We might note here how schools have traditionally operated to regulate scarcity of credentialed achievement, including literacies. This has maintained scarce "supply" and, to that extent, ensured high value for well-credentialed achievements.

In the economy of cyberspace, however, the opposite holds true. Barlow argues that with information it is familiarity, not scarcity, that has value. With information

> it's dispersion that has the value, and it's not a commodity, it's a relationship and as in any relationship, the more that's going back and forth the higher the value of the relationship. People don't get this if they're coming from the industrial-era model (Barlow in Tunbridge, 1995).

The point here is that if we approach the new space in "old" ways we risk missing out on options that are there to be had—which, in some instances, might mean missing out or losing altogether in the long run on the experience of alternative kinds of relations and economies. A "gift" economy was in strong evidence at GRUNT, based on a pervasive awareness that maximum "dispersion" was in everyone's interests. Experts gave freely of their knowledge, over long hours, and often without any payment beyond the compensations of building networks and practices grounded in shared pleasures, values, and reciprocity.

In this model, the network/project/idea runs as long (or as short) as energy, funding support, and goodwill last. It does not *endure* in the manner of a long-distance institution, like school. The time of GRUNT as a tangible project had passed by mid-1998. The model, however, continues as projects coordinated by MWK (see <http://mwk.thehub.com.au>), as do other specific projects and networks spawned during the time of GRUNT such as Digitarts.

Postmodern Tendencies

Lyotard's account of the postmodern condition pinpoints the deeply contradictory nature of our times. The very incredulity toward metanarratives that tends toward multiplicity and plurality meets with a crisis of legitimation that is momentarily "resolved" in the interests of capital by a regime of performativity which dictates: be operational (that is, commensurate) or disappear. All language games are to be subsumed under the logic of performance in conformity to its master principle of efficiency, of optimizing a system's overall performance. This is to reduce social practice to purely technological considerations: a logic that delivers up the shallow ubiquitous notion of information, reduces practice to technique, and competence to the most arid mechanical indicators. Lyotard's "report on knowledge" houses a trenchant critique of capitalism and its penetration of language and the way thought is managed, packaged, and commodified in the new postmodern technologies, insofar as they express the most recent application of capitalist rules to language.

At the same time, Lyotard wants to rethink politics and resistance in "minoritarian" terms, and to think justice in relation to conflict and difference that admit of no resolution. For Lyotard, "our role of thinkers" in the situation of postmodernity "is to deepen what language there is, to critique the shallow notion of information, to reveal an irremediable opacity within language itself" (van Reijen and Veerman 1988, 302).

The cases presented in this chapter provide glimpses of these contending tendencies—albeit at the risk of intimating dichotomized "ideal" models." This has not been our intention, although we *have* aimed to provide clear and concrete examples of how these tendencies play out in everyday routines. What technological literacies we develop and sustain; what subjectivities we admit and constrain; what possibilities for social practice and social identities we envisage, create and nourish; how, in short, we enact the right to education in the decades ahead; all these things, we believe, will have a lot to do with how we respond to precisely the kinds of "tendencies" portrayed here.

Curriculum in the postmodern condition is, to say the least, deeply contradictory. How we understand and respond to these contradictions is, however, as much now as it ever was, a matter for us to decide.[8]

Notes

1   Chris Bigum (personal communication) refers to the "sabre tooth curriculum" character of much computer-mediated classroom work (cf. Peddiwall 1939). Teachers learn a specific software application which then becomes the "model" for computer-based activity, and the original purpose of the software and/or the activity objectives may become lost in the process.

2   It is important to note here the considerable informal evidence of teachers doing their Internet learning and preparation at home, after hours, on weekends.

3   Chris Bigum wryly observes that the brand-specific character of much software-mediated learning—such as HyperCard—is a form of developing brand loyalty, "for which schools are innocent enough to pay when they really ought to be charging" (personal communication).

4   Much of this involves high intensity consumption—for example, role-play games that require computer software and large amounts of time on-line.

5   We are well aware of how this distinction has been used by racist and similar interests to define natives or immigrants as irreconcilably inferior to immigrants or natives respectively. No such implications are imputed here. As employed here they are adopted as useful markers for a powerful heuristic distinction which we believe is useful for underlining a critical blind spot in many educational accounts of literacy and technology. If readers wish, they may use the language of "insiders" for "natives", and "newcomers" for "immigrants" (see Lankshear and Bigum forthcoming).

6   This is, of course, an evolving historical process. New technologies slowly "bed down" in social practices and, eventually, become old. The automobile moved from being seen as a "horseless carriage" to being seen in the ways we perceive it today (cf. Marvin 1988 for an account of communications technologies). Indeed, many of the odd and seemingly counterproductive practices currently evident in classrooms—such as reducing a powerful technology to a "sophisticated pencil," valuing desktop applications as a means for fostering "pride in their work," etc.—are best seen as an inescapable aspect of this process. Teachers, like all "users" of new technologies, have to negotiate initial conceptions and uses that are often naive when seen from the standpoint of more established users.

7   As with the Black Voices Web material referred to previously, Justin's work no longer appears on the Web. For further information, contact MWK personnel at: <mwk@mwk.thehub.com.au> or via the web site at <http://mwk.thehub.com.au>.

8   This chapter owes much to the research and development activities of our colleagues Chris Bigum, Michael Doneman, Ludmila Doneman, Cal Durrant, Eileen Honan, Michele Knobel, and Joy Murray.

Bibliography

ABS (Australian Bureau of Statistics). 1997a. *Aspects of Literacy: Profiles and Perceptions—Australia 1996.* Canberra: Australian Government Publishing Service.

————. 1997b. *Aspects of Literacy: Assessed Skill Levels—Australia 1996.* Canberra: Australian Government Publishing Service.

Angel Maya, A. 1995. *Desarrollo Sostenible: Aproximaciones Conceptuales.* Quito: Fundación Natura-UICN.

Arditi, B. 1989. *El Deseo de la Libertad y la Cuestión del Otro. Ensayos Acerca de la Posmodernidad, el Poder y la Sociedad.* Asunción: CDE-RP Ediciones/Criterio.

————. 1992. "La totalidad como archipiélago. El diagrama de los puntos nodales." In *Conceptos. Ensayos sobre Teoría Política, Democracia y Filosofía,* ed. B. Arditi. Asunción CDE-RP Ediciones.

————. 1993a. "Drifting. El destino del nómada." Department of Government, University of Essex (mimeo).

————. 1993b. "Virtual Spaces: The Reinscription of the Public-Private Divide." Department of Government, University of Essex (mimeo).

————. 1996. "Notas personales del seminario 'Espacio público y universidad'. " México City: Centro de Estudios sobre la Universidad de la Universidad Nacional Autónoma de México, 7 al 9 de agosto.

Aronowitz, S. and H. Giroux. 1993. *Education Still under Siege.* Westport, Conn.: Bergin & Garvey.

Atran, Scott. 1990. *Cognitive Foundations of Natural History: Towards an Anthropology of Science*. Cambridge, England: Cambridge University Press.

Bachelard, Gaston. 1984. *The New Scientific Spirit*. Translated by A. Goldhammer. Boston: Beacon Press.

Baker, Alan. 1990. *New Zealand Whales and Dolphins*. Wellington, Biological Society, Victoria University.

Ball, S. J., comp. 1994. *Foucault y la Educación. Disciplinas y Saber*. 2nd ed. Madrid: Morata-Paideia. (Coleccion: Pedagogía. Educación Crítica).

Ballantyne, Roy and David Uzzell. 1993. Environmental Mediation and Hot Interpretation: A Case Study of District Six, Cape Town. *The Journal of Environmental Education* 24, no. 3: 4–8.

Barker, Alan. 1993. "The New Zealand Qualifications Framework: Practical Issues in Its Implementation." Paper presented at the conference "Successfully Managing Quality, Performance and Efficiency in Tertiary Education." 13–14 April, at NZQA House, Wellington.

Barnes, T. 1996. *Logics of Dislocation: Models, Metaphors and Meanings of Economic Space*. New York: Guilford Press.

Barry, A., T. Osborne, and N. Rose, eds. 1996. *Foucault and Political Reason: Liberalism, Neoliberalism and Rationalities of Government*. London: UCL Press.

Baudrillard, J. 1983. *El Extasis de la Comunicación en La Posmodernidad*. Barcelona: Editorial Kairós.

Beare, H. and W. H. Boyd. 1993. "Introduction." In *Restructuring Schools: An International Perspective on the Movement to Transform the Control and Performance of Schools*, ed. H. Beare and W. H. Boyd. London: Falmer Press.

Becker, G. 1964. *Human Capital; A Theoretical and Empirical Analysis, with Special Reference to Education*. New York: National Bureau of Economic Research.

Bell, Daniel. 1974. *The Coming of the Postindustrial Society: A Venture in Social Forecasting*. New York: Basic Books.

Bengoa, José. 1988. La educación para los moviemientos sociales. In *Educación Popular en América Latina*, ed. A. Puiggrós. Holanda: CESO.

Berzin, A. 1972. *The Sperm Whale*. Translated by E. Hoz and Z. Blake. Jerusalem: Israel Program for Scientific Translations.

Bifani, P. 1993. "Desarrollo sostenible, población y pobreza: algunas reflexiones conceptuales en educación ambiental y universidad." In proceedings of the *Congreso Iberoamericano de Educación ambiental. Una estrategia al porvenir*. México City: Universidad de Guadalajara.

Bigum, C. 1997. "Teachers and Computers: In Control or Being Controlled?" *Australian Journal of Education* 41, no. 3: 247–61.

Bigum, C. and B. Green. 1992. "Technologizing Literacy: The Dark Side of the Dream." *Discourse: The Australian Journal of Educational Studies* 12, no. 2: 4–28.

———. 1993. "Governing Chaos: Postmodern Science, Information Technology and Educational Administration." *Educational Philosophy and Theory* 25, no. 2: 79–103.

Birch, Charles. 1988. "Eight Fallacies of the Modern World and Five Axioms for a Postmodern Worldview." *Perspectives in Biology and Medicine* 32, no. 1: 12–30.

Bohm, David. 1980. *Wholeness and the Implicate Order*. London: Routledge and Kegan Paul.

———. 1985. *Unfolding Meaning: A Weekend Dialogue with David Bohm*, ed. D. Factor. Mickleton, England: Foundation House.

Bonfil Batalla, G. 1986. "La querella por la cultura." *Nexos* (Abril): 7–13.

Boston, Jonathan. 1991. "The Theoretical Underpinnings of Public Sector Restructuring in New Zealand. In *Reshaping the State*, ed. J. Boston. Auckland: Oxford University Press.

Brandon, S. 1998. "Workers as Thinkers in New Times: Critical Literacy Development in the Restructured Workplace." MEd Diss. Brisbane: QUT, Faculty of Education.

Buchanan, J. 1991. *Constitutional Economics*. Cambridge, Mass.: Blackwell.

Buchanan, J. and G. Tullock. 1962. *The Calculus of Consent: Logical Foundations of Constitutional Democracy*. Ann Arbor: University of Michigan Press.

Buenfil Burgos, R. N. 1995. "Horizonte postmoderno y configuración social." In *Posmodernidad y educación*, ed. A. de Alba. México City: Porrúa/CESU-UNAM.

Burchell, Graham. 1993. "Liberal Government and Techniques of Self." *Economy and Society* 22, no. 3: 267–82.

————. 1996. "Liberal Government and Techniques of the Self." In *Foucault and Political Reason*, ed. A. Barry, T. Osborne, and N. Rose. London: UCL Press.

————. 1997. "Liberalism and Government: Political Philosophy and the Liberal Art of Rule." In *Foucault: The Legacy*, ed. Clare O'Farrell. Brisbane: Queensland University of Technology.

Calderón, C. 1994. "Postmodern Horizon." Seminar at the Faculty of Philosophy and Letters. México City: National Autonomous University of México.

Campos, J. 1995. *Qué Hacemos con los Pobres? La Reiterada Querella por la Nación*. México City: Aguilar.

Canguilhem, Georges. [1977] 1988. *Ideology and Rationality in the History of the Life Sciences*. Translated by A. Goldhammer. Cambridge, Mass.: MIT Press.

Cardona, Patricia. 1996. "La lista negra?" *Unomásuno*. Suplemento Páginauno. Ecología. México. No. 784, domingo 13 de octubre. p. 14.

Caride, J. A., ed. 1991. *Educación Ambiental: Realidades y Perspectivas*. Santiago de Compostela: Tórculo.

Carnoy, M. 1995. "Structural Adjustment and the Changing Face of Education." *International Labour Review* 134, no. 3: 653–673.

Carrasco, L. and R. Hernández Puente. 1995. "Rumbo a la cumbre mundial de desarrollo social." *La Jornada* (Economic report). Monday, 20 February, México City ed., 57.

Cavailles, Jean. [1943] 1987. *Sur la Logique et la Theorie de la Science*. 4th. ed. Paris: Vrin.

CDMAALC (Comisión de Desarrollo y Medio Ambiente de América Latina y el Caribe). 1991. *Nuestra Propia Agenda sobre Desarrollo y Medio Ambiente*. México City: Banco Interamericano de Desarrollo,

Programa de las Naciones Unidas para el Desarrollo, Fondo de Cultura Económica.

Chalmers, Alan. 1990. *Science and Its Fabrication.* Milton Keynes, England: Open University Press.

Cheever, Henry. 1850. *The Whaleman's Adventures in the Southern Ocean.* Edited by W. Scoresby. London: Low.

Cherfas, Jeremy. 1989. *The Hunting of the Whale: A Tragedy that Must End.* Harmondsworth: Penguin.

Cherryholmes, Cleo. 1988. *Power and Criticism: Poststructuralist Investigations in Education.* New York and London: Teachers College Press.

Colby, M. E. 1990. *Environmental Management in Development: The Evolution of Paradigms.* Washington, D.C.: The World Bank (World Bank discussion papers no. 80).

Cooper, D. E. and J. A. Palmer, eds. 1995. *Just Environments: Intergenerational, International, and Interspecies Issues.* London: Routledge.

Cowan, J. 1998. "Destino Colombia: A Scenario Planning Process for the New Millennium." *Deeper News* 9, no. 1: 7–31.

Critchley, S. 1997. "What Is Continental Philosophy?" *International Journal of Philosophical Studies* 5, no. 3: 347–65.

Crocombe, G., M. Enright, and M. Porter. 1991. *Upgrading New Zealand's Competitive Advantage.* Auckland: Oxford University Press.

Dale, R. 1991. "International Comparisons or a 'Societal Approach' as Guidelines for New Zealand?" Paper presented to New Zealand Planning Council Seminar on Education Models from Overseas, April, Wellington.

Daniels, Peter. 1992. "Barriers to Sustainable Development in Natural Resource-Based Economies: Australia as a Case Study." *Society and Natural Resources* 5, no. 3: 247–62.

de Alba, A. 1991. *Curriculum: crisis, mito y perspectivas.* México City: CESU-UNAM.

————. 1993. "El curriculum universitario ante los retos del Siglo XXI: La paradoja entre posmodernismo, ausencia de utopía y determinación currricular." In *El curriculum universitario de cara al nuevo milenio,* ed. A. de Alba. México City: CESU-UNAM, 1993.

————. 1995a. *Expectativas Docentes ante la Problemática y los Desafíos del Curriculum Universitario en México.* Madrid: UNED.

————. 1995b. "Posmodernidad y educación. Implicaciones epistémicas y conceptuales en los discursos educativos." In *Posmodernidad y Educación,* ed. A. de Alba. México City: Porrúa/CESU-UNAM.

————. 1996. "Crisis y curriculum universitario: Horizontes postmodernos y utópicos." Paper presented at the International Congress of Education "Education, Crises and Utopias." 24–26 July, Buenos Aires, Argentina.

Dean, M. 1991 *The Constitution of Poverty: Toward a Genealogy of Liberal Governance.* London: Routledge.

DEET (Department of Education, Employment and Training, Australia). 1991a. *Australia's Language: The Policy Paper.* Canberra: Australian Government Publishing Service.

————. 1991b. *Australia's Language: Companion Volume to the Policy Paper.* Canberra: Australian Government Publishing Service.

DEETYA (Department of Employment, Education, Training and Youth Affairs, Australia). 1998. *Literacy for All: The Challenge for Australian Schools.* Canberra: Australian Government Publishing Service.

Deleuze, G. 1995. "Postscript on Control Societies." *Negotiations 1972–1990.* Translated by M. Joughin. New York: Columbia University Press.

Delgado-Gaitan, C. 1990. *Literacy for Empowerment.* London: Falmer Press.

Delors, J., ed. 1996. *Learning: The Treasure Within. Report to UNESCO of the International Commision on Education for the Twenty-first Century.* Paris: UNESCO.

Department of Social Welfare, New Zealand. 1996. *Strategic Directions: Post-Election Briefing Paper*. Wellington: Corporate Communications Unit.

DEQ (Department of Education, Queensland). 1995a. *The Year 2 Diagnostic Net*. Brisbane: Department of Education, Queensland.

————. 1995b. *English in Years 1 to 10 Queensland Syllabus Materials: English Syllabus for Years 1 to 10*. Brisbane: Department of Education, Queensland.

Doll, William. 1989. "Foundations for a Post-Modern Curriculum." *Journal of Curriculum Studies* 21, no. 3: 245–53.

————. 1993. *A Post-Modern Perspective on Curriculum*. New York: Teachers College Press.

Doneman, M. 1997. "Multimediating." In C. Lankshear, C. Bigum, C. Durrant, B. Green, E. Honan, J. Murray, W. Morgan, I. Snyder, and M. Wild. *Digital Rhetorics: Literacies and Technologies in Education—Current Practices and Future Directions*. Canberra: DEETYA.

Donzelot, J. 1979. *The Policing of Families*. Translated by R. Hurley, foreword by G. Deleuze. New York: Pantheon Books.

Driver, F. 1992. "Geography's Empire: Histories of Geographical Knowledge." *Environment and Planning: Society and Space* 10: 23–40.

Drucker, P. 1959. *Landmarks of Tomorrow*. New York: Harper.

————. 1993. *Post-Capitalist Society*. New York: Harper.

Duncombe, S. 1997. *Notes from Underground: Zines and the Politics of Alternative Culture*. London: Verso.

Education Queensland. 1997. *Schooling 2001: School Kit*. Brisbane: Education Queensland.

Eisenstadt, S. 1989. "Introduction: Culture and Social Structure in Recent Sociological Analysis." In *Social Structure and Culture*, ed. H. Haferkamp. Berlin and New York: de Gruyter.

Ermarth, E. D. 1998. "Postmodernism." In *Routledge Encyclopedia of Philosophy*, ed. E. Craig. London: Routledge.

Esteva, J. 1997. *Ambientalismo y Educación. Hacia una Educación Popular Ambiental en América Latina: Contribuciones Educativas para Sociedades Sostenables*. Pátzcuaro: Centro de Estudios Sociales y Ecológicos.

Esteva, J. and X. Reyes. 1997. *La Perspectiva Ambiental de la Educación Ambiental entre Personas Adultas: Contribuciones Educativas para Sociedades Sustentables*. Pátzcuaro: Centro de Estudios Sociales y Ecológicos.

Featherstone, Mike. 1989. "Toward a Sociology of Postmodern Culture." In *Social Structure and Culture*, ed. H. Haferkamp. Berlin and New York: de Gruyter.

Ferraris, M. 1988. "Problemas de los postmoderno." *Utopias* 2 (May–June): 58–64.

Ferré, Frederick. 1976. *Shaping the Future: Resources for a Postmodern World*. New York and San Francisco: Harper & Row.

Fortino, C. 1997. "Leaders in Environmental Education: The Cascade of Influence." *Environmental Education Research* 3, no. 2.

Foucault, Michel. 1980. *The History of Sexuality*, Vol. 1. New York: Vintage.

———. 1982. "Afterword: The Subject and Power." In *Michel Foucault: Beyond Structuralism and Hermeneutics*, ed. H. Dreyfus and P. Rabinow. Chicago: The Harvester Press Ltd.

———. 1991a. "Governmentality." In *The Foucault Effect: Studies in Governmentality*, ed. G. Burchell, C. Gordon, and P. Miller. Hemel Hempstead, England: Harvester Wheatsheaf.

———. 1991b. "Questions of Method." In *The Foucault Effect: Studies in Governmentality*, ed. G. Burchell, C. Gordon, and P. Miller. Hemel Hempstead, England: Harvester Wheatsheaf.

Frampton, K. 1987. "Towards a Critical Regionalism: Six Points for an Architecture of Resistance." In *Postmodern Culture*, ed. Hal Foster. London, Pluto Press.

Fraser, N. 1981. "Foucault on Modern Power: Empirical Insights and Normative Confusions." *Praxis International* 1: 272–87.

Friedman, Milton. 1962. *Capitalism and Freedom.* With the assistance of Rose D. Friedman. Chicago: University of Chicago Press.

García-Canclini, N. 1995. *Consumidores y Ciudadanos. Conflictos Multiculturales de la Globalización.* México City: Grijalbo.

Gee, J. P. 1996. *Social Linguistics and Literacies: Ideology in Discourses.* 2nd ed. London: Taylor and Francis.

————. 1998. "The New Literacy Studies and the 'Social Turn'." Madison: University of Wisconsin-Madison Department of Curriculum and Instruction (mimeo).

Gee, J. P., G. Hull, and C. Lankshear. 1996. *The New Work Order: Behind the Language of the New Capitalism.* Boulder, Colo.: Westview Press.

Gelernter, D. 1998. *Machine Beauty. Elegance and the Heart of Technology.* New York: Basic Books.

Giolitto, P. 1984. *Pedagogía del medio ambiente.* Barcelona: Herder.

Giolitto, P., ed. 1997. *Educación ambiental en la Unión Europea.* Luxemburg: CECA-CEEA.

Giroux, H. 1996. *Placeres Inquietantes. Aprendiendo de la Cultura Popular.* Barcelona: Paidós Ibérica.

Giroux, H., C. Lankshear, P. McLaren, and M. Peters. 1996. *Counternarratives: Cultural Studies and Critical Pedagogies in Postmodern Spaces.* London: Routledge.

Glasby, G. P. 1991. "A Review of the Concept of Sustainable Management as Applied to New Zealand." *Journal of the Royal Society of New Zealand* 21, no. 2: 61–81.

Gómez-Gutiérrez, J. M. and N. R. Ramos Álvarez. 1989. "Bases ecológicas de la educación ambiental." In *Educación Ambiental. Sujeto, Entorno y Sistema,* ed. N. Sosa. Salamanca: Amarú.

González-Gaudiano, E. 1993. *Hacia una Estrategia y Plan de Acción en Educación Ambiental.* México City: Instituto Nacional de Ecología/SEDSOL-UNESCO.

————. 1996. "From Apodictic to Paralogy. New Meanings of Environmentally Literate Citizenship: A View from México." *International Research in Geographical and Environmental Education* 5, no. 2: 140–43.

————. 1997a. *Educación Ambiental. Historia y Conceptos a Veinte Años de Tbilisi.* México City: SITESA.

————. 1997b. "En busca de la sustentabilidad de la educación ambiental." *Perspectivas Docentes* 21 (enero–abril): 3–14.

————. 1997c. "Glocalization and Sustainability." *Critical Forum* 5, nos. 1 and 2: 83–90.

————. 1998. *Centro y Periferia en la Educación Ambiental. Un Enfoque Antiesencialista.* México City: Mundi-Prensa.

González-Gaudiano, E. and Alicia de Alba. 1994. "Freire—Present and Future Possibilities." In *Politics of Liberation: Paths from Freire,* ed. P. McLaren and C. Lankshear. London: Routledge.

————. 1997. *Evaluación de Programas de Educación Ambiental. Experiencias en América Latina y el Caribe.* México City: CESU/ UNAM-Semarnap-UNESCO.

González-Muñoz, C. 1996. "Principales tendencias y modelos de la educación ambiental en el sistema escolar." *Revista Iberoamericana de Educación* 11 (mayo–agosto): 28–41.

Gordon, Colin. 1991. "Governmental Rationality: An Introduction." In *The Foucault Effect: Studies in Governmentality—With Two Lectures by and an Interview with Michel Foucault,* ed. G. Burchell, C. Gordon, and P. Miller. Hemel Hemstead, England: Harvester Wheatsheaf.

Gordon, C. 1996. "Foucault in Britain." In *Foucault and Political Reason,* ed. A. Barry, T. Osborne, and N. Rose. London: UCL Press.

Green, B. 1988. "Subject-Specific Literacy and School Learning: A Focus on Writing." *Australian Journal of Education* 32, no. 2: 156–79.

————. 1995. "Post-Curriculum Possibilities: English Teaching, Cultural Politics, and the Postmodern Turn." *Journal of Curriculum Studies* 27, no. 4: 391–409.

———. 1997a. "Literacy, Information and the Learning Society." Keynote address at the Joint Conference of the Australian Association for the Teaching of English, the Australian Literacy Educators' Association, and the Australian School Library Association. 8–11 July 1997, Darwin High School, Darwin, Australia.

———. 1997b. "Literacies and School Learning in New Times." Keynote address at the "Literacies in Practice: Progress and Possibilities" Conference. 1 May 1997, South Australian Department of Education and Children's Services and the Catholic Education Office, Adelaide, Australia.

Green, B. and Bigum, C. 1993. "Aliens in the Classroom." *Australian Journal of Education* 37, no. 2: 119–41.

Green, D. 1996. *From Welfare State to Civil Society: Towards Welfare that Works in New Zealand.* Wellington: NZ Business Roundtable.

Grene, Marjorie. 1985. "Perception, Interpretation and the Sciences: Toward a New Philosophy of Science." In *Evolution at the Crossroads: The New Biology and the New Philosophy of Science*, ed. D. J. Depew and B. H. Weber. Cambridge Mass.: MIT Press.

Griffin, David Ray. 1988a. "Introduction to SUNY Series in Constructive Postmodern Thought." In *The Reenchantment of Science: Postmodern Proposals*, ed. David Ray Griffin. Albany, N.Y.: State University of New York Press.

———. 1988b. "Preface." In *The Reenchantment of Science: Postmodern Proposals*, ed. David Ray Griffin. Albany, N.Y.: State University of New York Press.

———. 1988c. "Introduction: The Reenchantment of Science." In *The Reenchantment of Science: Postmodern Proposals*, ed. David Ray Griffin. Albany, N.Y.: State University of New York Press.

Guthrie, J. W. 1993. "School Reform and the 'New World Order'." In *Reforming Education*, ed. S. L. Jacobson and R. Berne. Thousand Oaks, Calif.: Corwin Press Inc.

Gutiérrez-Pérez, J. 1995. *La Educación Ambiental. Fundamentos Teóricos, Propuestas de Transversalidad y Orientaciones Extracurriculares.* Madrid: La Muralla.

Gutiérrez-Pérez, J., J. Perales, J. Benayas, and S. Calvo. 1997. *Lineas de Investigación en Educación Ambiental*. Granada: Junta de Andalucía-Universidad de Granada.

Habermas, J. 1972. *Knowledge and Human Interests*. Translated by Jeremy J. Shapiro. London: Heinemann Educational.

————. 1982. "New Social Movements." *Telos* 49: 33–37.

————. 1987. *The Philosophical Discourse of Modernity*. Translated by F. Lawrence. Cambridge, Mass.: MIT Press.

Hacking, I. 1991. "How Should We Do the History of Statistics?" In *The Foucault Effect: Studies in Governmentality*, ed. G. Burchell, C. Gordon, and P. Miller. Hemel Hempstead, England: Harvester Wheatsheaf.

Hall, S. 1996. "Who Needs 'Identity'?" In *Questions of Cultural Identity*, ed. S. Hall and P. Du Gay. London: Sage Publications.

Harding, Sandra. 1991. *Whose Science? Whose Knowledge? Thinking from Women's Lives*. Milton Keynes, England: Open University Press.

————. Ed. 1993. *The "Racial" Economy of Science*. Bloomington: Indiana University Press.

Harvey, D. 1989. *The Condition of Postmodernity*. Oxford: Blackwell.

Hawken, P. 1994. *The Ecology of Commerce*. New York: HarperBusiness.

Hayek, F. 1944. *The Road to Serfdom*. London: Routledge and Kegan Paul.

————. 1949a. *Individualism and the Economic Order*. London: Routledge and Kegan Paul.

————. 1949b. "Individualism: True and False." In *Individualism and the Economic Order*, ed. F. Hayek. London: Routledge and Kegan Paul.

————. 1960. *The Constitution of Liberty*. London: Routledge and Kegan Paul.

Heath, S. B. 1983. *Ways with Words: Language, Life and Work in Communities and Classrooms.* Cambridge: Cambridge University Press.

Heing, J., C. Hamnett, and H. Feigenbaum. 1988. "The Politics of Privatisation: A Comparative Perspective." *Governance* 1, no. 4: 442–68.

Henman, P. 1997. "Computers and Governmentality in Australia's Department of Social Security." In *Foucault the Legacy*, ed. Clare O'Farrell. Brisbane: Queensland University of Technology.

Hickling-Hudson, A. 1994. "The Environment as Radical Politics: Can 'Third World' Education Rise to the Challenge?" *International Review of Education* 40, no. 1: 19–36.

Hindess, B. 1996. *Discourses of Power: From Hobbes to Foucault.* Oxford: Blackwell.

Hirst, P. H. 1974. *Knowledge and the Curriculum.* London: Routledge and Kegan Paul.

Hodas, S. 1996. "Technology Refusal and the Organizational Culture of Schools." In *Computerization and Controversy: Value Conflicts and Social Choices*, ed. R. Kling. San Diego: Academic Press.

Holmberg, J. 1992. *Making Development Sustainable: Redefining Institutions, Policy, and Economics.* London: Earthscan Pub. Ltd.

Hood, Christopher. 1991. "A Public Management for All Seasons?" *Public Administration* 69 (Spring): 3–19.

Hood, Christopher and Michael Jackson. 1991. *Administrative Argument.* Aldershot: Dartmouth.

Huckle, J. and S. Sterling, eds. 1996. *Education for Sustainability.* London: Earthscan Pub. Ltd.

Hunt, A. and G. Wickham. 1994. *Foucault and Law: Towards a Sociology of Law as Governance.* London: Pluto Press.

Hunter, I. 1994. *Rethinking the School: Subjectivity, Bureaucracy, Criticism.* Sydney: Allen and Unwin.

Hutcheon, Linda. 1988. *A Poetics of Postmodernism: History, Theory, Fiction.* New York: Routledge.

Illich, I. 1971. *Deschooling Society.* New York: Harper & Row.

———. 1973. *Tools for Conviviality.* New York: Harper & Row.

IUCN/UNEP/WWF. 1991. *Caring for the Earth. A Strategy for Sustainable Living.* Gland, Switzerland: The World Conservation Union-United Nations Environment Programme-World Wide Fund for Nature.

Jameson, Fredric. 1983. *Posmodernismo y Sociedad de Consumo* en *la Posmodernidad.* Barcelona: Editorial Kairós.

Jencks, Charles. 1987. *The Language of Post-Modern Architecture.* London: Academy Editions.

Jones, A. 1986. *At School I've Got a Chance—Culture/Privilege: Pacific Islands and Pakeha Girls at School.* Palmerston North: Dunmore Press.

Jusidman, C. 1996. "Mujeres y Pobreza." *Problemas del Desarrollo. Revista Latinoamericana de Economía* 27, no. 106: 115–27.

Kearns, D. and D. Doyle. 1991. *Winning the Brain Race: A Bold Plan to Make Our Schools Competitive.* San Francisco: ICS Press.

Keat, R. 1991. "Consumer Sovereignty and the Integrity of Practice." In *Enterprise Culture,* ed. R. Keat and N. Abercrombie. London: Routledge.

Keat, R. and N. Abercrombie, eds. 1991. *Enterprise Culture.* London: Routledge.

Keating, M. 1993. *Cumbre para la Tierra. Programa para el Cambio. El programa 21 y los demás Acuerdos de Río de Janeiro en versión simplificada.* Tr. por Consuelo Nuñez. Ginebra-Suiza: Centro para Nuestro Futuro, Común.

Kell, C. 1996. "Literacy Practices in an Informal Setting in the Cape Peninsula." In *The Social Uses Of Literacy: Theory and Practice in Contemporary South Africa,* ed. M. Prinsloo and M. Breier. Amsterdam: John Benjamins.

Khanin, Dmitry. 1991. "The Postmodern Posture." *Philosophy and Literature* 14: 246–65.

Kirsch, I., A. Jungeblut, L. Jenkins, and A. Kolstad. 1993. *Adult Literacy in America: A First Look at the Results of the National Adult Literacy Survey.* Washington, D.C.: National Center for Educational Statistics, U.S. Department of Education.

Klotz, Heinrich. 1988. *The History of Postmodern Architecture.* Cambridge, Mass.: MIT Press.

Knobel, M. 1997. Language and Social Practices in Four Adolescents' Everyday Lives. Ph.D. Diss. Queensland University of Technology, Faculty of Education.

————. 1999. *Everyday Literacies: Language, Discourse, and Social Practice.* New York: Peter Lang.

Kuhn, Thomas S. 1962. *The Structure of Scientific Revolutions.* Chicago: University of Chicago Press.

————. 1970. "Logic of Discovery or Psychology of Research?" In *Criticism and the Growth of Knowledge*, ed. I. Lakatos and A. Musgrave. Cambridge: Cambridge University Press.

Kumar, K. 1978. *Prophecy and Progress: The Sociology of Industrial and Post-Industrial Society.* New York: Penguin.

Lacan, J. 1973. *The Four Fundamental Concepts of Psycho-Analysis.* London: Penguin.

Laclau, E. 1983. "The Impossibility of Society." *Canadian Journal of Political and Social Theory* 7, no. 1: 28–43.

————. 1988. Politics and the Limits of Modernity. Universidad de Essex, Inglaterra, mecanograma 15 p. (Documento inédito proporcionado por Ernesto Laclau a la Dra. Rosa Nidia Buenfil en la estancia académica que ella realizó en Essex durante 1994).

————. 1990. *New Reflections on the Revolution of Our Time.* London & New York: Verso.

————. 1993a. *Nuevas reflexiones sobre la revolución de nuestro tiempo.* Buenos Aires: Nueva Visión.

————. 1993b. "Discourse." In *A Companion to Contemporary Political Philosophy*, ed. R. Goodin and P. Pettit. Oxford: Blackwell.

Laclau. E. and C. Mouffe. 1985. *Hegemony and Socialist Strategy: Towards a Radical Democratic Politics.* London: Verso.

————. 1990. "Post-Marxism without Apologies." In E. Laclau, *New Reflections on the Revolution of Our Time.* London: Verso.

Lankshear, C. 1997. "Language and the New Capitalism." *International Journal of Inclusive Education* 1, no. 4: 309–21.

————. 1998. "Meanings of Literacy in Educational Reform Proposals." *Educational Theory* 48, no. 3: 351–72.

Lankshear, C. and C. Bigum. 1998. "Literacies and Technologies in School Settings: Findings from the Field." Keynote address, Joint National Conference of the Australian Association for the Teaching of English and the Australian Literacy Educators' Association, 5–7 July, Canberra.

————. Forthcoming. "Literacies and Technologies in School Settings." *Journal of Curriculum Studies.*

Lankshear, C., C. Bigum, C. Durrant, B. Green, E. Honan, J. Murray, W. Morgan, I. Snyder, and M. Wild. 1997. *Digital Rhetorics: Literacies and Technologies in Education—Current Practices and Future Directions.* 3 vols. Project Report. Children's Literacy National Projects. Brisbane: QUT/DEETYA.

Lankshear, C., M. Peters, and M. Knobel. 1996. "Critical Literacy and Cyberspace." In *Counternarratives: Cultural Studies and Critical Pedagogies in Postmodern Spaces*, by H. Giroux, C. Lankshear, P. McLaren, and M. Peters. New York: Routledge.

Latour, Bruno. 1987. *Science in Action: How to Follow Scientists and Engineers through Society.* Cambridge, Mass.: Harvard University Press.

Le Grand, J. and R. Robinson. 1984. "Privatisation and the Welfare State: An Introduction." In *Privatisation and the Welfare State*, ed. J. Le Grand and R. Robinson. London: Allen and Unwin.

Levett, A. and C. Lankshear. 1990. *Going for Gold: Priorities for Schooling in the Nineties.* Wellington: Daphne Brasell Associates Press.

Lilly, R. 1998. "Postmodernism and Political Philosophy." In *Routledge Encyclopedia of Philosophy*, ed. E. Craig. London and New York: Routledge.

Lyotard, Jean-François. 1979. *The Postmodern Condition: A Report on Knowledge.* Translated by G. Bennington and B. Massumi. Foreword by Fredric Jameson. Manchester: Manchester University Press.

————. 1984 [1979]. *The Postmodern Condition: A Report on Knowledge.* Translated by G. Bennington and B. Massumi. Foreword by Fredric Jameson. Minneapolis: University of Minnesota Press.

————. 1989. "Defining the Postmodern." In *Postmodernism: ICA Documents,* ed. L. Appignanesi. London: Free Association Books.

————. 1992. *The Postmodern Explained to Children: Correspondence 1982–1985.* Sydney: Power Publications.

————. 1993. "A Svelte Appendix to the Postmodern Question." In *Political Writings.* Translated by Bill Readings and Kevin Paul Geiman. Minneapolis: University of Minnesota Press.

MacDonald, M. 1997. "Professionalization and Environmental Education: Is Public Passion Too Risky for Business?" *Canadian Journal of Environmental Education* 2: 58–85.

Markeley, Robert. 1999. "After the Science Wars: From Old Bottles to New Directions in the Cultural Studies of Science." In *After the Disciplines: The Emergence of Cultural Studies,* M. Peters ed., Westport, Conn.: Bergin and Garvey.

Marshall, James D. 1995. "Foucault and Neoliberalism: Bio-power and Busno-power." In *Proceedings of The Philosophy of Education Society,* ed. N. Alven. Urbana-Champaign, Ill.: Philosophy of Education Society.

————. 1998. "Performativity: Lyotard, Foucault and Austin." Paper delivered to the American Educational Research Association's Annual Meeting. 11–17 April, San Diego.

Martins de Carvalho, H. 1994. "Padroes de sustenabilidade: Uma medida para o desenvolvimento sustentável." In *A Amazonia e a Crise du Modernizacao,* ed. M. A. D'Incao and Maciel da Silveira. Belém: Museu paraense Emilio Goeldi.

Marvin, C. 1988. *When Old Technologies Were New: Thinking About Communications in the Late Nineteenth Century.* New York: Oxford University Press.

Matthews, L. H., ed 1968. *The Whale.* London: Allen and Unwin.

Maxson, J. and B. Hair. 1990. *Managing Diversity: A Key to Building a Quality Workforce.* Columbus, Ohio: National Alliance of Community and Technical Colleges.

McCaffery, Larry. 1986. "Introduction." In *Postmodern Fiction: A Bio-Bibliographical Guide,* ed. Larry McCaffery. Westport, Conn.: Greenwood Press.

McCarthy, Thomas. 1987. "Introduction." In J. Habermas, *The Philosophical Discourse of Modernity.* Translated by F. Lawrence. Cambridge, Mass.: MIT Press.

McLaren, P. 1993. *Hacia una Pedagogía Crítica de la Formación Posmoderna.* Paraná, Argentina: Universidad Nacional de Entre Ríos.

———. 1994. *Pedagogía Crítica, Resistencia Cultural y la Producción del Deseo.* Buenos Aires: Instituto de Estudios y Acción Social.

McNeely, J. A. 1996. *Conservation and the Future: Trends and Options toward the Year 2025.* A discussion paper. Gland, Switzerland: ICUN. Congress Document CGR/1/96/8.

Mead, Aroha. 1992. "Cultural and Intellectual Property Rights of Indigenous Peoples—A History of Denial." *ASSR News* (October): 2–4.

Meister, Anton and Jeffrey Weber. 1991. "Sustainability: Myth or Reality?" *Sites* 22 (Autumn): 64–76.

Meyer, Leonard. 1967. *Music, the Arts, and Ideas: Patterns and Predictions in Twentieth Century Culture.* Chicago: Chicago University Press.

Michaels, S. 1981. "'Sharing Time': Children's Narrative Styles and Differential Access to Literacy." *Language in Society* 10: 423–42.

Ministry of Education. 1993. *The New Zealand Curriculum Framework.* Wellington: Ministry of Education.

MMA (Ministerio del Medio Ambiente). 1996. *Seminarios Permanentes de Educación Ambiental.* Madrid: Secretaría General Técnica/ Ministerio del Medio Ambiente.

Moll, L. 1992. "Literacy Research in Community and Classroom: A Sociocultural Approach." In *Multidisciplinary Perspectives on Lit-*

eracy Research, ed. R. Beach, J. Green, M. Kamil, and T. Shanahan. Urbana, Ill.: NCRE/NCTE.

Morales, C. 1988. "Roundtable: Postmodernity." (Round Table). October Seminar, México City: Facultad de Filosofía y Letras, National Autonomous University of México.

Morris, P. 1991. "Freeing the Spirit of Enterprise: The Genesis and Development of the Concept of Enterprise Culture." In *Enterprise Culture*, ed. R. Keat and N. Abercrombie. London: Routledge.

MoRST (Ministry of Research, Science and Technology, New Zealand). 1992a. *Long Term Priorities for the Public Good Science Fund: A Public Discussion Paper*, prepared by a Science and Technology Expert Panel, May. Wellington, MoRST.

———. 1992b. *Charting the Course*. Report of the Ministerial Task Group Reviewing Science and Technology Education. Wellington: MoRST and Ministry of Education, February.

Moser, J. 1997. "The Origins of the Austrian School of Economics." *Humane Studies Review* 11, no. 1: 15–21.

Mouffe, Chantal. 1988. "Radical Democracy: Modern or Postmodern?" In *Universal Abandon? The Politics of Postmodernism*, ed. A. Ross. Minneapolis: University of Minnesota Press.

Mrazek, R., ed. 1996. *Paradigmas Alternativos de Investigación en Educación Ambiental*. Guadalajara: Universidad de Guadalajara-NAAEE-Semarnap.

Nandy, Ashis, ed. 1988. *Science, Hegemony and Violence: A Requiem for Modernity*. New Delhi: Oxford University Press.

National Academy of Sciences Task Force. 1984. *High Schools and the Changing Workplace: The Employers' View*. Washington, D.C.: National Academy Press.

NBEET (National Board of Employment, Education and Training, Australia). 1996. *Literacy at Work: Incorporating English Language and Literacy Competencies into Industry/Enterprise Standards*. Canberra: Australian Government Publishing Service.

NCEE (National Commission on Excellence in Education). 1983. *A Nation at Risk: The Imperative for Educational Reform*. Washington, D.C.: U.S. Department of Education.

Negroponte, N. P. 1996. *Ser Digital*. Translated by D. Plácking. México: Océano.

Norval, A. 1990. "Carta a Ernesto." In *Nuevas Reflexiones sobre la Revolución de Nuestro Tiempo*, by E. Laclau. Buenos Aires: Nueva Visión.

Novo, M. 1986. *Educación y Medio Ambiente*. Madrid: UNED.

————. 1996. "La educación formal y no formal: Dos sistemas complementarios." *Revista Iberoamericana de Educación* 11 (May–August): 16–29.

O'Malley, P. 1996. "Risk and Responsibility." In *Foucault and Political Reason: Liberalism, Neoliberalism and Rationalities of Government*, ed. A. Barry, T. Osborne, and N. Rose. London: UCL Press.

Owens, C. 1987. "The Discourse of Others: Feminists and Postmodernism." In *Postmodern Culture*, ed. Hal Foster. London: Pluto Press.

Papadimitrou, V. 1995. "Professional Development of In-Service Primary Teachers in Environmental Education: An Action Research Approach." *Environmental Education Research* 1, no. 1.

Papert, S. 1993. *The Children's Machine: Rethinking School in the Age of the Computer*. New York: Basic Books.

Pardo-Díaz, A. 1995. *La Educación Ambiental como Proyecto*. Barcelona: Universitat Barcelona-Horsori.

Peddie, W. S. 1995. Alienated by Evolution: The Educational Implications of Creationist and Social Darwinist Reactions in New Zealand to the Darwinian Theory of Evolution. Ph.D. Diss. University of Auckland.

Peddiwall, J. 1939. *The Sabre-Tooth Curriculum*. New York: McGraw-Hill.

Peet, John. 1992. *Energy and the Ecological Economics of Sustainability*. Washington, D.C.: Island Press.

Perelman, L. 1992. *School's Out: The New Technology and the End of Education*. New York: Morrow.

Peters, Michael. 1991. "Postmodernism: The Critique of Reason and the Rise of the New Social Movements." *Sites* 22 (Autumn): 142–60.

————. 1993. "Postmodernism, Language and Culture." *Access* 12, nos. 1 & 2: 1–16.

————. 1994. "Governmentalidade Neoliberal e Educacao." In *O Sujeito Educacao, Estudos Foucaulianos*, ed. T. Tadeu da Silva. Rio de Janeiro: Editora Vozes.

————. 1995a. *Education and the Postmodern Condition*. Westport, Conn.: Bergin and Garvey.

————. 1995b. "The New Science Policy Regime in New Zealand: A Review and Critique." *New Zealand Sociology* 9, no. 2: 317–48.

————. 1996a. *Poststructuralism, Politics and Education*. Westport, Conn.: Bergin & Garvey.

————. 1996b. "Education and the Mode of Information: An Interview with Mark Poster." *New Zealand Journal of Educational Studies* 31, no. 1: 3–12.

————. 1997. "What Is Poststructuralism? The French Reception of Nietzsche." *Political Theory Newsletter* 8, no. 2: 39–55.

Peters, M. and C. Lankshear. 1996. "Critical Literacy and Digital Texts." *Educational Theory* 46, no. 1: 41–70.

Peters, M. and J. Marshall. 1995. "An Interview with Mark Poster." *New Zealand Journal of Media Studies* 2, no. 1: 45–53.

————. 1996. *Individualism and Community: Education and Social Policy in the Postmodern Condition*. London: Falmer Press.

————. 1999. *Wittgenstein: Philosophy, Postmodernism, Pedagogy*. Westport, CT: Bergin and Garvey.

Petitjean, Patrick, Catherine Jami, and Ann Marie Moulin, eds. 1992 *Science and Empire*. Dordrecht: Kluwer.

Pinar, W., W. Reynolds, P. Slattery, and P. Taubman. 1995. *Understanding Curriculum: An Introduction to the Study of Historical and Contemporary Curriculum Discourses*. New York: Peter Lang.

Pitelis, C. and T. Clarke. 1993. "Introduction: The Political Economy of Privatization." In *The Political Economy of Privatization*, ed. T. Clarkes and C. Pitelis. London: Routledge.

Plieck, G. and E. Aguado. 1995. *Educación y Pobreza. De la Desigualdad Social a la Equidad*. Zinacantepec, Estado de México: El Colegio Mexiquense/UNICEF.

PNUD (Programa de las Naciones Unidas de Desarrollo)/UNDP (United Nations Development Program). 1992. *Desarrollo Human: Informe 1992*. Santaféde Bogotá: Mundo Editores-PNUD.

—————. 1993. *Desarrollo Human: Informe 1993*. Madrid: PNUD-FCE.

—————. 1994. *Desarrollo Human: Informe 1994*. México City: PNUD-FCE.

—————. 1995. *Desarrollo Human: Informe 1995*. México City: PNUD-FCE.

PNUD-BID-FCE. 1991. *Nuestra Propia Agenda sobre el Desarrollo y Medi Ambiente*. México City: PNUD-BID-FCE.

Popkewitz, T. 1988. *Paradigma e Ideología en Investigación Educativa. Las Funciones Sociales del Intelectual*. Madrid: Mondadori.

—————. 1991. *A Political Sociology of Educational Reform: Power/ Knowledge in Teaching, Teacher Education, and Research*. New York: Teachers College Press.

Porter, M. 1990. *The Competitive Advantage of Nations*. London: Macmillan.

Poster, Mark. 1993. *The Mode of Information*. Chicago: University of Chicago Press.

—————. 1995. *The Second Media Age*. Cambridge, Mass.: Polity Press.

Prebble, M. 1990a. *Information, Privacy, and the Welfare State: An Integrated Approach to the Administration of Redistribution*. Wellington: VUW Press for Institute of Policy Studies.

—————. 1990b. *Integrated Circuit Cards: Is It Smart to Use a Smart Card?* Wellington: VUW Press for Institute of Policy Studies.

Prigogine, I. and I. Stengers. 1985. *Order Out of Chaos: Man's New Dialogue with Nature*. London: Flamingo.

Puiggrós, A. 1990. *Imaginación y Crisis en la Educación Latinoamericana*. México City: CONACULTA (*Los Noventa, 21*).

Quinn, D. 1995. *Ismael y la Salvación de la Tierra*. Buenos Aires: Emecé.

Rapalus, P. 1994. "Optimum Human Population about One-Third of Present Number." *Environmental Conservation* 21, no. 2: 176–77.

Readings, Bill. 1991. *Introducing Lyotard: Art and Politics*. London and New York: Routledge.

Reed, Edward. 1992. "Knowers Talking about the Known: Ecological Realism as a Philosophy of Science." *Synthese* 92, no. 1: 9–23.

Reich, R. 1992. *The Work of Nations*. New York: Vintage Books.

Richardson, R. 1991. *Budget 1991*. Wellington: Government Printer.

Ricoeur, Paul. 1965. "Civilization and National Cultures." In *History and Truth*. Translated by C. Kelbley. Evanston: Northwestern University Press.

Roa, Keehua. 1986. "Introduction." In *Symmes Hole*, by I. Wedde. Auckland: Penguin.

Rogoff, B. 1990. *Apprenticeship in Thinking: Cognitive Development in a Social Context*. New York: Oxford University Press.

―――. 1995. "Observing Sociocultural Activity on Three Planes: Participatory Appropriation, Guided Participation, Apprenticeship." In *Sociocultural Studies of Mind*, ed. J. Wertsch, P. del Rio, and A. Alvarez. New York: Cambridge University Press.

Rorty, Richard. 1979. *Philosophy and the Mirror of Nature*. Princeton: Princeton University Press.

―――. 1991. *Contingencia, Ironía y Solidaridad*. Barcelona: Paidós-Ibérica.

Rose, N. 1993. "Government, Authority and Expertise in Advanced Liberalism." *Economy and Society* 22, no. 3: 283–300.

―――. 1996. "Governing 'Advanced' Liberal Democracies." In *Foucault and Political Reason: Liberalism, Neoliberalism and Rationalities of Government*, ed. A. Barry, T. Osborne, and N. Rose. London: UCL Press.

Rosenau, Pauline. 1992. "Modern and Post-Modern Science: Some Contrasts." *Review* 15, no. 1: 49–90.

Ross, Andrew. 1988. "Introduction." In *Universal Abandon? The Politics of Postmodernism*, ed. Andrew Ross. Minneapolis: University of Minnesota Press.

Roszak, T. 1990. *El Culto a la Información. El Folclore de los Ordenadores y el Verdadero Arte de Pensar.* Translated by Jordi Beltrán. México City: Grijalbo-CONACULTA.

Rouse, Joseph. 1987. *Knowledge and Power: Toward a Political Philosophy of Science.* Ithaca: Cornell University Press.

Rowan, L. and C. Bigum. 1997. "The Future of Technology and Literacy Teaching in Primary Learning Situations and Contexts." In *Digital Rhetorics: Literacies and Technologies in Education—Current Practices and Future Directions*, Vol. 3, by C. Lankshear, C. Bigum, C. Durrant, B. Green, E. Honan, J. Murray, W. Morgan, I. Snyder, and M. Wild, Canberra: DEETYA.

Ryan, Michael. 1988. "Deconstruction and Social Theory: The Case of Liberalism." In *Displacement: Derrida and After*, ed. M. Krupnick. Bloomington: Indiana University Press.

Salmond, Anne. 1985. "Maori Epistemologies." In *Reason and Morality*, ed. J. Overing. London: Tavistock.

Santos, B. de Sousa. 1992. "A Discourse on the Sciences." *Review* 15, no. 1: 9–48.

Sauvé, L. 1996. "Environmental Education and Sustainable Development: A Further Appraisal." *Canadian Journal of Environmental Education* 1, no. 1: 15–32.

Schwartz, P. 1991. *The Art of the Long View.* New York: Doubleday.

Schwengel, H. 1991. "British Enterprise Culture and German *Kulturgesellschaft*." In *Enterprise Culture*, ed. R. Keat and N. Abercrombie. London: Routledge.

Scobie, Grant and Veronica Jacobsen. 1991. "Restructuring New Zealand's Research and Development Policy." *Policy*, Winter: 16–20.

Scollon, R. and S. Scollon. 1981. *Narrative, Literacy and Face in Interethnic Communication.* Norwood, NJ: Ablex.

Scott, Graham, Peter Bushnell, and Nikitin Sallee. 1990. "Reform of the Core Public Sector: The New Zealand Experience." *Governance* 3, no. 2: 138–67.

Semarnap (Secretaría de Medio Ambiente, Recursos Naturales y Pesca). 1996a. *México hacia el Desarrollo Sustentable: Bases de la Transición.* México City: Semarnap.

———. 1996b. *México: The Transition to Sustainable Development.* México City: Semarnap.

Shaw, Robert. 1990. *Purchasing Science.* Wellington: Ministry of Research, Science and Technology.

Sheldrake, Rupert. 1991. *The Rebirth of Nature: The Greening of Science and God.* New York: Bantam.

Silverman, H. J. 1996. "Modernism and Postmodernism." In *The Encyclopedia of Philosophy, Supplement*, ed. D. Borchert. New York: Simon and Schuster.

Slocombe, S. D. 1993. *What Works. An Annotated Bibliography of Case Studies of Sustainable Development.* Sacramento, Calif.: IUCN-CESP Working Paper, No. 5.

Smith, L. (Minister of Education, New Zealand). 1991a. "Speech Notes for Conference of the Secondary Schools Principals' Association of New Zealand." Sunday 28 April, Auckland, New Zealand.

———. 1991b. *Investing in People: Our Greatest Asset.* Wellington: Government Printer.

———. 1992. "Speech to the Education for Enterprise Conference." 12 February, Wellington.

Smyth, J. 1995. "Environment and Education: A View of a Changing Scene." *Environmental Education Research* 1, no. 1: 33–48.

Sosa, N. M., ed. 1989. *Educación Ambiental: Sujeto, Entorno y Sistema.* Salamanca: Amarú.

Sterling, S. and G. Cooper. 1992. *In Touch. Environmental Education for Europe.* London: WWF.

Stevenson, P. 1995. "Making Space: For Those Who Invent Tomorrow. A Report on the Feasibility of a Multi-Purpose Youth Facility for

Brisbane." Brisbane: Queensland Department of Tourism, Sport and Racing and Queensland University of Technology Academy of the Arts.

Street, B. 1984. *Literacy in Theory and Practice.* Cambridge: Cambridge University Press.

Sureda, J. and J. A. Colom. 1989. *Pedagogía Ambiental.* Barcelona: CEAC (Colección Educación y Enseñanza).

Te Awekotuku, Ngahuia. 1991. *He Tikanga Wakaaro: Research Ethics in the Maori Community.* Wellington: Manatu Maori, Government Printer.

Thomas, R. M. 1994. "Educational Reform." In *International Encyclopaedia of Education,* ed. T. Husén and T. Postlethwaite, eds. 2nd ed. Oxford: Pergamon Press.

Tinkler, D., B. Lepani, and J. Mitchell. 1996. *Education and Technology Convergence.* Commissioned Report No. 43. Canberra: Australian Government Publishing Service.

Toch, T. 1991. *In the Name of Excellence.* New York: Oxford University Press.

Toledo, V. M. 1996. "Latinoamerica: Crisis de Civilización y Ecología Política." *Gaceta Ecólogia* 38: 12–22.

Toulmin, Stephen. 1982. *The Return to Cosmology: Postmodern Science and the Theology of Nature.* Berkeley: University of California Press.

———. 1985. "Pluralism and Responsibility in Post-Modern Science." *Science, Technology, Human Values* 10, no. 1: 28–37.

———. 1990. *Cosmopolis: The Hidden Agenda of Modernity.* New York: The Free Press.

Trzyna, T. C., ed. 1995. *A Sustainable World. Defining and Measuring Sustainable Development.* Sacramento, Calif.: IUCN–The World Conservation Union.

Tunbridge, N. 1995. "The Cyberspace Cowboy." *Australian Personal Computer* (September): 16–20.

Ulmer, G. 1989. *Teletheory: Grammatology in the Age of Video.* New York: Routledge.

U.S. Congress. 1993. *Goals 2000: Education America Act*. Washington, D.C.: U.S. Congress.

U.S. Congress Office of Technology Assessment. 1993. *Adult Literacy and New Technologies: Tools for a Lifetime*. Washington, D.C.: U.S. Government Printing Office.

van der Heijden, K. 1996. *Scenarios: The Art of Strategic Conversation*. Chichester: Wiley.

van Reijen, W. and D. Veerman. 1988. "An Interview with Jean-François Lyotard." *Theory, Culture and Society* 5: 302.

Vattimo, G. 1992. *The Transparent Society*. Cambridge: Polity Press.

―――. 1996. *La Sociedad Transparente*. Barcelona: Paidós Ibérica-ICE/UAB.

Wack, P. 1985a. "The Gentle Art of Reperceiving." *Harvard Business Review* (Sept.–Oct.): 73–89.

―――. 1985b. "Scenarios: Shooting the Rapids." *Harvard Business Review* (Nov.–Dec.): 139–150.

Wallace, D. and M. Packer. 1998. "The Cultural Field in Foresight." Unpublished paper. Wellington: Knowledge Policy research group, Humanities Society of New Zealand.

Weizenbaum, J. 1984. *Computer Power and Human Reason: From Judgment to Calculation*. Harmondsworth: Penguin.

Welford, R. 1995. *Environmental Strategy and Sustainable Development: The Corporate Challenge for the 21st Century*. London: Routledge.

White, Stephen. 1991. *Political Theory and Postmodernism*. Cambridge: Cambridge University Press.

Wiggenhorn, W. 1991. "Motorola U: When Training Becomes an Education." *Harvard Business Review* (July–August): 71–83.

Winters, K. 1996. "America's Technology Literacy Challenge." Washington DC: US Department of Education, Office of the Undersecretary, posted on <acw-l@unicorn.acs.ttu.edu> 17 February 1996.

Wittgenstein, L. 1953. *Philosophical Investigations*. Translated by G. E. M. Anscombe. Oxford: Blackwell.

Worldwatch Institute. 1990. *El Mundo. Medio Ambiente 1990*. Un Reporte del Worldwatch Institute sobre el Avance hacia una Sociedad Sustentable. México City: Fundación Universo Veintiuno.

————. 1991. *La Situación en el Mundo, 1991*. Translated by R. Alonso. Madrid: Apóstrofe.

Zemelman, H. 1987a. *Conocimiento y Sujetos Sociales: Contribución al Estudio del Presente*. México City: Centro de Estudios Sociológicos-El Colegio de México.

————. 1987b. *Uso Critico de la Teoría: En Torno a las Funciones Analíticas de la Totalidad*. México City: Universidad de las Naciones Unidas-El Colegio de México.

Ziman, J. M. 1994. *Prometheus Bound: Science in a Dynamic Steady State*. Cambridge and New York: Cambridge University Press.

Žižek, S. 1990. "Beyond Discourse—Analysis." In E. Laclau, *New Reflections on the Revolution of Our Time*. London and New York: Verso.

Index